Treasure

in

Louisiana:

A Treasure Hunter's Guide to the Bayou State.

By

John Edward Miller

P.-93
P.95

P.107 TO 109
- P-112
- P.-117

P-225-*opals*

Published by John Miller

Front cover photographed by Carmel L. Miller, map by
Harold E. Brayton.

Additional copies may be obtained by sending $20.45 (price
includes applicable tax and postage), check or money order to:

John Miller
P. O. Box 3764
Bay St. Louis, Ms 39521-3764

Special rates are available for volume orders.

First Edition
First Printing 1,000 copies

Library of Congress Card Catalog Number: 96-94445

ISBN 1-57502-237-0

Printed in the USA by

*M*ORRIS
PUBLISHING

3212 E. Hwy 30
Kearney, NE 68847
800-650-7888

This book is dedicated to all of those who believe, especially my wife Carmel, and my friend Carol Bogolin, for all of their time and effort. Thank you.

TABLE OF CONTENTS

INTRODUCTION

There is no doubt that the state of Louisiana has enjoyed a long and colorful history. It was first settled by Indians in prehistoric times. In 1528, Panfilo de Naravez's expedition found itself shipwrecked on Timbalier Island, and Alvar Nunez Cabaza de Vaca and three other survivors explored their way to the Pacific Ocean. In 1541, Hernando de Soto's company of men were the second known party of Europeans to explore the Louisiana territory. By the mid 1600's the Spanish had established a settlement in what is now New Orleans. Robert Cavalier, sieur de La Salle took possession of the territory in 1682, and named it Louisiana. In 1687 the first French colony was started south of New Orleans with the building of a fort by Pierre Le Moyne, sieur d'Iberville. By 1711, Louisiana had become an independent French colony and established its first school in 1720. On April 30, 1812, it became the 18th state to join the Union. Louisiana seceded from the Union in 1861, and joined the Confederate States of America.

These dates and names can be found in any Louisiana History textbook. But, there is "more to the story." Some items included in this book have never before appeared in print. There are also some points of history that necessitated correcting or should at least be brought to light.

Throughout Louisiana's long and colorful history, many treasures have been amassed, buried, and lost. What I have attempted here is to list a small portion of the possible treasures that await discovery by the right person. A person with enough perseverance, savvy, and time to realize his or her dreams, or perhaps a person with just good old-fashion luck. Some of you may even find the stories a treasure in themselves.

My collection of treasure stories began in the 1940's as I listened to endless tales of treasure while growing up in Louisiana. My maternal grandmother came to Louisiana in a covered wagon. My maternal grandfather was born in Louisiana and was a riverboat captain. In the early 1960's, I began a serious collection of stories and reference material on lost treasure and have most of it to this day. I have found a few treasures of my own, some of which I had no idea of their real value until it was too late. Some of these treasures were given to my children as they grew up. Others now lay in cardboard coffins stacked in darkened tombs within my home. Other treasures consisted of a combination of persons, places and things and could not be taken away from their place in time, except as precious memories. As you may learn, there are plenty of treasures of all types left to find. You may not be rewarded financially, but you will be rewarded nonetheless. The beauty and splendor of Louisiana is constantly changing, creating new and different treasures for us all to enjoy.

What is treasure? Treasure takes many different forms, objets d'art, a persons good name, money, curios, antiques, bric-a-bracs, novelties, pirate booty, outlaw loot. The list is endless and varies from person to person. I have found that nothing makes the adrenaline pump like the glint of gold in a shovelful of dirt. It may be a gold nugget, ring, chain or coin. All have the same effect on the system.

I have panned for gold in California and searched for diamonds in Arkansas. I have hunted for treasure throughout the United States. But the two finds that brought the most joy were found within minutes of my home. Using a $35 metal detector I found a *circa* 1890's gold pocket watch 250 feet from my front door. Using a $650 metal detector my wife found a very old solid brass fire nozzle within two miles of our home. She wanted to throw the nozzle away. I think some people would rather find diamond rings, gold coins, or just hard cash, and do not see the beauty in an object's uniqueness.

I eventually came to the realization that I could never search every known site in the state of Louisiana and decided to pass the information on to you with the sincere hope that everyone finds at least something worthwhile. Should the following information help you find what you consider a real treasure, please let me know. I will keep all finds strictly confidential.

WARNING:

The facts stated herein are believed to be true, accurate, and involve some forty years of research, but are given only for reference and entertainment. Nothing stated or implied should be considered to be a right to trespass or break any of the laws of the United States of America, the State of Louisiana, any parish, city or township. Most of the treasures listed will be on property owned by some entity. It would behoove you to learn the names of the owners and any applicable laws where you intend to search. Often a written agreement can be reached prior to the searching of any treasure. This will save time, trouble, and legal fees. It is recommended that you always state the truth and never attempt to circumvent the law. Some sites listed are on government lands where treasure hunting may be illegal, but these sites often extend onto private property where permission to search may be obtained. If access to the property is denied by the owner, the offer of a percentage of any treasure found often clears the way. The Unmarked Burial Sites Preservation Act of 1991, makes it illegal to knowingly disturb an unmarked burial site or any human remains. Without proper authorization from the United Stated government, it is illegal to remove or possess artifacts from a sunken Confederate or United States ship.

ONE LAST BIT OF ADVISE:

Make yourself familiar with the latest ruling of the United States Archaeological Resources and Protection Act of 1978. As of February 27, 1995, the rule expands the list of prohibited acts to include attempts to excavate, remove or damage archeological resources on federal lands. Attempts are being made by some to have the rule apply to private as well as federal lands.

CHAPTER I

MAXIMS FOR THE TREASURE HUNTER

MOST TREASURES ARE FOUND BY CHILDREN

Over the years I have found that most treasures are found by children. Why? Children have a lot of time on their hands and can get into all kinds of things. Children love to explore the world around them. My brothers and I grew up on what was the original Chalmette Plantation, the site of the Battle of New Orleans, and later a Civil War training area. The finds were unbelievable. We found, lost and, just plain threw away things that I would give anything to have today, now that I know their value. We beat copper enameled British unit crests with hammers to free the copper. We tossed Cannon balls into the Chalmette Canal just to see the splash. We turned over an old pistol found in Rodriquez Canal to the Chalmette National Historic Park. Swords, belt buckles, minie balls and musket balls, coins, our list of finds is endless and our carelessness very painful. I have since gone back with a state of the art metal detector and found a lot of junk. I guess that is the price of civilization.

MOST TREASURES ARE FOUND BY ACCIDENT

If you live in Louisiana or read the newspapers, you must know at least one story of a shrimp or oyster boat crew who has pulled up a Treasure Chest.

Let us take a look at Mel Fisher, one of the most successful Treasure Hunters in the world. Mel Fisher searched twenty years for the Spanish treasure galleon, *Nuestra Senora de Atocha*. He dedicated his life to the search for the *Atocha's* 901 silver ingots, 250,827 silver coins, 161 pieces of gold bullion, jewels, and 582 copper planks. He did not expect to find the

Spanish treasure galleon *Santa Margarita*, 20+ million dollars. Oh! Sorry, wrong ship, it was an accident. See what I mean.

NOTE: Even after finding the *Santa Margarita*, Fisher continued to search, and did eventually find the *Atocha*.

X MARKS THE SPOT

There are countless real treasure maps and a zillion fake ones. Just because a map exists, do not think for a minute that if it were real, someone would surely have found the treasure by now. In 1967, I was invited by friends to accompany them on a treasure hunt in another state. The group had been searching for a lost gold mine every weekend for months. They had a copy of a map that came from the state archives. The map was public record. I had car trouble and could not make the search. Early Monday morning, I received a telephone call and was told that they had found the mine within the first hour. It seems that they had been reading the map upside down.

Question: When is a map not a map? Answer: When you do not know it is a map. Maps take all types of shapes, sizes and forms. You make a map to insure that you can find a certain place or object. Not all treasure maps are made by a cartographer. Most of them are crude. Many look like sketches. Some treasure maps consist of signs, symbols, numbers, letters or whatever. But, all maps have a meaning to the person who made them. It only stands to reason that they would want the map to help them find the treasure, not someone else.

I found this map in my wallet. "L HEWES RRT R L OAK 3BLKS 28TH 3RD ON R." It is directions to a friends new house. Left on Hewes Avenue, after the Railroad tracks, turn right, then left at Oak Street, go three blocks to 28th Street, he lives in the third house on the right. When I wrote the instructions I was in a hurry, it makes sense to me and might have made sense to you.

NOTE: If you are interested in treasure maps you may want to order a copy of the following:

A Descriptive List of Treasure Maps and Charts in the Library of Congress, compiled by Richard S. Ladd, (Glorieta, New Mexico 87535: The Rio Grand Press, Inc., 1988), $5.95, originally published by the Map Division, Reference Department, Library of Congress, Washington: 1964. An Addendum to A Descriptive List of Treasure Maps and Charts in the Library of Congress, may be obtained without charge from the Library of Congress, Geography and Map Division, Washington, DC 20540.

TELLING TRUTH FROM FICTION

Never believe anything you see in movies or on television. For example Jean Lafitte was not at the Battle of New Orleans. Lafitte was at Barataria during the actual battle. Lafitte supplied information about the British invasion, 366 cannons, 6,400 kilograms of gunpowder, 300,000 flints, and 1,515 men. Lafitte's men at the battle were under the command of the worlds greatest cannoneer Dominique You, considered by most historians as the real hero of the Battle of New Orleans.

Have you ever played the game of telephone. This is the game where ten people stand in a line and the first person is given a card to silently read. Person number one then whispers what was written on the card into the ear of person number two. Person number two whispers what they heard to person number three. This is continued on down the line to person number ten. By the time the story gets to person number ten it has become so distorted that it no longer resembles what was written. The same is true with treasure stories.

Most treasure hunters are like most fisherman. The size of a treasure lost or found, like the size of a fish, has a tendency to grow as time passes and the stories are retold. Minor treasures often evolve into larger treasures. Let's say that the original story began in the year 1800 with 50 ounces of gold. The price of gold was established by the United States Congress in the original Mint Act of April 2, 1792, putting the price of gold at approximately $15 a troy ounce. At the time the treasure was lost it was worth $750. On June 28, 1834, Congress went on the Gold Standard, and the price was raised to $19.39 a troy ounce. Our treasure is now worth $969.50. In 1965, at $35 a troy ounce, that 50 ounces of gold was worth $1,750. At that time the story could honestly be told of a $1,750 treasure. By January of 1980, the price of gold reached $850 a troy ounce, and the true value of the treasure may have grown to around $42,500. The next teller of the story may think that the original treasure was $42,500 in gold coins. It could have been in $20 Double Eagles. Today we are talking about coins worth $400 each, 2,125 coins, or $850,000. The actual value of the treasure today would be $18,500, due to the drop in the price of gold. No one meant to tell a lie, it just happened. Always try to find the original source of the story.

If an expert says that a treasure story is a myth, the story could in fact be true. I have read tens of thousands of stories of lost and found treasures over the years, and it always makes me smile to read of a treasure found after an expert has labeled it a myth. Most treasure stories have a factual base. Do some research and find out what is based on fact and what is fiction.

WHERE TO LOOK

Prior to 1933 banks were few and far between and most were unstable. Many a man hid his cash and other valuables, then died or went off to the war never to return. There were two places where a person could cache his cash and other valuables, inside or outside his house. "Never put all of your eggs in one basket". That goes for inside as well as outside.

INSIDE

One could never tell when he might need a little cash, so some money would have to be kept close. The money should not be hidden where he could be seen making a withdrawal or a deposit by someone from the inside or outside of his home. Try door moldings, baseboards and floors. If the money was in the mattress, bedpost, cookie jar or tin can, it may be long gone. I will never forget the day my wife went shopping and left me a list of "honey-dos." Two of the grandchildren were coming for the summer and she wanted some beds setup for them. The bed frames were old and in the house when we purchased it. As I moved one of the headboards I heard a rattle. Upon inspection I found approximately one dozen coins. All were old and some were silver. It made my day.

OUTSIDE

A person would hide coins, because paper money rots. He would put the coins in a container to keep from losing any. He'd bury the cache where it could be seen from his bedroom window. He may have buried his cache in a remote location on his property, near a prominent landmark, but he would not be able to keep an eye on that area. The place where he buried the cache would have to be found at night without the aid of a lamp. Light carries a long distance, and he would not want anyone to see any unusual actives. The best place to bury his valuables would be near an animal pen. Chickens, pigs, geese, horses, cows, dogs, whatever, all make noise when disturbed at night. Animals are old fashion burglar alarms. Fence postholes make good hiding places. At night he could go out and count to the twenty-fifth post, pull it up, reach into the hole, and retrieve his cache. To help in your search of treasure think about where you would have hidden your valuables.

NOTE: During the construction and repair of ships, coins were placed under the mast, to bring good luck to those placing the coins. This practice was later followed in the construction of plantation homes, and coins were placed within the base of the fireplaces, to bring good luck to the residence. The coins were usually placed under the top layer of stone near the center.

HUNTED OUT LOCATIONS

There is no such thing as a hunted out location. I hunted a location with a metal detector throughout the 1970's. During that time there were always seven or eight other people in that same park. The park had been the site of military camps during the War of 1812 and the Civil War, and over the years produced some nice finds. Eventually the finds were few and far between, and mostly new junk. Over the years, I would often see people sweeping that same park with metal detectors. In 1988 I purchased my fifth metal detector and, with the park being only a few blocks, I went there to try it out. I was certain the park was hunted out, but maybe there would be a new coin or two to be found. To my astonishment, I began to find minie balls at ten inches in the ground. My friend, the one that sold me the metal detector, told me not to tell anyone about his secret place. He had been going to the park on rainy days and finding coins from the 1850's and 60's. The coins were all beautiful, rare, and in very fine condition. About a month later he found a five dollar gold piece in of all places Audubon Park. Every year new metal detectors come on the market. As I write this, new generation detectors can alert the operator as to what an object may be and how far down into the ground it rests. Garrett Metal Detectors has a model that can even talk. The next one that I buy may be able to dig up the object, keep my soft drinks cold, have an AM/FM stereo and a three speed synchromesh transmission with overdrive. Who knows?

THE TRUE TREASURE HUNTER

The test of the true treasure hunter can be measured by the amount of trash he digs up. As the old saying goes, "You have to kiss a lot of frogs, before you get a prince." When you are not finding trash, it is because your discrimination is too high. If you take the time to go treasure hunting do not risk passing up the treasure. Dig up everything, fill in your holes, and dispose of your trash properly. A better metal detector may be invented tomorrow, and you could be back at the same spot digging the same trash. Always respect the property of others and **OUR** environment.

ALWAYS USE THE PROPER TOOL TO DO THE PROPER JOB

At the time of this writing their at least a dozen companies that make very good metal detectors. Over the years I have owned a few, some I had to build myself. I have never owned a White's metal detector, but I know people who will swear they are the best. Others will swear that Fisher, Tesoro, Bounty Hunter, Hays, Keene, or Minelab is the best. Some prefer the fork of a willow branch. I have never owned any of those either. I do own a Compass metal detector and I like it. I own several Garrett detectors and I like them the best. I guess that it why most of the equipment I own is from Garrett. This is not a paid advertisement for Garrett, I like their products for several reasons.

Number 1: Charles Garrett is an electrical engineer, but he his first a treasure hunter. If his produces can be improved he will improve them, to make it easier to find more treasure.

Number 2: I have never had to read their warranty, much less use it. I do not know anyone personally who has had a problem, but I did read about one person that did. He had nothing but praise for Garrett Metal Detectors.

Number 3: Garrett Metal Detectors come in a wide range of types and prices. This allows you to purchase the detector you need at a price you can hopefully afford. Good metal detectors are expensive, but why pay for features you will never use. Why purchase a detector that is water proof to 200 feet, if you are not diving for treasure.

I had intended to list all of Garrett's products and prices, but I could not do them justice, without adding another chapter to my book. You can obtain a current catalog by writing Garrett Metal Detectors, 1881 West State Street, Garland, Texas 75042-6761, or by calling (214) 494-5151.

If you would like information on all of the better detectors, you may write to Metal Detectors of Minneapolis, 3746 Cedar Avenue South, Minneapolis, Mn 55407, or call (612) 721-1901. I have purchase my last four detectors from them, and I do not think the price or service can be beat. I do not think that they sell divining rods, but I could be wrong.

RESEARCH

A lot of research is usually needed before you run out and start digging for treasure. This can often be done at or through your local library. Often what is needed is something special, like an 1886 map of Bastrop, Louisiana. Where do you look for that map?

K. B. Slocum Books, P. O. Box 10998 #620, Austin, Texas 78766, (512) 833-8449. Slocum has hundreds of old maps and hard to find books on treasure. That map of Bastrop is $5.95. Their address on the Internet is: HTTP//WWW.HALCYON. COM/TREASURE/KBSLOCUM/

You are walking around in the woods near Winnfield when you trip over a large bolder. You look at it and notice someone has chiseled designs on it. After carefully taking note of the area around the bolder, you feel you can find your way back with no problems, and you beat feet to your local library. Once at the library you learn their are no books on old signs to be found. What do you do?

Try Carson's Bookstore, Carson Enterprises, drawer 71, Deming, New Mexico, 88031, (505) 546-3252. Treasure Signs and Symbols ($6.95), or Treasure Signs, Symbols, Shadows, and Sun Signs, ($19.95). These are just two of the many books on

Spanish treasure signs readily available from Carson's Bookstore. They also have many old, hard to find treasure books that are now out of print. The store is owned and operated by renown experts in the field of Treasure Hunting.

THE TREASURE HUNTERS CODE OF ETHICS

Yes, even treasure hunters have a code of ethics, some do not follow them very well, but in just about every treasure book and magazine you should find a code of ethics. Having often been called difficult and sometimes called different, I am to old to change. Here is my code of ethics:

1. "Do unto others as you would have them do unto you."

2. I will always respect private property and never hunt without the owner's permission. (This permission should be in writing.)

3. I will always respect a friend's digging spot. Once a spot is shown to me by a friend I will never return without the knowledge and consent of that friend.

4. I will always respect the law.

5. I will always respect the property of others. I will never touch or use another's property without their permission. If allowed to touch or use someone's property, I will treat it better than I would my own property.

6. I will always fill my holes as well as those left by others.

7. I will always respect the environment and remove all trash carried in by myself or found within the area I am searching.

8. I will always be considerate and courteous to others at all times.

9. I will only build fires in a designated or safe area.

10. I will always leave gates as I found them.

11. I will never knowingly disturb any human remains. If human bones are found, I will report it to the proper authorities at once.

12. I will remember that my actions represent those of all treasure hunters. The carelessness of one negligent person will reflect badly on all treasure hunters.

CHAPTER II

TREASURE FOUND

Here is a list some of the treasures already found within the state of Louisiana. Please keep in mind that for various reasons Treasure Hunters are a secretive lot. Some have found the treasure on private property, without the owner's permission. Some may wish to avoid the "Tax Man", while others wish to avoid the notoriety and all that it brings. Whatever the reason, you must take whatever information you can get and be thankful that you are among the people in the know.

Aside from the obvious, a treasure that has been obtained legally has other rewards. Often a treasure with a certification will demand a higher value. Taxes are paid on a treasure only after it is sold. Transactions involving Unites States gold and silver coins, Canadian 1 ounce gold maple leaf coins, 1 ounce Krugerrands, and gold and silver ingots must be reported by the dealer to the Internal Revenue Service. When you sell a treasure you have found, you become a professional treasure hunter and can claim your expenses on your taxes. A good tax lawyer can get back all you paid in taxes. You get bragging rights. You get paid to appear on all of those talk shows. A movie could be made about your adventure, with some really big star playing you. Do you know who the technical advisor would have to be?

ALLEN PARISH

In 1929 unusually low waters of the Calcasieu River exposed a chest containing $75,000 in gold and silver coins. The coins were reportedly Spanish and the finders believed that it was one of Jean Lafitte's treasures.

ASCENSION PARISH

Darrow: l'Hermitage (Hermitage Plantation) built in 1812 by Marius Pons Bringier. During the Civil War the plantation owner, Colonel Bringier received word of the approaching Union Army and buried three chests filled with gold coins, a silver service, and the family jewels, in three locations about the plantation. After the war ended the owner could only locate two of the chests. In 1928 a large oak tree that stood in front of the plantation was blown over in a storm. Upon examination the family found the third chest. It had become embedded within the trunk of the tree.

ASSUMPTION PARISH

Napoleonville: In 1933 a small cache of coins was found at Woodlawn Plantation, giving rise to the theory that more treasure exists.

AVOYELLES PARISH

Bunkie: On March 3, 1930, a farmer named Forrest Normand plowed up an iron pot filled with American and Spanish silver coins dated between 1763 and 1805. The treasure was believed to be one of Jean Lafitte's caches.

Marksville: A farmer near Marksville uncovered an Iron pot containing over 3,000 silver coins.

Marksville: In 1976 a cache containing 27 rifles, 19 pistols, and a large quantity of ammunition, swords and knives were unearthed by treasure hunters. The cache was said to have been one of three made by an outlaw gang. It is believed that the treasure hunters may have possessed a map to the location.

BEAUREGARD PARISH

Texas state line: In 1972 it was reported that a $4,000,000 treasure consisting of gold and silver coins, and jewels was recovered near the Texas state line. The cache had been housed within a stone and log vault and was believed to have been placed there in the 1860's by an outlaw gang who had been operating in the area.

CALCASIEU PARISH

Contraband Bayou: In the 1890's one gold bar was found along Contraband Bayou. It is believed that the bar may have been part of one of the many Jean Lafitte treasure caches made within that area.

Edgerly: In 1929 a work crew was digging through a dry river bed and found $75,000 in gold coins dated in the 1840's and 1850's. Some people believe this was a $75,000 Jayhawkers' treasure rumored to have been buried in this area. Others believe it to be a $75,000 cache planted by a wealthy plantation owner during the Civil War. If it was not one it was the other, but since only one has been found a $75,000 cache still remains.

CAMERON PARISH

Coca Island: $1,000,000 in gold ingots is believed to be buried on the island by an unknown pirate. An additional $900,000 in silver was said to have been buried by Jean Lafitte. To date only $1,500 in gold doubloons has ever been reported found.

Grand Chenier: In 1981, in the waters just off of Grand Chenier, a Spanish Treasure ship was found. The ship is believed to have been sunk in a 1766 storm. No value was given for the treasure found.

Rockefeller Wildlife Preserve: In October of 1990, a shrimp boat pulling a trawl in fifteen feet of water snagged part of a sunken treasure ship. The treasure was at first valued at $250,000, but the value of the gold and artifacts will probably be in the millions. The treasure was part of the cargo carried by the *El Constante*, which sunk in 1766 during a hurricane. The ship was returning to Spain from Veracruz loaded with gold, silver, Chinese pottery, copper, and cases of silver handled knives.

EAST BATON ROUGE PARISH

Baker: In 1973 Herbert Babin found a 1652 British shilling while metal detecting around an old home site. That may not seem like much of a treasure but that one coin could be worth $3,200.

Baton Rouge: A Civil War cache of weapons was a nice find, but add in the chest containing gold, silver and jewels found with them, and you have a REALLY NICE FIND. The cache was only one of several in the area, with the main cache consisting of $500,000 in gold and silver coins. The search continued for the other caches, but as of 1995 they have not seen daylight.

Baton Rouge: In 1929 Clyde Pickett was reading some of his old family records when he learned that during the Civil War his ancestors cached the family silverware. Mister Pickett went to the location of the plantation ruins and began to search for the silverware. What Mister Pickett found was a cache of pre-Civil War gold and silver coins. At that point, Mister Pickett stopped looking for the silverware.

IBERIA PARISH

Jefferson Island: In 1921 several Spanish gold doubloons dated 1754 were found on Jefferson Island. In that same year, three pots of gold and silver coins were found in an area called the Lafitte Oaks on Jefferson Island.

In 1923, while digging a trench, a laborer found a large quantity of Spanish and Mexican gold and silver coins.

In 1928, while digging in an area known as "Voodoo Land", a work crew uncovered three triangular boxes. Each box was constructed of baked clay with lead covers. It was reported that the boxes contained as much as $40,000 in English, French and Mexican gold and silver coins.

In 1933 a man digging for a culvert found Spanish gold doubloons and silver pieces-of-eight.

In 1952 what has been described only as a "Bushel of Coins" was found on Jefferson Island.

JEFFERSON PARISH

Gretna: In 1960 two small chests were found containing more than $1,300 in gold coins.

Gretna: In 1963 approximately $65,000 in gold coins was found. It was reported to be a Jean Lafitte treasure cache.

Grand Isle: It is rumored that treasure hunters have found $1,600,000 in Spanish gold coins at Caminada Pass. The parties involved did not wish to be known, but they believe there find is only part of a much larger cache. It has been estimated that over the years more then $4,000,000 in gold, silver and jewels have been found in the area of Barataria Bay alone.

NOTE: This find would match the story of a Jean Lafitte treasure cache of reportedly $1,500,000 being buried at Caminada Pass.

Grand Terre Island: Treasure hunters have recovered a large number of gold and silver coins as well as Civil War relics and artifacts from the area around Fort Livingston. It is believed that the coins are washed ashore during storms.

LAFAYETTE PARISH

Lafayette: In 1923 a cache of Mexican Gold and Silver coins, believed to be one of Jean Lafitte's many caches, was reported found.

LIVINGSTON PARISH

Amite River: In 1956 a farmer unearthed several hundred Spanish Gold doubloons while plowing his field near the Amite River and Lake Maurepas.

ORLEANS PARISH

New Orleans: In 1915 a worker uncovered an old chest containing more than 1,500 Spanish gold doubloons dated between the late 1700's and early 1800's.

New Orleans: In 1948 a 6 year old girl was playing in front of a neighbor's house on Ursuline Street. Digging under the front steps she uncovered approximately 20, "shiny yellow coins." The girl showed the coins to the 9 year old boy who's family was renting the house. The boy brought the coins in and showed his mother. The mother came out and questioned the girl as to the exact location of the find, told her that they were just worthless old tokens and sent her home. A short time later the family moved out of the rented house and into their own home. The girl never saw the family again, but never forgot the "shiny yellow coins."

New Orleans: During the construction of the Louisiana Superdome, hardly a week would go by without someone finding a treasure. The Central Business District would grind to a halt when a back hoe would turn up gold or silver coins. People from blocks away would make a mad dash to the site. Gold, silver and copper coins of almost any nation were found. Jewelry and gun caches were also found. This was repeated over and over again, during the 1960's and 1970's.

New Orleans: During the construction of the new Tad Gormley Stadium track in City Park, pre Civil War silver coins were found in the dirt being used as fill. An effort was made to locate the site where the dirt had come from, but because of the enormity of the project the dirt had been trucked in from many locations. It is not known how much was found, but the coins were beautiful and looked like they had just been minted.

PLAQUEMINES PARISH

Island #82: A large number of gold and silver coins have been found on Island #82. It is believed that the coins are being washed in from the wreck of the *Oregon*, which sank in the Mississippi River on March 2, 1871.

Island #83: A large number of gold and silver coins were also found on Island #83. These coins are believed to be from the *John Adams*, which sank in the Mississippi River on February 27, 1871.

POINTE COUPEE PARISH

Batchelor: It has been rumored that a treasure cache consisting of Spanish silver and gold coins was found near Batchelor.

RAPIDES PARISH

Bunkie: $11,000 worth of old coins were found by a farmer plowing his field.

Bunkie: 3,000 silver coins with a value of $120,000 were found by a farmer plowing his corn field.

SAINT BERNARD PARISH

Arabi: In 1955, a man was having a lot graded on Perrin Drive in preparation for the building of his new house. After the equipment was shut down for the day and the workers departed the property, children in the area would begin finding gold coins in the freshly turned dirt. The man attempted to purchase some of the coins, but the children refused to sell any. The man hired a fellow with a metal detector to search the area. The fellow was unable to find a single coin. After the fellow departed the children returned and found more coins. The man who owned the property put a for sale sign on it and has refused to even pass the location ever since.

Chandeleur Island: It has been reported that in 1942 a fisherman found a large cache of Spanish pieces-of-eight near the northern tip of Chandeleur Island. The island was a favorite resting spot for pirates of all nations.

Chandeleur Island: In 1989 two Swedish cannons, dated between 1689 and 1750, were found near Chandeleur Island by a Biloxi, Mississippi, charter boat captain. It is believed that after several centuries of being covered with sand wave action from a hurricane exposed the cannons.

New Harbor Island: Several finds of coins have been reported on New Harbor Island. The island was frequented by pirates.

North Harbor Island: Coins have also been found on North Harbor Island. This island like the rest of the islands in Chandeleur Sound was often visited by pirates.

SAINT TAMMANY PARISH

Honey Island: Honey Island is located between the East and West Pearl Rivers, and can be reached by land at United States Interstate Highway 59. The eastern shore of the East Pearl River constitutes the Mississippi State border. It is estimated that as much as $4,000,000 was hidden within the Honey Island Swamp by James Copeland, Calico Dick, Jean Lafitte, John Murrell, Pierre Rameau, and others. A conservative estimate of the treasure found to date would have to be approximately $1,000,000, leaving treasure hunters around $3,000,000 to dream about.

Honey Island Swamp: In 1907 two hunters found an old chest containing more than $1,000 in pre 1830's Mexican coins.

Honey Island Swamp: It has been rumored that in 1943 a fisherman found a rusty old chain wrapped around a tree in the swamp. The fisherman followed the chain as it led into the water. After some effort he raised an iron chest from the water. The chest was taken away unopened and the contents were never made public, but was said to contain "just gold coins."

Honey Island Swamp: Over the years many finds of gold coins have been made and most of these have not been reported by the media. It is believed that these coins are washed free during the yearly spring flooding of the Pearl River which covers the Honey Island Swamp.

Covington: Hunters investigating an old abandon plantation home found more than they bargained for, almost $10,000 in pre-Civil War gold and silver coins. At the time the find was worth an estimated $60,000. Today it would be worth over $100,000.

Covington: Divers have found the remains of a sunken ship in a creek near Covington. To date they have brought up several cannon, a large amount of coins and other artifacts.

Madisonville: It has been reported that a treasure hunter searching for a mysterious $500,000 treasure has had at least some luck. The man found several gold coins and believes he is now on the right track. There was never a report about finding the $500,000.

TENSAS PARISH

Lake Bruin, Lakewood Plantation: The Lakewood Plantation was built in 1854, by Albert C. Watson. In 1861 Captain Watson withdrew $80,000 from the bank. He cached $30,000 in several locations on the grounds of his plantation and went off to join the Confederate Army. With the remaining $50,000, Watson outfitted his unit, known as Watson's Battery. After the war ended Watson returned to his home and found all but $5,000. In 1928, while working in the plantation garden, one of Watson's descendants found the last jar of coins containing $5,000 in pre-Civil War gold coins. Now that the entire $20,000 has been accounted for, new stories have spread that more is still buried at the plantation. This may have been caused in 1952, when yet another jar containing $5,000 in pre-Civil War gold coins was reported found. The Lakewood Plantation is located on Lake Bruin Road, Louisiana State Highway 606.

Waterproof: A iron bound, wooden keg filled with Spanish coins was plowed up on the plantation of James Miller.

TERREBONNE PARISH

Caillou Island: Over the years several treasures have been found on the island, but it is believed that the main treasure still awaits. In 1851, $20,000 in Spanish gold doubloons was found.

A second treasure of $2,000 in Spanish doubloons was said to have been found. Both of these treasures have been attributed to Jean Lafitte.

VERMILION PARISH

Pecan Island: In 1925 reports of a large treasure being found on Pecan Island started a gold rush resulting in person or persons unknown blowing up parts of the island with dynamite.

Abbeville: Two vases filled with gold were found near a swamp.

Abbeville: What has been called "a large hoard of silverware" was found in Abbeville. The discovery was made in 1906 and was part of a Civil War plantation cache.

Abbeville: A copper kettle filled with coins was discovered by workman repairing an old sidewalk in Abbeville. The kettle was found in 1955, but the source and amount of the coins is unknown.

WASHINGTON PARISH

Bogalusa: In 1977 a large cache of Civil War weapons and two kegs of silver coins were recovered from a closed in water well on a farm near Bogalusa. This cache was discovered by a professional treasure hunter.

WEST FELICIANA PARISH

Old Port Hudson: It was reported that in December of 1977 a large cache of Civil War weapons was found near Old Port Hudson. The cache consisted of many rare and exotic weapons, but was reported as being worth only $6,000. At today's prices (eighteen years later) that cache should be worth at least $100,000.

West bank of the Mississippi River: Two pots of gold were reported to have been found near the west bank of the Mississippi River, across from the Louisiana State Prison at Angola.

GULF OF MEXICO

In 1973, a shrimp boat crew from Mobile, Alabama, found $30,000 in Spanish silver coins in their nets. The coins have a value of approximately $60 each, making the haul worth $180,000.

CHAPTER III

JEAN LAFITTE

Jean Lafitte was born on April 22, 1782 in Port-au-Prince, Santo Domingo, now Haiti. The exact date of his death will most likely remain a mystery. Most sources list 1826 at Dzilam de Bravo (Silan), Yucatan, Mexico as the date and place of Lafitte's death. Some sources list his death in 1854 at Alton, Illinois. There are numerous mysteries surrounding the life and death of Jean Lafitte.

Lafitte was undoubtedly the most successful pirate who ever lived. There are thousands of treasure sites throughout Central and North America that are attributed to Jean Lafitte, and most may be true. It was the custom for the Pirate Captain to take a large portion of the booty from captured ships, with the remainder being split among the crew. In order to make room on the ship for more booty, the captain and crew would put to shore and use various sites to cache their individual treasures. This practice would alleviate the need to return to their base every time a ship was taken. It was not always feasible to return for the treasure, and it would be put off until the next time they were in the area. Some pirates were killed, some forgot the exact location of their treasure, and some for whatever reason could not return.

It is written that before coming to Louisiana, Jean Lafitte was a captain in the French Navy and a close friend of Napoleon Bonaparte. While serving in the navy his ship was captured by the English and Lafitte was imprisoned. Because of the treatment he received during his incarceration, Lafitte hated the British and vowed revenge.

Because the Spanish were responsible for the death of his first wife, Lafitte also hated the Spanish and vowed revenge.

In 1806 Jean Lafitte and his brother Pierre arrived in New Orleans aboard the *La Soeur Cheri* and opened a blacksmith shop on the corner of Bourbon and Saint Philip Streets. The shop was a cover for their smuggling operations. Jean Lafitte attempted to keep his life of piracy a secret and as such could learn what ships, as well as their cargos, were due in and out of the port. The pirates were based on Grand Terre Island and were under the command of Dominique You (Alexandre Frederic Lafitte), Renato "Oncle" (Uncle) Beluchai (Beluche, Bluche), Louis "Nez Coupe" (Split Nose) Chighizola, Paul Lacombe, Joni Benuit and Vincent Gambi. It did not take long before their association grew to over 5,000 men. At that time Grand Terre Island measured six miles in length and only three miles at its widest point and was only twenty-five miles from New Orleans. A messenger would be sent to Grand Terre with the news of shipping, and it was from this base that the pirates would conduct their raids.

Lafitte had several warehouses built to hold all the booty that began pouring in. One of the warehouses was at New Orleans, a second at Barataria, the third at Donaldsonville and the fourth warehouse was located at "The Temple."

The Temple, was located at the mouth of Bayou Des Allemands, along the shores of Lake Salvadore, approximately twenty miles from New Orleans. Originally the mound was a Chawasha Indian burial mound. The Temple received its name because of the large quantity of human bones found on the island, and it was believed that the mound was the site of a sacrificial alter.

It did not take long before the residences of New Orleans were mesmerized by Jean's persona. He wore the right clothes, said all the right things and most importantly, he moved in all the right circles.

Shortly after his arrival Jean Lafitte established himself as a gambler in New Orleans. Legend has it that he won $40,000 in gold from Colonel John R. Grimes, a New Orleans attorney, and it was cached in the Barataria Bay area, just north of Lafitte's headquarters on Grand Terre Island.

Until 1810 the Lafitte brothers were only acting as representatives for the pirates. As the Baratarians prospered and grew in number, problems began to arise. The pirates split into several groups and began stealing from one another. The Baratarians were now living on three islands in the bay, Grande Terre, Grande Isle and Chenier Caminada, and each had its own leader and set of laws. In October 1810, a truce was declared, and Pierre Lafitte was called upon to bring unity to the area. Pierre was the logical choice since he was the older, and stronger of the brothers. When Pierre suffered a stroke which left the left side of his face paralyzed, Jean became the man of the hour. Jean met with leaders of the respective pirate crews and became their leader or "Boz" (boss). Lafitte established a uniform set of laws which everyone had to sign. He then departed for Carthagena where he obtained letters of marque, thereby making the pirates privateers.

Once Lafitte's secret was made public most of the people were surprised, but not as surprised as Lafitte, himself. The people became more enchanted with him. He could at last go public.

Most of Lafitte's interest was in slaves. In 1804 when the importation of slaves became illegal in the Louisiana Territory, the going rate for slaves ranged between $200 and $1,000 each. Lafitte's slave market was a few miles southwest of New Orleans at The Temple and was run by Dominique You.

Most of the other goods such as clothes, hardwares and household items were smuggled into New Orleans by the pirates and sold at the French Market. Lafitte was filling a demand for a shortage that he and his crew helped to create. Also, the pirates were able to sell the goods for less then market value, because they did not have to pay customs charges and had very little overhead. The pirates, therefore, were getting more money by selling most of their booty and, thereby, enjoying greater profits. Everyone was happy . . . well, almost.

Lafitte, it was said, had his way with many of the women of New Orleans' upper class. In fact, he may have had his way with the wife of Governor William Charles Cole Claiborne. It has been written that Lafitte and Mrs. Claiborne had rendezvoused at the plantation home of a mutual friend, Jean Noel d'Estrehan. Governor Claiborne was determined to run

Lafitte out of Louisiana. Claiborne offered a reward of $500 for the arrest of Jean Lafitte and had Pierre Lafitte thrown into jail. In turn, Jean Lafitte offered a $1,500 reward for the head of Governor Claiborne.

On September 3, 1814, a British envoy approached Lafitte at his Barataria headquarters and offered him a Land Grant in North America, protection of his person and property, $30,000 in gold, and the rank of captain in the Royal Navy, if he would join them in the attack on New Orleans. Lafitte told the British that he would have to think over the offer. Lafitte then wrote Claiborne telling him of the British offer, enclosing the documents to prove his story, along with an offer to help defend the city. Claiborne refused Lafitte's offer.

With the help of some of the New Orleans elite Pierre Lafitte escaped from jail and returned to Barataria Bay. Claiborne increased the reward on Pierre to $1,000 and pushed for the destruction of the pirate stronghold.

On September 11, 1814, Lafitte received word that the order to attack the Baratarians was given and that Commodore Daniel T. Patterson of the United States Navy and Colonel George T. Ross, Commander of the 44th United States Infantry, were in route via the Mississippi River aboard six gunboats, a launch and the *Carolina*.

Lafitte began emptying his Barataria warehouse and sending munitions to The Temple. Most of the other valuables were loaded aboard ships. Jean and Pierre departed the island and Dominique was left in charge.

On September 16, 1814, Colonel Ross and Commodore Patterson's troops attacked Barataria for three days. Dominique You gave the order to retreat, and approximately 500 Baratarians escaped into the swamps. The remainder stayed with You. Without a shot being fired by the Baratarians, Dominique and 80 of his men surrendered and were taken prisoner. Patterson seized 26 ships and treasure with an estimated valued at that time of over $2,500,000. Upon Patterson's return to New Orleans he claimed all of the seized contraband for himself.

Again, Lafitte offered to help defend the city from the British attack. The avoidance of a conflict on Barataria coupled with Lafitte's offer to help defend the city may have made an impression on Claiborne. More likely, though, it was the pressure brought about by the citizens of New Orleans who liked Lafitte and knew that the British were preparing to attack the city at any time that made Claiborne change his mind. On October 30, 1814, Claiborne wrote to the United States Attorney General recommending clemency for Lafitte and his followers. This time Lafitte's offer was refused by General Andrew Jackson.

In a move of desperation, the District Attorney, John Randolph Grymes, and an unknown judge had Dominique You and the other Baratarians released from the Cabildo.

The British were started up the Mississippi River, and General Andrew Jackson, realizing the hopelessness of the situation without much needed munitions, finally accepted Lafitte's offer. Two artillery detachments were formed under the command of Dominique You and Renato Beluche. The other Baratarians were assigned to man the guns at Fort Petite Coquilles (little shells) at The Rigolets, Fort Saint John on Bayou Saint John, and Fort Saint Philip on the Mississippi River near its mouth. Lafitte was attached to Brigadier General Morgan guarding the southern approach through Barataria during the Battle of New Orleans. There is no record of any engagements involving Lafitte.

After the Battle of New Orleans, Lafitte and his men were pardoned by President Madison. Dominique You went from being a pirate to being a New Orleans politician which was an easy transition. Renato Beluche became an admiral in the Venezuelan Navy. Some of Lafitte's men became law abiding citizens of Barataria, but most eventually returned to piracy.

After Lafitte was pardoned he attempted to have the property seized by Patterson during the raid on Barataria returned. Lafitte had a lawsuit filed against the United States Government. During the time that the suit was in litigation, Patterson and Ross held an auction in contempt of the suit, and the property was sold for $1,500,000. Lafitte had no receipt for any of the seized property and eventually lost his lawsuit.

In April of 1816, it is believed that Jean Lafitte gathered up part of his fortune and returned to piracy. He began operating out of a base on Campeachy, now Galveston Island, Texas. During his tenure at Campeachy, Lafitte and his men are credited with the capture of over 100 Spanish ships and over two dozen ships of assorted nations including the United States. The prize capture of the Spanish ships was the *Santa Rosa*.

Lafitte and his crew attacked the *Santa Rosa* in Matagorda Bay, after removing $2,000,000 in silver, gold and jewels, sank the ship to dispose of all evidence of the attack. The treasure was taken first to Campeachy until it could be transferred to an inland site. Some sources say that the Spanish got word of the attack and dispatched 200 Mexican soldiers from San Antonio to retrieve the treasure. Lafitte entrusted Gasper Trammel to transport the booty taken from the *Santa Rosa* along with other accumulated treasure to Saint Louis, Missouri.

Trammel, accompanied by some of Lafitte's men, headed north with the wagons. The route taken would lead Trammel through Nacogdoches, Carthage, Marshall and Texarkana, Texas, and then on to Saint Louis. At Hendricks Lake, Harrison County, Texas, members of the wagon train observed the approach of the Mexican soldiers and pushed the six wagons containing the treasure into the lake before the Mexicans attacked. It is more than likely that the Mexican troops were just in the area and had no idea that Trammel was transporting the treasure. During the battle, the Mexicans killed Trammel and most of Lafitte's men and captured the rest of the wagon train. A witness to the battle saw two men escaping. Some sources say only one man escaped. There has been some evidence uncovered which shows that Lafitte had been shipping a lot of his treasure to Saint Louis, and that this was only the last of the many runs made by Trammel for Lafitte.

NOTE: In 1920, three silver bars were found at Hendricks Lake, lending credence to the story. Since then there have been numerous attempts to retrieve the treasure from Hendricks Lake. The Lake was even dredged in the 1950's, but nothing else has ever been reported found. It is believed that the treasure may have been removed by Lafitte or someone else. (See Chapter IV, Thomas Beale.)

By December 1, 1819, Lafitte's crew sunk a few too many American ships, namely the *Hampton Queen*, carrying $750,000 in gold and silver, and the *Helen Fry*, carrying $1,500,000 in assorted treasure. Once again, Lafitte ran afoul of the United States Government. Two of Lafitte's officers and sixteen men were captured while plundering a ship near the mouth of the Mississippi River. People everywhere were demanding that a stop be put to the piracy in the Gulf of Mexico.

On Saturday, January 7, 1821, the United States Navy warship *Enterprise* arrived at Campeachy. Lafitte was given three months to vacate Galveston. On Saturday, March 3, 1821, the *Enterprise* returned as promised.

Here stories vary. Some say Lafitte had everything of value placed in one location where it was divided equally among the entire commune. At 4:00 p.m. everyone left the island as Campeachy burned.

Other stories relate that Lafitte had his vast treasure loaded onto his ship, the *Pride*, and before the navy could fire a shot, Lafitte and his men burned the village to the ground. Lafitte boarded the *Pride* and sailed up the Lavaca River. When he could sail his ship no further, Lafitte unloaded his treasure and allowed his men to take as much as they could carry. Lafitte and two of his most trusted men stayed behind and buried the remainder of the treasure. Lafitte and the two men then walked in the direction of Austin, Texas. Just outside of Austin, both of Lafitte's men became very ill. Lafitte sought the aid of an Austin resident, and the two men were left in his care. Lafitte instructed the men to return to New Orleans once they had recovered and not to return for three years to the spot where the treasure had been buried. If after three years the treasure was still there, they could have it. The last thing Lafitte said to the men was that he was headed north of the Red River. Lafitte then departed into American History and disappeared as mysteriously as he arrived.

By 1823 England and the United States had united forces in an effort to drive all of the pirates from the Gulf of Mexico.

By 1825 there were no more privateers, and very few pirates were left in the Gulf of Mexico.

Most sources believe that Lafitte went to Central America and continued his life of piracy until his death in 1827. This story originated with the Indians of Central America. After the Battle of New Orleans several of Lafitte's men became pirate leaders in their own right. It is possible that one of Lafitte's men may have been the pirate who died in the Yucatan. There were numerous documented sightings of Jean Lafitte in Louisiana during the 1830's. These sightings were made by people who had known Lafitte personally for many years.

According to Lafitte's journals, he spread the stories of his own death, then changed his name to John Lafflin, married Emma Mortimore of Charleston, South Carolina and moved to Saint Louis, Missouri. Lafflin became a manufacture and dealer of gunpowder. His business was located at 29 North Water Street and his residence was for awhile at 24 Collins Avenue. John Lafflin died on Friday May 5, 1854 of pneumonia in Alton, Illinois. Could it be that Lafitte merely decided to enjoy the fruits of his labors and died as John Lafflin in his own bed at the age of 77?

JEAN LAFITTE TREASURE PROFILE

It has been estimated that Lafitte may have cached as much as $100,000,000 between the years of 1806 and 1821. Since that time it is doubtful that as much as $4,000,000 has ever been reported found. If Lafitte would have lived to be 177 years old, he could not have spent it all.

Lafitte did not keep maps of all his caches, but he did keep journals of his activities. The Journals were translated from French and published in 1958 by Vantage Publishing Company.

The original journals and his Bibles are in the Sam Houston Regional Library and Research Center at Liberty, Texas. What is also interesting is that before the journals were translated into English, two of the pages were removed by an unknown person. The two missing pages were said to contain a description of Lafitte's hidden treasures.

NOTE: If you are thinking of acquiring a copy of The Journal of Jean Lafitte, it was reprinted by Dogwood Press, Woodville, Texas, in 1994. The journal is based on fact, but I believe it to be a fraud. The last entry made by Jean Lafitte was on Monday, December 2nd, 1850, and had predictions of many major events that occurred between that date and the date it was published in 1958. There were no predictions of anything after 1958. Among the entries of Tuesday, December 1, 1846, Lafitte writes, "Engraved on Silver Coins is the Sacred inscription: In God We Trust. But illiterate citizens are taught to adore money and blindly neglect the laws of humanity..." The Congressional Act of April 22, 1864, was the first to authorize the motto "In God We Trust." There was never a coin issued with the motto "In God We Trust," before 1864. Lafitte died in 1854, ten years before the first coin appeared with that motto.

It has been reasoned that Lafitte converted the receipts received for his slave trade into silver and gold and made numerous cashes within a $40,000 to $60,000 range. This theory is based on facts. Several treasures believed to have been caches by Lafitte have been recovered, and they all fit into a pattern or profile of a minor Lafitte treasure. All the coins date between 1765 and 1810. All of the treasures were within two sailing days of Barataria. It seems that Lafitte took a small sloop and went off alone. He was never away for more then four days, usually only a day or two. The area of these caches would have been along the Gulf of Mexico between Galveston, Texas, and Pensacola, Florida.

It would be difficult to profile a major Lafitte treasure because there may only be one ever reported found. The dates of the gold and silver coins would be in all likelihood between 1765 and 1817. The amount would have to be at least $290,000, the smallest amount known to be cached by Lafitte. This cache was made somewhere between Bay Saint Louis, Mississippi and Barataria. A major Lafitte treasure cache would most likely contain jewels.

CALCASIEU PARISH

Big Lake: Once called Calcasieu Lake, Big Lake has been an area of many searches for Lafitte's treasure. Nothing has ever been reported found on any of the islands in this area.

Contraband Bayou: This area has long been the site of many treasure hunts, due to the fact that Lafitte was an often visitor to the area. Lafitte was said to have held auctions along the banks of the bayou, and that he had a base on Contraband Bayou.

One story was told by a former slave named Wash. It seems that Wash observed three of Lafitte's men remove a portion of treasure from a large grassy knoll in a wooded area near Contraband Bayou. Only two men departed the area, using the third man's horse to transport two sacks of treasure. The third man was found dead in the bayou and was buried on the same knoll where the treasure was found. It is not known if all the treasure was ever removed.

Hackberry Island: Located south of Lake Charles, Hackberry Island has been mentioned as a Lafitte treasure site, though nothing has ever been reported found.

Iowa: The site of the Old LeBleu Plantation is a location given by many as a Lafitte treasure site. It seems that Lafitte was known to visit the plantation and use the barn for clandestine meetings. Arsene LeBleu was a retired pirate and close friend of Lafitte's. The plantation is located where the Old Spanish Trail crosses the Calcasieu River. Lafitte was said to have stated that he had left part of his treasure in the care of LeBleu.

Lake Charles: A log hut that is rumored to have been built for Jean Lafitte is believed to be the key to another treasure site. Some stories claim that Lafitte was at this site as a Spanish war ship approached, while other stories state that Lafitte was being pursued by an American gunboat. Lafitte ordered the treasure and cannons removed from his ship and the ship scuttled. The treasure was then buried between three Oak trees which once stood in front of the hut and a small fort was constructed from a nearby shell mound. This treasure has never been reported found.

Lafitte was a regular visitor of Charles and Catherine LeBleu Sallier, sometimes called Savoyard, the man for whom the lake and city are named. It was Sallier who had the cabin built for Lafitte. The site of the old hut may be at 204 Sallier Street, the present site of the Imperial Calcasieu Museum. If you are in the area, the museum has an excellent Lafitte exhibit including a copy of his journal. After your visit to the museum step out back and look at the Sallier Oak, believed to be over three hundred years old. I do not think the proprietors of the museum allow digging on their grounds, but one can dream.

The site of Lafitte's makeshift fort was called "Money Hill" by the locals, and was said to be near the old Calcasieu River Bridge built around 1920. Also in front of the fort was a very low spot that always held water. This was referred to as "Dead Man's Lake." The cabin was very near the fort and may have long since disappeared.

Another story states that two Frenchmen found two chests filed with silver and gold in the wreckage of the scuttled ship. The two men moved the chest down the Calcasieu River to Contraband Bayou and re-buried them, but never reclaimed them.

Starks: Jean Lafitte is said to have made two treasure caches in the area of Starks. One cache consisted of Spanish gold doubloons, and the other cache consisted of a mixture of Spanish gold, silver and jewels.

Vinton: Nibletts Bluff is located 8 miles west of Vinton on Louisiana State Highway 3063. Rumors have persisted for years that one of Lafitte's treasures of $1,000,000 in gold, silver and jewels is buried within the area of Nibletts Bluff under a Gum Tree. The value of this treasure today would be more like $100,000,000.

Could this treasure be Lafitte's "Napoleon Treasure?" The story goes like this: A close friend of Lafitte's, Michel de Riviere, adopted the name of the man who reared him, Pithon. Eventually Michel Pithon settled in Calcasieu Parish and told of Lafitte's attempt to rescue Napoleon before he was exiled to Saint Helena. Pithon said that Lafitte was unable to rescue Napoleon, but was able to bring most of Napoleon's treasure to Louisiana. Pithon purchased a slave named Catalan from Lafitte. The slave had been one of Lafitte's cooks and may have told Pithon the general location of Lafitte's "Napoleon Treasure" cache. It is believed by some people that this is the treasure buried at Nibletts Bluff. It is also believed by others that Napoleon's treasure may have been buried in Mississippi.

There is another version of this story. The tale passed down among the long time families of the area is that Jean Lafitte did not remove the "Napoleon treasure" from the ship. The ship was scuttled and its treasure sent to the bottom of Old River.

CAMERON PARISH

Coca Island: $900,000 in silver is said to have been buried by Jean Lafitte. The cache was said to have been made in two caskets. It is believed that a map to this treasure was at one time in the hands of a man named Clarke.

NOTE: There is also a second treasure allegedly on Coca Island, said to be $1,000,000 in gold ingots. This treasure cache was made by some unknown pirates.

To date only $1,500 in gold doubloons has ever been reported found on Coca Island, and since neither cache is alleged to contain gold doubloons, there is reason to believe that more may exist.

Grand Chenier Island: In 1930 a brick vault was found which many believed once housed a rather large Lafitte treasure cache. Nearby there was a very large oak tree with what was described as treasure signs carved in the trunk. If a treasure was recovered from this location, it was never reported.

Johnson Bayou: Near the early homestead of Henry Griffith is reportedly the spot of another Lafitte treasure cache.

Kelso Island: The site of a $35,000,000 Lafitte treasure cache is believed to be on Kelso Island. The treasure consists of 70,000 gold Spanish doubloons and is said to be buried on the island near the Calcasieu, Cameron Parish line.

Lake Misere: The site of another Jean Lafitte sunken treasure ship is Lake Misere, north of Chenier Ridge near a shell bank.

Sabine River: It is believed that members of Lafitte's crew buried several individual caches in the area of the mouth of the Sabine River. Lafitte allegedly used this site to make emergency repairs to one of his ships. The repairs took several weeks. Some of these caches are rumored to have been found by a farmer in the area and reburied near his home.

EAST BATON ROUGE PARISH

Little Chenier: What has been called an authentic Lafitte treasure map is believed to be in the area of Little Chenier. It is not known who has the map or how it came to be in their possession.

East Baton Rouge Parish: The bluffs of the Mississippi River near Baton Rouge is yet another alleged site of a $1,000,000 Lafitte treasure.

IBERIA PARISH

Jefferson Island: Some treasure has been found on Jefferson Island, but it is not known for certain which came first, the story of a Lafitte treasure or the treasure its self.

After removing $4,000,000 in gold, silver and jewels and then sinking the *Santa Elena*, Lafitte put to shore on Jefferson Island and buried the treasure.

Grand Coteau in Saint Landry Parish has also been suggested as a burial site for the *Santa Elena* treasure.

JEFFERSON PARISH

Grand Terre Island and Grand Isle: Because of the fact that Lafitte operated from Barataria Bay, the two islands are believed to hold many treasures. It is believed that the Lafittes alone left $7,000,000 at Grand Terre when they departed for Galveston, Texas. The islands have been the site of many searches over the years, and most sources say nothing has ever been reported found. It is, however, rumored that between $1,500,000 and $4,000,000 in treasure has been removed from the area. Most treasure hunters think that as much as $4,500,000 in treasure awaits some fortunate person. Remember there is no such thing as a hunted out location.

Caminada Pass: For years the story has circulated of a Jean Lafitte treasure cache of reportedly $1,500,000 being buried at Caminada Pass.

NOTE: It is rumored that treasure hunters have found $1,600,000 in Spanish gold doubloons at Caminada Pass. The parties involved did not wish to be known, but they believe the find is only part of a much larger cache. It has been estimated that over the years more then $4,000,000 in gold, silver and jewels have been found in the area of Barataria Bay alone.

Lafitte: It has long been rumored that treasure had been buried within the cemetery at Lafitte. In all likelihood this was started in all likelihood because of the pirate activity in Barataria Bay. The cemetery is located on an Indian mound making it a prime site for a cache. Some treasure has been removed from the cemetery and more is suspected hidden among the graves.

NOTE: The last time I was at the cemetery it was in danger of eroding away and iron coffins could be seen at the waters edge. I would hope that steps have been made to prevent any further deterioration of the cemetery. Also, it is illegal to disturb this site.

LIVINGSTON PARISH

Amite River and Bayou Manchac: Across the Amite River from the site of Old Galvez Town, one of Jean Lafitte's treasure ships is rumored to have sunk with $2,000,000 in gold and silver. There is no record of any treasure being removed from this wreck.

Another version of this story is that Lafitte removed the treasure and buried it near the mouth of the Amite River.

ORLEANS PARISH

New Orleans, 941 Bourbon Street: Lafitte's blacksmith shop is thought to be the site of another treasure. It is believed that a tunnel was built from the shop to the residence at the rear of the shop, should the Lafitte brothers need to escape capture. In this tunnel, it is claimed, lies one of the Lafitte's treasures.

NOTE: Growing up in the area, I find it impossible to believe the tunnel story. The city of New Orleans is five feet below sea level. If you have ever tried to dig a hole in New Orleans you would know that it fills with water. Because of the water table, people are buried above the ground, coffins pop out of the ground.

New Orleans: The story of the 1810 wreck of one of Lafitte's ships has been around since the 1950's. The ship was said to be carrying $1,500,000 and was sunk during a storm or was scuttled, depending on which story you have heard. In an area between Irish Bayou and the railroad bridge to the west along the shore of Lake Pontchartrain, gold and silver discs were found in the late 1950's and early 1960's after storms. It is possible that in this case the treasure came first and the story of a sunken Lafitte ship followed. (See Chapter X, Civil War Treasures, The New Orleans Mint Treasure.)

PLAQUEMINES PARISH

Calillan Island: $1,000,000 was said to have been cached by Lafitte on Calillan Island.

English Turn: It has been written that Jean Lafitte buried a treasure along a bayou that leads from English Turn to Barataria Bay.

SAINT BERNARD PARISH

Lake Borgne: An uncharted island in Lake Borgne is the reported resting spot of another Lafitte treasure cache. The treasure had a value of $500,000 at the time of its burial. It is quite possible that it was buried on one on the many Indian mounds within the area.

Lake Borgne, Malheureux Island: Stories persist of a $2,000,000 cache being made by Lafitte and his men on Malheureux Island. Since Malheureux Island can not be found on most maps, over the years the story has changed to the cache being made on an uncharted island off of Malheureux Point.

NOTE: If you have ever looked at an old map and compared it to a new map you can see only some similarities. Old maps were usually made by taking sightings of the stars, putting dots on paper and later connecting the dots. These sightings were sometimes made from the deck of a rolling ship. Needless to say old maps were not very accurate. Over the years equipment improved and so did the maps. Along came the Wright brothers and Mr. Eastman and the advent of aerial photography. During World War II, photographs of areas were laid out like a giant puzzle and maps of an area were made without actually setting foot on the ground. In 1966 the Pageos satellite was launched, allowing pictures of greater areas to be photographed at one time. In 1976 Landsat satellites allowed more precise locating of points on the Earth's surface. One may purchase a hand held, battery operated, Loran receiver that will pinpoint your position using the correct longitude and latitude almost anywhere on Earth. Maps are now generated by computers and the next step may be a hand held holographic map.

Also the names of places have been changed over the years. Should it happen that you were the first person to be in the area you could name a place anything you wanted. You could name places for your favorite saints, kings, bankers or your brother-in-law. Twenty years later someone from another country comes along making a new and improved map. If no one is there to tell him the name you had chosen for the location, he names it what he wants and shapes the world as he sees it. It must have been fun participating in the making of history.

Another reason for name changes could be language differences. If you were looking for Bay Spirito Sante on a map, would you look for Holy Ghost Bay, Holy Spirit Bay, Saint Spirit Bay or Chandeleur Sound? When the Spanish explorer Alonzo Alvarez de Pineda found the Mississippi River he named it "Rio del Espiritu Santo," River of the Holy Spirit, and the large body of water near it "Bay del Espiritu Santo." When the French came along the name of the bay was changed to "Bay Spirito Sante," and the rivers name was changed to the Mississippi. When the next Frenchman came along it was on the day of "The Feast of Candlemas," and he named the island and sound Chandeleur in honor of the feast.

So, where is Malheureux Island? Malheureux Island would probably be Grand Island in the Mississippi Sound. After checking old and new charts of the area, it was determined that Malheureux Island appeared on charts made in 1815 as a large island off of Point Claire. To confuse matters more, Malheureux Point did not appear on the 1815 charts. It does appear on the newer charts but on the other side of Lake Borgne and could possible have been called Point Saint Malo on the 1815 chart. Grand Island was not on the charts of 1815, but is on the newer charts in the approximate location of where Malheureux Island would have been. Grand Island has been searched for other reasons, but no known attempts have been made since the new age of metal detectors. Grand Island would be a very good place to check on a sunny winter day.

SAINT CHARLES PARISH

Destrahan, d'Estrehan Plantation: Jean Noel d'Estrehan was a wealthy merchant and good friend of the Lafitte brothers. Jean Lafitte is said to have buried one of his many treasures here. The treasure was buried in 1814 and was said to be $40,000 in gold, silver and jewels. It is also said that the ghost of Jean Lafitte haunts the plantation house. The d'Estrehan Plantation is often referred to as the only site of a documented Jean Lafitte treasure.

The Destrehan Plantation home is located at 9999 River Road, Louisiana State Highway 48, approximately four and one half miles west of the junction at Louisiana State Highway 50. In 1972 the plantation was donated to the River Road Historical Society and is now open to the public.

Des Allemands: It has been reported that Jean Lafitte buried a treasure cache valued at $400,000, near the junction of Bayou Des Allemands, and United States Highway 90.

Lake Cataouatche: Jean Lafitte is said to have also made a treasure cache where Cataouatche Bayou joins with Lake Cataouatche.

Lake Salvadore: Between Lakes Salvador and Cataouatche lies Couba Island. It is believed that Lafitte may have made several treasure caches on Couba Island.

Lake Salvadore: The Temple was located at the mouth of Bayou Des Allemands along the shores of Lake Salvadore and was used by the Lafitte brothers as a storehouse for treasure. It has long been suspected that many treasure caches were made on this island.

SAINT JAMES PARISH

Vacherie: The Valcour Aime Plantation is located off of Louisiana State Highway 18 near the Oak Alley Plantation. The Refinery Plantation was built in the late 1700's by Don Francisco Aime. It is said that Lafitte cached a treasure of $50,000 somewhere on the plantation. The mansion was burned to the ground in 1920, but the site is marked with a historical marker.

SAINT LANDRY PARISH

Sunset: The Chretien Point Plantation has been given as the location of several Jean Lafitte treasure caches. It has been said that Lafitte and Hippolyte Chretien were the best of friends and that Lafitte was a frequent visitor to the plantation. Hippolyte's son, Hippolyte II, is rumored to have buried $625,000 at this site. Felicite, the wife of Hippolyte II, is also rumored to have made a Treasure cache or two. The plantation is located three miles southwest of Sunset. From Sunset, drive west on Louisiana State Highway 93 to Louisiana State Highway 356 (Bristol-Bosco Road) and then turn right. After approximately 100 yards, turn right again onto Chretien Point Road. The plantation is located approximately one mile down this road on the left.

SAINT MARY PARISH

Bayou Teche: At the mouth of Bayou Teche was the wreck of one of Lafitte's treasure ships. During periods of unusually low tides, parts of the superstructure could be seen lying just beneath the water. Over the years sand began to collect in and around the wreck and eventually an island was formed. Today the ship is completely under ground.

NOTE: This was the first treasure story that I ever remember being told, and comes from my grandfather Captain John Edward Stinson via my grandmother Marcus Carter "Dinkey" Stinson.

SAINT TAMMANY PARISH

Honey Island: Jean Lafitte is said to have buried one of his many treasures on Honey Island. This could have been the Napoleon Bonaparte treasure, also rumored to be buried in Mississippi's Hancock County.

TERREBONNE PARISH

Caillou Island: This island is reported to be the location of another Jean Lafitte treasure. Over the years several treasures have been found, but it is believed that the main treasure still awaits. In 1851, $20,000 in Spanish doubloons were found. Another time $2,000, also in Spanish doubloons, was said to have been found. Both of these treasures have been attributed as once belonging to Jean Lafitte.

Isle Dernier: It has been reported that the spoils from the Spanish treasure ship *Laguna Roja* were buried on the Isle Dernier. The island has been searched many times over the years, but if any part of the $1,250,000 in silver was ever found, it was not reported.

Timbalier and East Timbalier Islands: The two islands were used at one time or another by pirates, and it is believed that Lafitte and his crew cached some of their treasures here. Though searched many times, there have not been any finds reported.

VERMILION PARISH

Pecan Island: Always a favorite spot for treasure hunters, the island is reported to be another site of a Lafitte treasure. It has been said that Lafitte stated he visited the island shortly after removing $500,000 in treasure from the *Reya del Mar*. Also mentioned was an "oak-covered ridge."

NOTE: When Pecan Island was first explored, the ground was covered with human bones. The Island is believed to have been used as an Indian burial ground, but all of those bones being found on the island may have been the reason for the following story.

As the story goes, one of Lafitte's crews captured a small-pox-infected Spanish treasure ship. The ship and its crew were taken to Pecan Island. A short time after reaching the island the crews of both ships, along with the Indians who lived on the island, came down with small-pox. It was not long before all but one of Lafitte's crew and one Indian were the only two people who had not died from the disease.

The two men attempted to cross the marsh to Grand Chenier. Only the Indian reached the French settlement. The Indian could not speak French, but after he learned the language the story was passed on.

Pecan Island: One of Lafitte's treasure ships sank just west of Pecan Island. It has been said that over the years, because of the ship trapping sand and silt, the wreck now lies under the western side of the island.

Pecan Island: There has been an unconfirmed report that two farmers found a treasure chest containing Spanish coins, lending some credence to the islands treasure stories.

NOTE: There may be some confusion caused by the fact that there is also a Little Pecan Island in Cameron Parish. Little Pecan Island is part of the Rockefeller Wildlife Refuge and may in fact be a Lafitte treasure site. The wreckage of the Spanish merchant ship *El Nuevo Constant* was found just offshore and artifacts can be seen at the Rockefeller Wildlife Refuge Visitors' Center.

Schooner Island: Legend has it that Schooner Island received its name because one of Lafitte's ships was scuttled there and the island formed around the sunken ship.

Vermillion Bay: Lafitte is said to have made a treasure cache near the mouth of the Vermillion River. Before Lafitte could return to reclaim his treasure, a flood washed his markers away.

White Lake: Somewhere along the shores of White Lake, Lafitte and his crew constructed a vault of ballast stones. The vault was said to have been filled with Spanish gold, silver, and jewels.

In 1908, a hunter discovered the vault and removed several of the gold doubloons. The hunter then returned to his home in order to enlist the aid of a few friends. With the doubloons as proof, the hunter had no trouble finding help or friends. By the time everything needed was obtained, it was dark. As the men awaited daylight, most no doubt, had figured out at least one way to spend his fortune.

At first light the party was on the water, and by eight o'clock the site was spotted. The hunter was sure it was the spot, just as sure as he was about the next ten spots. For several weeks the hunter made trips to White Lake, but he could never again find the stone vault.

Wine Island: This site is believed to contain another Lafitte treasure. This cache was valued at $750,000.

UNKNOWN PARISH

In 1851, a Mister Newell aided an old sailor and in return was given a map. The map was said to be of a Lafitte treasure cache. Newell died and his son began a search for the treasure that lasted his lifetime. The map was alleged to be of an island in the Gulf of Mexico off the Louisiana coast. The island had no name which made the task impossible, especially at a time when metal detectors had not yet been invented. While still searching, young Newell died during a storm, at which time, it is believed, the map was lost forever.

Lake Pontchartrain: Legend has it that in 1810 one of Lafitte's ships sank somewhere in Lake Pontchartrain during a sudden storm. It was supposedly loaded with $1,725,000 in gold.

Catouche Bayou: Rumors persist of a letter written by Jean Lafitte which tells of a $250,000 treasure consisting of Spanish gold and silver coins somewhere along Catouche Bayou.

SHAKE YOUR FAMILY TREE AND MAYBE A PIRATE WILL FALL OUT

The following is a list of known officers, associates and financial backers of Jean Lafitte. If you find a member of your family on this list, you may have a treasure map laying around the old homestead.

A

Andre Abelard, John Amigone (Captain), Pierre Ampere (Captain), Antoine Angelette, Antonio Angelo (Captain), Jules Arceneaux (Agent), Benito De Ariza (Agent), John B. Arnaud (Agent), Salvator Artique, Louis De Arury (Agent).

B

Alexandre Barrival, Manuel Bazo (Captain), Ellis Polk Beanne (Agent), Antoine Beaudelaire (Captain), Antoine Beluchai or Beluche or Bluche, (Captain), Felix Beluchai or Beluche or Bluche (Captain), Reyne "Oncle" Beluchai or Beluche or Bluche (Captain), Henri Bentley, Joni Benuit (Captain), Jules Beratte, Daldir Berret (Captain), Irygoyen Berretera (Captain), John Betabcourt (Captain), James Black (Captain), John Blanque (Advisor, Financier), Joseph Bonaparte (Agent, Advisor), Antoine Bormette, Jacques Bornier, James Bowrie, John Bowrie, Francois Boysnet (Captain), Ernest Bramlit (Captain), Louis Brion (Agent, Financier), Antoine Bronte (Carpenter), John Brossiere (Captain), Joseph Broutin (Lawyer), Narcisse Broutin (Advisor), James Brown (Captain), Alexandre La Bruyere.

C

Pierre Cadet (Captain), James Campbell (Captain), James Cannon, Jules Cartier (Captain), John Caurrier (Carpenter), John Celard (Captain), John Champlain (Captain), Ross Chapman, Francois Chevraud, Louis P. Chenier, Louis "Nez Coupe" (Split Nose) Chighizola (Captain), James Clark (Captain), Joseph Clemente (Captain), Amon Clozelle (Captain), William Cochrane (Captain), Auguste Commines (Captain), Alcida Gervin Conchol, John Constant (Captain), John M. Converse (Carpenter), Andre Como Coppee, Antoine Corbiere (Captain), Antoine Cordier, Sevren Courtais, John Cousins, Tomas Cox (Captain).

D

Alexandre Daguerre (Captain), Louis Dalhier, John Davez, Auguste Davezac (Advisor, Agent), Jose DeHuerrera, Jean and/or John Desfarges (Captain), John Irenne Deveraux, Charles Dickinson, Antoine Dubois (Captain), John Ducoing (Captain), Abner L. Duncan (Agent), Vincent Dupare, Francois Dupuis (Agent), Antoine Durieux (Captain), Louis Durieux (Captain), John Dutrieux, Gustave Duval (Captain).

E-F

Evan Epps, Raymond Espagnol, also known as Raymon Vagnol (Captain), John Fannette (Agent), John Faquare, John Farrel (Captain), Octave Fenelon, Claude Forain (Captain), David De Forrest or Fores (Agent, Financier), John Leal De France (Captain), Aurelio Fuentes (Captain).

G

John Gallardo (Captain), Vincent "Johnny" Gambi or Gambai (Captain), someone known only as Garrot (Financier), Manuel Guerra Garcia, Jose Gasparilla (Captain), Henry Geme (Captain), John Gentille (Captain), Pierre Gilotte, John Giovannini (Agent), Nicholas Girod (Financier), Paul Gounod (Captain), Herman Grammaton (Captain), Nunzio Granato, Andre Grannette (Captain), Troyan Gravier (Captain), John Grimes (Lawyer, Financier), Pierre Gual (Captain/Doctor/Lawyer), John Guerin (Captain), someone known only as Guestier (Financier), John De Gutierrez (Captain).

H

William Hall (Captain), John Hamette (Captain), Wade Hampton (Captain), Jose Manuel De Herrera (Officer), John Hervien, Calvin Hillman (Captain, Financier), Claude Hudspeth,

Samuel Huette (Captain), John A. Humbert (Advisor, "Principal Officer").

I-J

Louis Iturribarria (Captain), Jose De Iuana (Captain), Eugene De Jammes, Michel J. Joffre, Rene' Joffre (Captain), Robert Johnson or Johnston (Captain), Etienne Evan Jones (Agent), John R. Jones (Captain), John Juanillio (Captain).

K-L

John Kluson, James De LaBorde (Captain), Reyle Lacassier (Captain), Paul Lacombe (Captain), Alexander Frederic Lafitte, also known as Dominique You, Alexander Youx, Captain Alexander, Generals Jontelle, Johnston, and Jossenet (Captain), Jean Lafitte, also known as Theodore Lucas, William Whiteridge, and John Lafflin (Pirate King), Pierre Lafitte, also known as Ricardo De Leon (Captain), Barthelemy Lafo, (Captain), Pierre LaMaison, Edward LaPorte (Captain), Eugene De LaPorte (Captain), James De LaPorte (Agent), Jean De LaPorte (Captain), Jerome De LaPorte (Captain), John De LaPorte, Arsene L. Latour, also known as John Williams (Agent), Pierre Clement Laussat (Advisor), Benjamine Laveau, Antoine Laverge, Arsene Lebeau (Captain), John L. Leclerc (Agent), Constant LeClercq, Clemente Lellande (Captain), Pierre Liguet (Captain), Rafel De Lisa (Captain), Francis Little (Captain, Son-in-law), John Little (Captain), Edward Livingston (Lawyer, Financier), Antoine L'Lallemande, Charles Lominne (Captain), Juan Lopez, Manuel Lopez (Captain), Louis Louaillier (Advisor).

M

Euthelere Maire (Captain), Laurent Maire (Captain), Pierre La Maison (Captain), Bernard Mandeville, Edouard Marcelin, Henri Marguere (Captain), Bernard Marigny (Advisor), John Marotte (Captain), Jose A. Martina or Martino (Captain), John

Masaleri (Captain), John Mayier, William McClure, John McGhee, Gregory McGregor (Agent), John McHenry (Captain), Polito Medina (Captain), William Mitchell (Captain), Antoine M. De Montaque, Pierre Morel (Lawyer), Manuel Moreno (Captain), Gerald Mortimore (Captain).

N-O-P

Fransis Neely (Captain), Louis Noel, Vincent Nolte (Agent), Henri Corne Nunez, Philippe Orozco, Herman Ortiz (Captain), Henry Peire, John Pereneau (Captain), Lucia Perez (Captain), John Perez (Carpenter), Manuel Perrin (Captain), Henry Perry, Louis Philippe, John M. Picornelli or Picornell, Jesse Pina (Carpenter), Antoine Piromeace (Captain), Antoine Pironeaux (Agent), Joseph De Place, Laurens Pages Ponsard, Martin Pouse (Captain).

R

Angel Raballo, John Antoine Ranchier, Raymond Ranchier, George Ratti, also known as George Brown, Theodore Rawlins (Captain), Eugene Renard (Captain), Andre Renaud, Vincent Rensand (Captain), John Reynier, Andre Rieux, Francois De Rieux (Captain), Francois De Rieuvre (Agent), Francois Rigaud (Captain), Andre Robin, John Rodofo, Joseph Roffignac (Advisor, Agent), Rewnne Roland, Nicholas Roquette (Agent), James Rousselin (Captain), John B. C. Rousselin (Captain), Pierre Rousselin (Agent), John Guerre De Rueda, Francois Rugaud.

S

Dumay Saint Martin (owned an interest in four of Lafitte's vessels, and received a percentage of their captures), Joachim Sautas, John Sauvinet (Agent, Financier), Antoine De Savarier, Jules Sedonier, J. S. Seleik (Captain), Antoine Sennette, Henri Seybasdier, Henri Chez Seymore, Pierre Sicard (Captain),

Daniel Smith, John B. Soulize, Alexandre Saint Elmo, John Stelsas.

T

Pierre Terrain (Captain), Andre Thiacus (Iron Worker), Ignace Thiacus (Iron Worker), John Thiacus (Agent), Jules Thiacus (Captain, Financier), Dennis Thomas, Eugene De Thomas, Ephraim Thompkins, Tyron Thompson, Isaac Tillette, Gregory Toeye (Captain), Joseph De Toledo, Francois Tomas or Thomas (Captain), Richard Touzias (Captain), John Trickert, John Tucker (Agent).

V-W

Jose Valliert, John West (Agent), Samuel Williams (Advisor, Lieutenant), Andre Whitman, John Whitman, Lancer Woodring.

The game is worth the candle and we will play it to the end.

Thomas Beale, 1822.

CHAPTER IV

THOMAS BEALE

The following story of buried treasure and puzzling codes comes with a warning from the unknown author of The Beale Papers, Containing Authentic Statements Regarding the Treasure Buried in 1819 and 1821, Near Bufords, in Bedford County, Virginia, and Which Has Never Been Recovered with good reason:

Before giving the papers to the public, I would say a word to those who may take an interest in them, and give them a little advise, acquired by bitter experience. It is, to devote only such time as can be spared from your legitimate business to the task, and if you can spare no time, let the matter alone. Should you disregard my advise, do not hold me responsible that the poverty you have courted is more easily found than the accomplishment of your wishes, and I would avoid the sight of another reduced to my condition. Nor is it necessary to devote the time that I did to this matter, as accident alone, without the promised key, will ever develop the mystery. If revealed by accident, a few hours devoted to the subject may accomplish results which were denied to years of patient toil. Again, never, as I have done, sacrifice your own and your family's interests to what may prove an illusion; but, as I have already said, when your day's work is done, and you are comfortably seated by your good fire, a short time

devoted to the subject can injure no one, and may bring
its rewards.

By pursuing this policy, your interests will not suffer,
your family will be cared for, and your thoughts will not
be absorbed to the exclusion of other important affairs.
With this admonition, I submit to my readers the papers
upon which this narrative is founded.

Many have speculated as to the identity of the unknown
author of the <u>The Beale Papers . . .</u>, since its publication in 1885,
however, that is only one of the mysteries surrounding the Beale
Treasure.   Beale's story was at first confined to the Robert
Morriss family beginning in 1845. The unknown author learned
of the story in 1862 from Robert Morriss. In 1885 James B.
Ward had the story published for the author who wanted to
remain anonymous. Only a few of the books were ever sold,
and the print shop was burned to the ground by person or
persons unknown in order to prevent anyone else from ever
learning the story. After 110 years, only three of the original
copies are known to exist. Over the years Beale's story has been
told and retold. People have dug, dynamited and bulldozed the
area. Zillions of hours have been spent in trying to crack Beale's
code.   Today there are thousands of people in pursuit of
information regarding every aspect of the story with the hopes
that they will one day say, "I was the one who cracked the Beale
Cypher."

With all the effort spent on this pursuit more information has
been gained, but without the "key", the Beale treasure may be
lost forever. The unknown author felt that since he deciphered
the second code by accident, the other two codes would also be
solved by accident. Today the treasure would have a value of at
least $20,000,000. That is a lot of "candles" as Beale may have
put it.

Like Jean Lafitte, little is known about the life of Thomas J.
Beale. It has been said that his middle name was Jefferson, but
that seems to be only speculation and did not appear in print
until 1927. A few people who know the story say that Beale

never existed. They say that because a code using the Declaration of Independence is involved and the name Thomas Jefferson was used, the Beale papers must be fake. Thomas Jefferson was the author of the Declaration of Independence and coincidentally was fond of codes. Also, it is alleged that Beale was the name of the person who first brought word of the California gold strike and started the great Gold Rush of 1849. The gold rush would have been after Beale wrote to Morriss conferring the story, but before the papers were printed, thus making the papers a fake.

In The Journal of Jean Lafitte, Lafitte stated that he used codes. Lafitte further stated that the greatest and most sacred of all the documents ever composed and written by men were the great Declaration of Independence and the great Constitution of the United States. It has also been speculated that Thomas J. Beale was really an alias of Jean Lafitte's.

THE STORY UNFOLDS

In 1773, one Thomas J. Beale is born to Colonel Tavener Beale and Betty Hite Beale of Lynchburg, Virginia.

In 1790, the Beale family moves to Fincastle, Virginia. Fincastle is only twenty miles from the city of Montvale, formerly Bufords.

In 1806, Beale fights a duel and, believing he has killed the man, departs the Blue Ridge Mountains of Virginia with little or no money in his possession. Beale's destination is New Orleans, considered the fastest growing city at the time.

Some time after his arrival, Beale marries Celeste Grand Pierre (de Grandpre) and becomes the owner and operator of a small hotel on Chartres Street.

At approximately the same time, Jean Lafitte and his brother Pierre arrive in New Orleans and open a blacksmith shop not far from Beale's hotel.

(There were a lot of similarities between Beale and Lafitte. Both men were said to be tall, dark and handsome, usually in the company of beautiful women, well educated, likeable, often in trouble and rogues. Both Beale and Lafitte were over six feet tall with black hair and dark brown eyes.)

In 1814, Captain Thomas J. Beale is commissioned by the Governor of Louisiana, William Charles Cole Claiborne. During the Battle of New Orleans, Beale commands the military unit formally known as the New Orleans Rifleman of the Louisiana Militia. This unit is composed entirely of Louisiana citizens and best known as "Beale's Company Rifleman." During the Battle of New Orleans, Beale and his unit fight next to the Baratarian unit commanded by Dominique You.

(It is believed that between their arrivals in 1806 and the Battle of New Orleans a union may have been formed between Lafitte and Beale. What is almost certain is that they knew each other. What is most uncertain is where Beale acquired his wealth.)

In 1816, Lafitte departs Louisiana and returns to piracy, operating first out of Padre Island, Texas and later at Campeachy, now Galveston Island, Texas.

In 1817, Lafitte entrusts Gasper Trammel and several of his own men to transport $3,000,000 in gold, silver and jewels to Saint Louis, Missouri.

As the wagon train reaches Hendricks Lake, Harrison County, Texas, members of the train observe the approach of 200 Mexican soldiers. Before the Mexicans can attack, the six wagons containing the treasure are pushed into the lake where they quickly sink. During the battle Trammel and most of his men are killed and the remaining wagons in the train are captured. A witness to the battle saw one man escaping. Some stories relate that two men escaped. (Could Beale have been with Trammel on this ill-fated trip and escaped? It was not uncommon for members of New Orleans society to accompany Lafitte and his crew on their raids. Many went for the money, others for the thrill, and some went for both.)

In 1817, Thomas J. Beale purchases a plantation eight blocks wide and three miles long, bordering what is now Nashville Avenue in New Orleans. This same year, the Thomas J. Beale of our story is reported seen with numerous other men departing Virginia.

In 1818, a Thomas J. Beale, born out of wedlock to Thomas J. Beale and Chloe Delaney in Fincastle, Virginia, arrives in New Orleans, and takes up residence with his father and step-mother.

Shortly after the arrival of his son the older Beale, facing financial difficulties, puts everything in young Thomas' name. The older Beale had neglected to pay an old debt, probably out of spite, and the note holder was trying to seize all of Beale's assets.

In November of 1819, the young Thomas Beale and ten men bury the first cache of 1,014 pounds of gold and 3,812 pounds of silver in Bedford County, Virginia.

In January of 1820, young Thomas Beale arrives at the Washington Hotel, Lynchburg, Virginia. During the next month and a half, Beale develops a friendship with the innkeeper Robert Morriss, also spelled Morris. During Beale's stay at the Washington Hotel, James Beverly Risque is also in residence. Risque is the man the older Beale had shot and believed he had killed. The two men do not recognize each other, thus confirming that it is the younger Thomas Beale staying at the hotel.

In mid February of 1820, young Beale departs Virginia and returns to New Orleans.

On Tuesday, September 5, 1820, the elder Thomas Beale dies and is buried in New Orleans.

In July of 1821, Thomas Beale completes construction on the Planters and Merchants Hotel located at number 15 Canal Street, New Orleans.

In December of 1821, Thomas Beale returns to Virginia with the second load of treasure, 1,907 pounds of gold, 1,288 pounds of silver, and jewels valued at $13,000. This load of treasure is cached with the first load. Beale again stays at the Washington Hotel.

In January of 1822, before returning to New Orleans, Beale leaves a locked strongbox with Robert Morriss for safekeeping. Beale tells Morriss that the box contains only important personal papers.

In May of 1822, Morriss receives a letter from Beale. The letter is postmarked Saint Louis, Missouri. The letter states that inside the strongbox are documents that can not be understood without the aid of a key. The letter further states that the key was placed within an envelope addressed to Mossis and left in Saint Louis with instructions to a friend not to mail the letter until June of 1832. Morriss never hears from Beale again, and the strongbox is put away and forgotten.

On October 22, 1823, the younger Thomas Beale dies at the Merchants and Planters Hotel in New Orleans.

After the death of her stepson, Celeste lives on the plantation, but later moves to Baton Rouge.

THE SAGA CONTINUES

Most stories end when the main character dies, but not this one. Both Beales were gone, but the mystery of Thomas J. Beale was only in its infancy.

In 1845 Morriss stumbles across the old strongbox and, believing that Beale will never return, breaks the lock off. Inside Morriss finds two letters addressed to him, some papers covered with numbers and some old receipts. One letter dated January 4, 1822, states that Beale and twenty-nine others went out west on a hunting expedition. That, in March of 1818, 250 to 300 miles north of Santa Fe, New Mexico, they found a gold and silver mine. That, in 1819, Beale and ten of the men journeyed to Virginia and buried their treasure. That the men returned to New Mexico and eventually brought another load of treasure to the site.

(What Beale would not have said was: "Look, a group of guys and I stole some treasure from Jean Lafitte and hid it in the woods near you. We would like you to make sure our families get our share." Instead, he would make up a story about finding gold and silver in the same mine and then, "Oh yeah, we traded some of our gold for jewels in Saint Louis.")

The other letter dated January 5, 1822, states that the numbered pages represents three cyphers: One telling the location of the treasure, another detailing the contents of the treasure, and the last listing the names and addresses of the persons the treasure is to be divided among.

(The three cyphers were in fact "book codes." A book code is made by choosing a document, book or just a page in a book as the key. Once the key is chosen, the encoder numbers the words 1, 2, 3, etc... The numbers then represent the first letter of the corresponding word. One then starts at the top of the page and works down, or starts at the bottom and works up. The only person who should be able to decipher the code is the person who knows the key and the direction. Another variation is to choose a book. The first or last number of the cypher could represent the page number and direction. The numbers in the cypher could also represent each letter in the key. The possibilities are virtually endless. Remember that in 1822 there were less books to chose from then today.)

In 1862, Morriss gives the coded letters to a friend, (the unknown author) who works on them until he has broken one of the codes using the Declaration of Independence as the key.

He substituted the numbers on the document for the first letter of that corresponding numbered word. Number 1 stood for a **W**, number **2** represented the letter **I**, and a number **3** stood for **T**, as in, **When In The**.

In 1884 the author decides that he is never going to be able to break the other cyphers and is near poverty from neglecting his other duties. The unknown author contacts James Beverly

Ward and persuades him to act as his agent in the publishing of the papers.   Ward has <u>The Beale Papers, Containing Authentic Statements Regarding the Treasure Buried in 1819 and 1821, Near Bufords, in Bedford County, Virginia, and Which Has Never Been Recovered</u> published, and thus starts one of the world's longest treasure hunts in terms of man hours spent trying to break the codes.

(Because Ward is listed as the copyright owner of <u>The Beale Papers . . .</u>, most people believe he is also the author.   Other people believe that the true author is Newton Hyde Hazlewood. Some even think that Morriss, himself, is the author.)

THE CYPHERS

Keeping in mind that the Declaration of Independence has no words that begin with the letters X and Y, it is presumed that Beale used the 994th word "sexes," for X, and the 822nd word, "fundamentally," for the Y.   Beale abbreviated the months.   A close translation of code number two follows:

> I have deposited in the county of Bedford about four miles from Bufords in an excavation or vault six feet below the surface of the ground the following articles belonging jointly to the parties whose names are given in number three herewith the first deposit consisted of ten hundred and fourteen pounds of gold and thirty eight hundred and twelve pounds of silver deposited November eighteen nineteen the second was made December eighteen twenty-one and consisted of nineteen hundred and seven pounds of gold and twelve hundred and eighty-eight pounds of silver also jewels obtained in St. Louis in exchange to save transportation and valued at thirteen thousand dollars the above is securely packed in iron pots with iron covers the vault is roughly lined with stones and the vessels rest on solid stone and are covered with others paper number one describes the

exact locality of the vault so that no difficulty will be had in finding it.

Code number one, describes the exact location of the treasure vault:

71, 194, 38, 1701, 89, 76, 11, 83, 1629, 48, 94, 63, 132, 16, 111, 95, 84, 341, 975, 14, 40, 64, 27, 81, 139, 213, 63, 90, 1120, 8, 15, 3, 126, 2018, 40, 74, 758, 485, 604, 230, 436, 664, 582, 150, 251, 284, 308, 231, 124, 211, 486, 225, 401, 370, 11, 101, 305, 139, 189, 17, 33, 88, 208, 193, 145, 1, 94, 73, 416, 918, 263, 28, 500, 538, 356, 117, 136, 219, 27, 176, 130, 10, 460, 25, 485, 18, 436, 65, 84, 200, 283, 118, 320, 138, 36, 416, 280, 15, 71, 224, 961, 44, 16, 401, 39, 88, 61, 304, 12, 21, 24, 283, 134, 92, 63, 246, 486, 682, 7, 219, 184, 360, 780, 18, 64, 463, 474, 131, 160, 79, 73, 440, 95, 18, 64, 581, 34, 69, 128, 367, 460, 17, 81, 12, 103, 820, 62, 116, 97, 103, 862, 70, 60, 1317, 471, 540, 208, 121, 890, 346, 36, 150, 59, 568, 614, 13, 120, 63, 219, 812, 2160, 1780, 99, 35, 18, 21, 136, 872, 15, 28, 170, 88, 4, 30, 44, 112, 18, 147, 436, 195, 320, 37, 122, 113, 6, 140, 8, 120, 305, 42, 58, 461, 44, 106, 301, 13, 408, 680, 93, 86, 116, 530, 82, 568, 9, 102, 38, 416, 89, 71, 216, 728, 965, 818, 2, 38, 121, 195, 14, 326, 148, 234, 18, 55, 131, 234, 361, 824, 5, 81, 623, 48, 961, 19, 26, 33, 10, 1101, 365, 92, 88, 181, 275, 346, 201, 206, 86, 36, 219, 320, 829, 840, 68, 326, 19, 48, 122, 85, 216, 284, 919, 861, 326, 985, 233, 64, 68, 232, 431, 960, 50, 29, 81, 216, 321, 603, 14, 612, 81, 360, 36, 51, 62, 194, 78, 60, 200, 314, 676, 112, 4, 28, 18, 61, 136, 247, 819, 921, 1060, 464, 895, 10, 6, 66, 119, 38, 41, 49, 602, 423, 962, 302, 294, 875, 78, 14, 23, 111, 109, 62, 31, 501, 823, 216, 280, 34, 24, 150, 1000, 162, 286, 19, 21, 17, 340, 19, 242, 31, 86, 234, 140, 607, 115, 33, 191, 67, 104, 86, 52, 88, 16, 80, 121, 67, 95, 122, 216, 548, 96, 11, 201, 77, 364, 218, 65, 667, 890, 236, 154, 211, 10, 98, 34, 119, 56, 216, 119, 71,

218, 1164, 1496, 1817, 51, 39, 210, 36, 3, 19, 540, 232,
22, 141, 617, 84, 290, 80, 46, 207, 411, 150, 29, 38, 46,
172, 85, 194, 36, 261, 543, 897, 624, 18, 212, 416, 127,
931, 19, 4, 63, 96, 12, 101, 418, 16, 140, 230, 460, 538,
19, 27, 88, 612, 1431, 90, 716, 275, 74, 83, 11, 426, 89,
72, 84, 1300, 1706, 814, 221, 132, 40, 102, 34, 858, 975,
1101, 84, 16, 79, 23, 16, 81, 122, 324, 403, 912, 227,
936, 447, 55, 86, 34, 43, 212, 107, 96, 314, 264, 1065,
323, 428, 601, 203, 124, 95, 216, 814, 2906, 654, 820, 2,
301, 112, 176, 213, 71, 87, 96, 202, 35, 10, 2, 41, 17, 84,
221, 736, 820, 214, 11, 60, 760.

Code number two states the contents of the vault:

115, 73, 24, 807, 37, 52, 49, 17, 31, 62, 647, 22, 7,
15, 140, 47, 29, 107, 79, 84, 56, 239, 10, 26, 811, 5, 196,
308, 85, 52, 160, 136, 59, 211, 36, 9, 46, 316, 554, 122,
106, 95, 53, 58, 2, 42, 7, 35, 122, 53, 31, 82, 77, 250,
196, 56, 96, 118, 71, 140, 287, 28, 353, 37, 1005, 65,
147, 807, 24, 3, 8, 12, 47, 43, 59, 807, 45, 316, 101, 41,
78, 154, 1005, 122, 138, 191, 16, 77, 49, 102, 57, 72, 34,
73, 85, 35, 371, 59, 196, 81, 92, 191, 106, 273, 60, 394,
620, 270, 220, 106, 388, 287, 63, 3, 6, 191, 122, 43, 234,
400, 106, 290, 314, 47, 48, 81, 96, 26, 115, 92, 158, 191,
110, 77, 85, 197, 46, 10, 113, 140, 353, 48, 120, 106, 2,
607, 61, 420, 811, 29, 125, 14, 20, 37, 105, 28, 248, 16,
159, 7, 35, 19, 301, 125, 110, 486, 287, 98, 117, 511, 62,
51, 220, 37, 113, 140, 807, 138, 540, 8, 44, 287, 388,
117, 18, 79, 344, 34, 20, 59, 511, 548, 107, 603, 220, 7,
66, 154, 41, 20, 50, 6, 575, 122, 154, 248, 110, 61, 52,
33, 30, 5, 38, 8, 14, 84, 57, 540, 217, 115, 71, 29, 84, 63,
43, 131, 29, 138, 47, 73, 239, 540, 52, 53, 79, 118, 51,
44, 63, 196, 12, 239, 112, 3, 49, 79, 353, 105, 56, 371,
557, 211, 505, 125, 360, 133, 143, 101, 15, 284, 540,
252, 14, 205, 140, 344, 26, 811, 138, 115, 48, 73, 34,
205, 316, 607, 63, 220, 7, 52, 150, 44, 52, 16, 40, 37,
158, 807, 37, 121, 12, 95, 10, 15, 35, 12, 131, 62, 115,

102, 807, 49, 53, 135, 138, 30, 31, 62, 67, 41, 85, 63, 10, 106, 807, 138, 8, 113, 20, 32, 33, 37, 353, 287, 140, 47, 85, 50, 37, 49, 47, 64, 6, 7, 71, 33, 4, 43, 47, 63, 1, 27, 600, 208, 230, 15, 191, 246, 85, 94, 511, 2, 270, 20, 39, 7, 33, 44, 22, 40, 7, 10, 3, 811, 106, 44, 486, 230, 353, 211, 200, 31, 10, 38, 140, 297, 61, 603, 320, 302, 666, 287, 2, 44, 33, 32, 511, 548, 10, 6, 250, 557, 246, 53, 37, 52, 83, 47, 320, 38, 33, 807, 7, 44, 30, 31, 250, 10, 15, 35, 106, 160, 113, 31, 102, 406, 230, 540, 320, 29, 66, 33, 101, 807, 138, 301, 316, 353, 320, 220, 37, 52, 28, 540, 320, 33, 8, 48, 107, 50, 811, 7, 2, 113, 73, 16, 125, 11, 110, 67, 102, 807, 33, 59, 81, 158, 38, 43, 581, 138, 19, 85, 400, 38, 43, 77, 14, 27, 8, 47, 138, 63, 140, 44, 35, 22, 177, 106, 250, 314, 217, 2, 10, 7, 1005, 4, 20, 25, 44, 48, 7, 26, 46, 110, 230, 807, 191, 34, 112, 117, 44, 110, 121, 125, 96, 41, 51, 50, 140, 56, 47, 152, 540, 63, 807, 28, 42, 250, 138, 582, 98, 643, 32, 107, 140, 112, 26, 85, 138, 540, 53, 20, 125, 371, 38, 36, 10, 52, 118, 136, 102, 420, 150, 112, 71, 14, 20, 7, 24, 18, 12, 807, 37, 67, 110, 62, 33, 21, 95, 220, 511, 102, 811, 30, 83, 84, 305, 620, 15, 2, 108, 220, 106, 353, 105, 106, 60, 275, 72, 8, 50, 205, 185, 112, 125, 540, 65, 106, 807, 188, 96, 110, 16, 73, 33, 807, 150, 409, 400, 50, 154, 285, 96, 106, 316, 270, 205, 101, 811, 400, 8, 44, 37, 52, 40, 241, 34, 205, 38, 16, 46, 47, 85, 24, 44, 15, 64, 73, 138, 807, 85, 78, 110, 33, 420, 505, 53, 37, 38, 22, 31, 10, 110, 106, 101, 140, 15, 38, 3, 5, 44, 7, 98, 287, 135, 150, 96, 33, 84, 125, 807, 191, 96, 511, 118, 440, 370, 643, 466, 106, 41, 107, 603, 220, 275, 30, 150, 49, 53, 287, 250, 208, 134, 7, 53, 12, 47, 85, 63, 138, 110, 21, 112, 140, 485, 486, 505, 14, 73, 84, 575, 1005, 150, 200, 16, 42, 5, 4, 25, 42, 8, 16, 811, 125, 160, 32, 205, 603, 807, 81, 96, 405, 41, 600, 136, 14, 20, 28, 26, 353, 302, 246, 8, 131, 160, 140, 84, 440, 42, 16, 811, 40, 67, 101, 102, 194, 138, 205, 51, 63, 241, 540, 122, 8, 10, 63, 140, 47, 48, 140, 288.

Code number three tells the names of persons involved and their next of kin:

317, 8, 92, 73, 112, 89, 67, 318, 28, 96, 107, 41, 631,
78, 146, 387, 118, 98, 114, 246, 348, 116, 74, 88, 12, 65,
32, 14, 81, 19, 76, 121, 216, 85, 33, 66, 15, 108, 68, 77,
43, 24, 122, 96, 117, 36, 211, 301, 15, 44, 11, 46, 89, 18,
136, 68, 317, 28, 90, 82, 304, 71, 43, 221, 198, 176, 310,
319, 81, 99, 264, 380, 56, 37, 319, 2, 44, 53, 28, 44, 75,
98, 102, 37, 85, 107, 117, 64, 88, 136, 48, 151, 99, 175,
89, 315, 326, 78, 96, 214, 218, 311, 43, 89, 51, 90, 75,
128, 96, 33, 28, 103, 84, 65, 26, 41, 246, 84, 270, 98,
116, 32, 59, 74, 66, 69, 240, 15, 8, 121, 20, 77, 89, 31,
11, 106, 81, 191, 224, 328, 18, 75, 52, 82, 117, 201, 39,
23, 217, 27, 21, 84, 35, 54, 109, 128, 49, 77, 88, 1, 81,
217, 64, 55, 83, 116, 251, 269, 311, 96, 54, 32, 120, 18,
132, 102, 219, 211, 84, 150, 219, 275, 312, 64, 10, 106,
87, 75, 47, 21, 29, 37, 81, 44, 18, 126, 115, 132, 160,
181, 203, 76, 81, 299, 314, 337, 351, 96, 11, 28, 97, 318,
238, 106, 24, 93, 3, 19, 17, 26, 60, 73, 88, 14, 126, 138,
234, 286, 297, 321, 365, 264, 19, 22, 84, 56, 107, 98,
123, 111, 214, 136, 7, 33, 45, 40, 13, 28, 46, 42, 107,
196, 227, 344, 198, 203, 247, 116, 19, 8, 212, 230, 31, 6,
328, 65, 48, 52, 59, 41, 122, 33, 117, 11, 18, 25, 71, 36,
45, 83, 76, 89, 92, 31, 65, 70, 83, 96, 27, 33, 44, 50, 61,
24, 112, 135, 149, 176, 180, 194, 143, 171, 205, 296, 87,
12, 44, 51, 89, 98, 34, 41, 208, 173, 66, 9, 35, 16, 95, 8,
113, 175, 90, 56, 203, 19, 177, 183, 206, 157, 200, 218,
260, 291, 305, 618, 851, 320, 18, 124, 78, 65, 19, 32,
124, 48, 53, 57, 84, 96, 207, 244, 66, 83, 119, 71, 11, 86,
77, 213, 54, 82, 316, 245, 303, 86, 97, 106, 212, 18, 37,
15, 81, 89, 16, 7, 81, 39, 96, 14, 43, 216, 118, 29, 55,
109, 136, 172, 213, 64, 8, 227, 304, 611, 221, 364, 819,
375, 128, 296, 11, 18, 53, 76, 10, 15, 23, 19, 71, 84, 120,
134, 66, 73, 89, 96, 230, 48, 77, 26, 101, 127, 936, 218,
439, 178, 171, 61, 226, 313, 215, 102, 18, 167, 262, 114,
218, 66, 59, 48, 27, 19, 13, 82, 48, 162, 119, 34, 127,

139, 34, 128, 129, 74, 63, 120, 11, 54, 61, 73, 92, 180,
66, 75, 101, 124, 265, 89, 96, 126, 274, 896, 917, 434,
461, 235, 890, 312, 413, 328, 381, 96, 105, 217, 66, 118,
22, 77, 64, 42, 12, 7, 55, 24, 83, 67, 97, 109, 121, 135,
181, 203, 219, 228, 256, 21, 34, 77, 319, 374, 382, 675,
684, 717, 864, 203, 4, 18, 92, 16, 63, 82, 22, 46, 55, 69,
74, 112, 135, 186, 175, 119, 213, 416, 312, 343, 264,
119, 186, 218, 343, 417, 845, 951, 124, 209, 49, 617,
856, 924, 936, 72, 19, 29, 11, 35, 42, 40, 66, 85, 94, 112,
65, 82, 115, 118, 236, 244, 186, 172, 112, 85, 6, 56, 38,
44, 85, 72, 32, 47, 73, 96, 124, 217, 314, 319, 221, 644,
817, 821, 934, 922, 416, 975, 10, 22, 18, 46, 137, 181,
101, 39, 86, 103, 116, 138, 164, 212, 218, 296, 815, 380,
412, 460, 495, 675, 820, 952.

If you attempt to use a newer version of the Declaration of Independence there are a few things you should know:

As the years passed our language has changed. Newer versions of the Declaration of Independence carry those changes. A copy of the Declaration of Independence that I have has omitted word number 386, "HE". The next word is "HAS", since both words start with an "H" the problem would not be noticed until later in the translation.

The 95th word in the newer Declaration of Independence is "INALIENABLE", originally the word was "UNALIENABLE".

The original The Beale Papers . . ., contains a copy of the Declaration of Independence that is numbered, but there are mistakes in the numbering. The most notable mistake occurs at number "480", ten numbers later the number "480" was repeated.

In 1897 Clayton I. Hart acquired copies of what may have been the original Beale cyphers from Newton Hyde Hazlewood. Mr. Hart and his brother George L. Hart did extensive research into the subject, and in 1952, George Hart sent an essay on the papers to the Libraries of Lynchburg and Roanoke, Virginia. In the Hart version of the cypher many of the numbers are different. Many people believe that the list of numbers provided in the Hart works are in fact the true cyphers and that Hazlewood changed some of the numbers before giving the cyphers to Ward. This was done so that if anyone did discover the key they would only be able to solve part of the cypher, and Hazlewood would then have the key. With the key known, Hazlewood would have the only true cyphers and a clear shot at the treasure.

EPILOGUE

Could Jean Lafitte have assumed the name of Thomas J. Beale and buried part of his treasure in Virginia? Is it possible that the older Beale may have accompanied Lafitte on several of his voyages and made maps of various treasure locations? Could the younger Beale have found the maps after his father's death and hid several of Jean Lafitte's treasures in Virginia?

Young Beale was born in Fincastle, Virginia, only twenty miles from where the treasure is buried. Young Beale did live in New Orleans and returned from Virginia only to die on October 22, 1823. The older Thomas and Celeste Beale had four legitimate children, Eliza, Celeste, James William, and Octavine. All four of these children were born in New Orleans, and after the death of the younger Thomas, moved to Baton Rouge with their mother. One of their descendents may have some of young Thomas' belongings. Perhaps, stored away in an attic near Nashville Avenue, or in Celeste's home in Baton Rouge, or possibly at your neighborhood Salvation Army Store is Thomas J. Beales' favorite book. A book with a page marked by an old copy of the Declaration of Independence or a letter addressed to Robert Morriss, Lynchburg, Virginia. Beale intended to give that letter to a friend, but was unable to do so at the time. Beale may have thought he would leave the letter with his friend upon his return to Saint Louis.

Anyone who is interested in pursuing the Beale Treasure may contact Robert E. Caldwell c/o Beale Cypher Association, P. O. Box 975, Beaver Falls, Pennsylvania 15010. Copies of all reference material may be purchased through the Association.

CHAPTER V

INDIANS

No one knows with any certainty when the Indians first appeared in Louisiana. That they were here first cannot be denied. Like a snowball rolling down hill increasing in size and speed comes the proof that Indians may have been on this continent from 35,000 to over 100,000 years. Archaeological research has shown that during the Ice Age Indians were nomadic hunters following large herds of mammoths and huge buffalo. As the great glaciers inched their way north exposing more solid ground, some tribes of Indians became regional hunter gathers. Later in the Indian prehistory some tribes began to form settlements where they lived, farmed, fished, hunted and traded with other tribes year-round.

So far Indian prehistory has been traced back about 20,000 years. Beginning with the Paleo Period occurring between 12,000 B. C. to 8,000 B. C.. The Indians of the Paleo Period were the Ice Age nomadic hunters. Their technology, called Upper Paleolithic, was merely functional and consisted of the atlatl (a short stick with a hook at one end, used to launch spears), stone points, scrapers, choppers, and bone tools.

The second period, known as the Early Archaic Period, occurred between 8,000 B. C. and 4,000 B. C. Some of the Indian tribes of this period began regional living, while others continued to follow the mammoths and huge buffalo. The regional tribes hunted game such as deer and bear and gathered available food within a given area. The Early Archaic people had their beginnings in the warm gulf coast areas, but as the glaciers moved northward so did the hunter gatherers. Artifacts from this period have a more esthetic quality than those of the Paleo Period. The Indians polished stones for use as ornamental pendants and gorgets. The atlatl was still in use, but a bannerstone was added to increase momentum. Along with the atlatl and bannerstone, scrapers and choppers, the Indians of this period added tools such as flaked and grooved axes, drills, and bola stones.

The Late Archaic Period ranges between 4,000 B. C. and 2,000 B. C. with the only difference being the dwindling number of nomadic hunting tribes, the increasing number of regional hunter gatherers, and the amount of land exposed by the receding glaciers.

The Transitional Period (2,000 B. C. to 500 B. C.) was a time of change. The tribes evolved from the regional hunter gathers of the Archaic Period into the permanent villagers of the Woodland Period. Artifacts from this period included steatite ware and ceramic pottery along with the introduction of the bow and arrow.

The Woodland Period (500 B. C. to 1,500 A. D.) closes out the prehistory, ending in what has been called the Contact Era. This Woodland period (also known as the Mississippian Period) saw the zenith of Indian advancement. By the end of this period Indian Nations had settlements along almost every waterway on the North American Continent. It was the time of the mound builders. Artifacts found from that period include etched shells, delicate gorgets, delicate flint blades three feet in length, carved platform animal effigy pipes, figurines, and ceramic bowls. These relics have been described as "the finest artifacts in the world."

The Contact Era marked several milestones in history. It marked the true beginning of the United States of America and the first written history of the Indians. This era also marked the end of the Indians.

Acolapissa, Adai, Alibamons, Atakapa (Attakapas [*Cannibals*]), Avoyel (*Flint People*), Bayou Goula (Bayougoula [*River People*]), Biloxi, Caddo (Kadohadacho [*Principal*]), Chawasha, Choctaw, Chitimacha, Doustiony, Houma (*red*), Keachi (Kisatchie [*Reed Brake River*]). Koroa, Muskogee, Natchez, Natchitoches, Ofo, Okelousa, Opelousa (*Appalousa* [*Black Legs*]), Quinipissa, Tangipahoa (*Cornstalk Gatherers*), Tensas, Tunica (*The People*), Washa, Washita, Yatasi, Yazoo and others known and unknown were living in Louisiana, before the Europeans knew they were Europeans. (The Chitimacha Indians are the only tribe in Louisiana still living on their original territory.) As the Indians were driven from their lands, they left many beautiful artifacts for us to find. Many archaeological sites in this country are being destroyed each day, not by "Grave Robbers" or "Treasure Hunters," but by ignorance and neglect. There are not enough professional archaeologist in the United States to work the large number of known sites.

In no way should this be interpreted to mean that the removal of any items from an Indian Burial Ground is condoned. Burial Grounds are sacred no matter who is buried there and are protected by the laws of a civilized nation. No one with any amount of decency would want their relative's grave disturbed, no matter what the monetary reward may be. The Unmarked Burial Sites Preservation Act of 1991 makes it illegal to knowingly disturb an unmarked burial site or any human remains.

Some Indian mounds were monuments to their gods. These sites should not be disturbed but restored and preserved. Some of the largest and most beautiful of these mounds were in the state of Louisiana and were destroyed in the name of progress or by neglect. For example; during the early 1700's, the number of Indian mounds in Barataria Bay was estimated at over 100. In the 1730's, Claude Joseph Villars Dubreuil Sr. had a canal dug from the Mississippi River to Bayou Fatma, a branch of Bayou Barataria, giving him access to the Gulf of Mexico. In the 1740's, Dubreuil began using the canal to remove timber and clam shells from the Barataria Bay area. The clam shells came from the Indian mounds and were used in the manufacture of cement.

In 1841, construction was begun on Fort Livingston at Grand Terre Island in Barataria Bay. The walls of the fort were constructed with cemented clam shells from Indian mounds in the area and faced with brick. As a result of the need for construction material, only a few Indian mounds can be found in that area today.

Most Indian mounds or middens were nothing more than a garbage dump where the remains of broken pottery and the scraps of last night's meal were discarded. A lot can be learned from a garbage heap, but by the time a professional archaeologist gets around to investigating a site it could be gone. The only time archaeologist are driven into action is when the site is in the way of construction. At this point they come in, survey the site, take a few objects and let the bulldozers roll. What is needed is education for the would-be amateur archaeologist. There are some impressive, private collections of Indian artifacts displayed in a very professional manner. Before digging on your own, made yourself familiar with the latest ruling of the <u>United Sates Archaeological Resources and Protection Act of 1978</u>.

NOTE: My interest in Indian mounds began Wednesday, September 21, 1972, when I performed my weekly ritual of reading Paul Serpas' "Rendezvous" column in the Saint Bernard News. It is not that I remember the date, but that I have saved every article of his I have seen in print. Over the years I have purchased all of his books. They had to be purchased several times, as Serpas' books have a habit of walking off under their own power or falling apart after being read only a few thousand times.

THE KNOWN INDIAN TRIBES IN LOUISIANA OF 1700

The Indians of Louisiana are divided into two major groups, historic and prehistoric, with 1700 being the dividing line. In 1700 the explorers began a crude history of the Louisiana Indians. Because the explorers usually had Choctaw guides, many of the Indian Nations and tribes, cities, rivers, lakes and other locations within Louisiana have Choctaw names. Atchafalaya (*Long River*), Bayou Fanny Louis (*Black Squirrel River*), Bayou Goula (*River People*), Bogalusa (*Black Creek*), Bogue Chitto (*Big Creek*), Catahoula (*Beloved Lake*), Chacahoula (*Beloved Home*), Choupique (*mud fish*), Coushatta

(*White Reed Brake*), Houma (*red*), Istrouma (*Red Stick*), Kisatchie (*Reed Brake River*), Manchac (*rear entrance*), Opelousas (*Black Legs*), Ponchatoula (*Hanging Hair/Spanish moss*), Shongaloo (*Cypress Tree*), Tangipahoa (*Cornstalk Gatherers*), Tchoupitoulas (*Pine Rest*), and Whiskey Chitto (*Big Cane Creek*). The Choctaw Indians did not settle in Louisiana until after they were forced off their lands by the whites in the early 1800's. Most Indian settlements were located along rivers, bayous and streams. Louisiana Indians visited gravel pits for stones and rocks to make their tools and beads. When looking for Indian artifacts, look for areas abundant with clam shells, as the Indians of Louisiana ate a lot of clams. In Southern Louisiana, an Indian mound resembles an island in a sea of grass or marsh.

In 1700 the Indians living in what is now Louisiana were divided into six major groups: The Atakapa, Caddo, Chitimacha, Muskogee, Natchez and Tunica tribes.

The <u>Atakapa Indians</u> had four known settlements in the state of Louisiana. One was located along the Calcasieu River, the second along the Mermentau River, the third along the Vermilion River, and the fourth, settled by a tribe known as the Opelousa, was located near Opelousas.

The <u>Caddo Indians</u> consisted of six known tribes in Louisiana. An Adai settlement was located near Robeline, the Doustiony near Campti. The Kadohadacho Tribe settled near Shreveport, the Natchitoches Tribe near Natchitoches. The Washita Tribe was near Columbia, and the Yatasi Tribe near Coushatta.

The <u>Chitimacha Indians</u> consisted of five tribes. Two Chitimacha Tribes were located along the Lower Bayou Teche, and the Bayou Grosse Tete and the Grand River. A third Chitimacha Tribe was located along the Upper Bayou Lafourche. The Chawasha and Washa Tribes lived in the areas along the Middle Bayou Lafourche and the Lower Mississippi River.

The Muskogee Indians consisted of six tribes. The Acolapissa tribe was located along the Lower Pearl River, the Bayougoula Tribe near Bayou Goula, and the Houma Tribe near Angola. The Okelousa Tribal settlement was along the Upper Atchafalaya River, the Quinipissa Tribe near Hahnville. The Tangipahoa Tribe was located in various sites around Lake Pontchartrain.

The Natchez Indians consisted of three tribes. The Tensas Tribe settled along Lake Saint Joseph. The Avoyel Tribe split, with one tribe settling near Alexandria and the second near Marksville.

The Tunica Indians (originally Quizquiz) were based mostly in Mississippi with the Koroa Tribe being the only known tribe in Louisiana. The Koroa Tribe settled near Winnsboro.

THE KNOWN INDIAN TRIBES AFTER 1700

As the Europeans settled the east, the Indians were forced to move west. Two groups of Choctaw settled in Louisiana, one near the town of Jena and the other near Lacombe. A Creek tribe of Koasati (Coushattas) was forced from Alabama and settled in Allen Parish. As the Tunica were forced to move, they in turn forced the smaller Houma to relocate to an area along the Mississippi River near Donaldsonville. When the whites reached Donaldsonville, the Houma were forced to the area south of Houma. When the whites reached Houma, most of the tribe adapted to the ways of the white man and remained in that area. Over the years the Houma accepted members of other tribes fleeing the white man, and today they are considered the largest tribe in Louisiana. The Tunica Indians eventually settled in the area of Marksville, along with the Ofo, Biloxi, and Avoyel Indians.

WHAT TO LOOK FOR

The types of Indian artifacts are vast and varied. Entire books have been devoted to this subject, but they only scratch the surface of what can be found. I will only attempt to identify the most common finds.

Projectile points were the basic tool of the most primitive man and are divided into two groups--spearpoints and arrowheads. Most of projectile points are spear points because they were in use long before the bow and arrow. The main difference between spear points and arrowheads is size. Arrowheads are smaller, lighter and more delicate. Spear, lance, and dart points are often confused with prehistoric knives. This may be due to the fact that the only difference was the length of the stick it was tied to. The most common material used for projectile points was quartz, both crystalline and cryptocrystalline. Presently, prices range from several dollars for a small common point to in the hundreds of dollars for the larger common points. The price of some of the longer points ranges into the tens of thousands of dollars.

Crystalline quartz points are the rarest and most beautiful of all points, because they were the hardest to make. They will bring a higher reward, being made from crystal quartz (clear), white quartz, rose quartz, blue quartz, amethyst and quartzite. Other materials used included argillite, chalcedony, chert, flint, jasper, novaculite, petrified wood. rhyolite and slate. Prices range from several dollars to hundreds of dollars.

Drills resemble projectile points, but are narrow and were used to bore holes into wood or stone. Drills used for stone usually show signs of wear and are dull. Needles were smaller and thinner than drills. Awls were smaller than drills, but shorter and sturdier. Prices range from several dollars to hundreds of dollars.

Axes come in a variety of shapes and sizes with some resembling very large, heavy projectile points. Some axes have notches or groves along the sides where the handles were attached. Prices range from the hundreds of dollars to the thousands of dollars.

Celts and adzes resemble axes, but are smaller and very sharp. The difference in celts and adzes is the edge that was sharpened. Celts were sharpened along the narrow edge, while adzes were sharpened along the broad edge. Small handheld adzes are known as choppers. Prices range from tens of dollars to thousands of dollars.

Gouges are like celts, but the blade has been hollowed to make a scoop. Gouges were used to scoop out wood like a chisel, as in the construction of early boats carved from a single tree. Prices range from tens of dollars to thousands of dollars.

Hoes look like an axe except they are thinner and wider. Prices range into the hundreds of dollars.

Hammerstones resemble axes, but are very dull and blunt. Hammerstones are always pitted to aid in gripping. Prices range into the hundreds of dollars.

Mortars resemble hollowed out stones (bowl shaped). Prices range from a few dollars to the hundreds of dollars.

Pestles are usually oblong and smooth on the ends. Prices range from a few dollars into the hundreds of dollars.

Stone discs or discoidals are found throughout North America. There are as many varieties as there are locations where they are found. It is believed that the disc may have been used as a game piece in an Indian version of checkers or hopscotch. Prices generally range well into the hundreds of dollars.

Sinkers were made from flat pebbles and notched on each side for the attachment of a cord or net. Prices are generally in the tens of dollars range.

Bolas are egg size or larger stones that were grooved around the center so they could be attached to the hide straps. Bolas are rare and, as such, much sought after by collectors. Prices range into the hundreds of dollars.

Bannerstones are among the rarest and most prized of Indian artifacts. Bannerstones were weights used on atlatl to help propel spears farther and faster. Most bannerstones were drilled, but some were grooved and are works of art, resembling a highly polished stone propeller without the blades being pitched. The price of whole bannerstones will range from $200 to $6,000, while broken bannerstones sell for between $20 to $140.

Gorgets are small, flat drilled stones that were worn as ornaments. Gorgets were usually made of slate, shells or clay and are commonly rectangular and have two holes. Some gorgets, however, are round and some are intricately carved effigies. Gorget effigies are priced into the thousands of dollars.

Pendants are similar to gorgets except they have only one hole. Some were grooved or notched and made to be worn around the neck. The rarest of pendants were made from fossilized shark teeth. Pendants are priced up into the tens of thousands of dollars.

Pipes, the smoking variety, are found in almost every location in North America and in endless variations. Most pipes were carved from steatite or catlinite, some were carved from slate. In later years pipes were made from clay. The rarest pipes are effigy pipes and are considered among the finest examples of Indian art. Priced from a few dollars up to the tens of thousands of dollars.

Effigies are symbolic images of animals, gods and man, produced for ceremonial religious or superstitious reasons. It is the goal of many collectors of Indian artifacts to find at least one effigy in their lifetime. Some of the subjects of effigies are beavers, ducks, eagles, humans, and turtles. Prices range from the hundreds to tens of thousands of dollars.

Beads made of catlinite, slate and steatite are among the oldest beads to be found. Shell beads are the most abundant to be found in Louisiana. Copper and clay beads were being made by the Indians when the Europeans arrived with their glass beads. Glass trade beads also have a value to collectors. Prices are in the tens of dollars, rarely going into the hundreds, unless they are carved.

This brings us to what has been called the most diversified of all Indian artifacts, pottery. Made from local, natural resources, pottery can be found everywhere, and prices go as high as the sky. Pottery shards will sell for several dollars. The Caddo/Mississippian pottery is considered the most elaborate of all pottery and, as such, commands a nice price. Clay pots from Louisiana are often found in the form of brightly colored effigies of animals and humans.

NOTE: Keep everything you find even fragments and shards.

INDIAN MOUNDS AND MIDDENS

Areas of known Indian mounds are listed separate from Indian settlements because they were usually located some distance from any single village, yet close enough to many villages to allow all the tribes equal access. Like the Indian settlements, temple mounds were usually located near the rivers, larger bayous and streams of Louisiana.

Indian mounds were usually made of earth, some were made from clam shells, and a few were made of a combination of shells and earth. The mounds are usually dome shape--round at the base and rounded at the top. Some mounds were cone shaped--round at the bottom rising to a peak at the top. These were usually burial mounds. Other mounds resemble pyramids with their tops sliced off. They were square or rectangle at the base and flat on top. These were temple mounds. A very few of the mounds were built to represent their gods. A giant bird can be found at Poverty Point. Giant alligators could be found in Cameron and Saint Bernard Parishes. Over the years nature has changed the shape of most mounds. What was once sharp edges have been rounded off. What was once crisp details have faded into a mass of earth and shells. When looking at Indian mounds today a good imagination is usually required.

Along with earth and shells, various artifacts can be found within most Indian mounds. Anything that had to do with the early Indian life can be found within a mound--arrowheads, beads, drills, knives, pipes, clay pots and sherds, stone axes, human and animal bones, stone and clay effigies.

Middens resemble mounds except for their shape. Middens are irregular in shape. Middens were the Indian garbage dumps. They are composed of rich earth and clam shells. Many of the same items found within the mound can also be found within the midden, but the items are usually broken. Even broken bits of pottery and tools can bring a price of over $25.

NOTE: At the time the Europeans arrived on this continent the Indians were enjoying their golden age. There were more Indians and more mounds and temples being built then at any other time in Indian history. Unfortunately for the Indians, the Europeans brought smallpox, chicken pox and measles with them. Most of the Indians were killed by the foreigners without a shot being fired. Most of the Indians who died had only heard of the whites from other Indians and never saw them at all. Whole villages were wiped out by these new diseases. It is no wonder that islands were found covered with human bones.

The following is a list of known Indian sites arranged according to parishes:

ASCENSION PARISH

Donaldsonville: An Indian village was located along Bayou Lafourche, approximately two miles south of Donaldsonville.

AVOYELLES PARISH

Marksville, The Tunica-Biloxi Regional Indian Center and Museum: If you are ever in the area of Marksville visit the museum, which contains an extraordinary collection of artifacts valued at over $5,000,000. You will not be allowed to dig anywhere on the 134 acre reservation, but just looking at the objects will be reward enough. The museum is located on Louisiana State Highway 1, in Marksville, near the Grand Casino Avoyelles.

Also in the area is the Marksville State Commemorative Area/Prehistoric Indian Park and Museum where you will be able to see six prehistoric Indian mounds. The park is located in Marksville at the end of Martin Luther King Avenue.

There are numerous Indian mounds in this area which are located on private property.

CADDO PARISH

Mooringsport: It is believed that the Caddo Indians were working a lead mine in the area of Black Bayou before they were forced from their land by the "white-eyes."

CALCASIEU PARISH

Lake Charles: A log hut that was once on what is now Shell Beach Drive was rumored to have been built for Jean Lafitte. It was said that Lafitte constructed a small fort near the hut from a Chawasha Indian shell mound.

DeQuincy: The Lost Indian Mine of Wyndham Creek:
Pioneers arriving in the area noticed that the local Indians were
wearing gold ornaments.   When questioned as to the origin of
the gold, the Indians refused to divulge the source.   Rumors
began to spread that the Indians had a gold mine in the area.

An unknown white woman was said to have wandered into
the pine forest and lost her way.   When she came to a creek, she
thought she could follow the stream and eventually reach
civilization.   As the lady walked downstream she heard the
sound of Indians talking and stopped.   She looked in the
direction of the sound and observed several Indians working in
front of what appeared to be a small cave opening.   When the
Indians entered the cave, the woman continued downstream.
After several hours she came to a road and made her way home.
It was later learned that the creek was Wyndham Creek.   When
she told the story, it was surmised that the location was the site
of the Indian gold mine.   She attempted several times to lead
others to the mine, but she was never able to relocate it.

Around 1905, three men began a meticulous search along
Wyndham Creek for the mine.   The three men were later found
brutally murdered.   Area residents suspected that the three may
have found the mine and were butchered by the Indians as a
warning to others.

NOTE: "The Lost Indian Mine of Wyndham Creek" may be
located in Beauregard Parish.

CARROLL PARISH

Goodrich's Landing: Fort Mound was a Union Army
fortification of 1863.   The fort was located on top of an Indian
mound near Goodrich's Landing on the Mississippi River.

CATAHOULA PARISH

Clayton: Numerous Indian relics and artifacts have been
found in the area along the Tensas River, between Clayton and

Foules. Several Indian mounds are said to be located in this area.

Ditto Lake: The Natchez Indians fought a battle with the French at a bluff along Ditto Lake. Many relics and artifacts of the battle have been found in the area of the bluff.

Jonesville: Anilco was an Indian Village that once stood on the site of present day Jonesville. Numerous Indian relics and artifacts have been found in this area.

Jonesville: Three Indian mounds were located at the southwest junction of the Black, Little, Washita, and Tensas Rivers.

Sicily Island: In 1716, the French established Fort Rosalie near Natchez, Mississippi. In 1729, the Natchez Indians, in retaliation for treatment received at the hands of the French, attacked Fort Rosalie and killed all the males at the fort. After the Massacre at Fort Rosalie, the Natchez Indians reportedly buried all of the valuables taken during the raid at Cash Knob. On January 20, 1731, the French attacked and burnt the Indian settlement known as Fort Natchez, killing everyone at the settlement in retaliation for the early Indian massacre. The site of Fort Natchez is believed by many to be located on the grounds of the Battle Ground Plantation. The plantation is located on the eastern edge of Sicily Island, one-half mile north of the town of Sicily Island and east of Louisiana State Highway 15.

Sicily Island: The Ferry Plantation was constructed in the late 1830's in the area of what was once a Chickasaw, Choctaw, Natchez, and Tensas Indian hunting ground. Indian relics and artifacts have been found in the area of Sicily Island, but the most by far have been found on the plantation grounds. There are several Indian mounds on the plantation. After the French were massacred by the Indians at Fort Rosalie in 1729, the

French retaliated by attacking the Natchez Indians. It is believed by many that the Ferry Plantation was the site of the last stand of the Natchez Indians in 1731. The Ferry Plantation is located on Louisiana State Highway 1017, approximately one and one-quarter miles south of Louisiana State Highway 8.

CONCORDIA PARISH

Clayton: Numerous Indian relics and artifacts have been found in the area along the Tensas River between Clayton and Foules. Several Indian mounds are said to be located in this same area.

EAST BATON ROUGE PARISH

Baton Rouge: Stone or brick-like walls averaging two to three feet in height were found south of Baton Rouge. It is believed that these walls were created by an unknown prehistoric Indian tribe. The exact location has been lost over the years. The walls may have been dismantled and the stone used for building materials.

Baton Rouge: The Louisiana State Capitol Building was constructed in an area that was the location of many Indian mounds. It is believed that the legendary "Red Stick" (Baton Rouge) was located at this site. A small Indian mound once stood near the intersection of North Boulevard and Lafayette Streets.

NOTE: The name Baton Rouge is French for "Red Stick." Legend has it that when the French first came to this area they observed a tall red pole. Stories of the origin of the pole differ slightly. One story suggests that the pole was used by the Istrouma Indians to hang game. The game would be cleaned in preparation for cooking, and the pole became red from the blood. Other stories state that the "Red Stick" only served to mark the Istrouma's territory. It should also be mentioned that the word Istrouma means "Red Stick" in Choctaw.

IBERIA PARISH

Avery Island: Avery Island is believed to be the site of the first Indian settlement in Louisiana. This site may be as old as 8,500 to 12,000 years.

Baldwin: Twenty miles south of Baldwin near Weeks Island an Indian settlement believed to be over 3,000 years old has been discovered. Morton Shell Mound is over 700 feet in length, 90 feet wide and 12 feet high. This mound would seem to be a midden as it is composed mostly of refuse.

IBERVILLE PARISH

Bayou Goula: In the 1600's the Bayougoula Indians established a fort. The fort was located northeast of the present site of Bayou Goula. There are several Indian mounds located in this area.

Carville: The Indian Camp Plantation, also known as Woodlawn, was built in 1857 on what was once the site of a Houma Indian village. Today it is the site of the United States Public Health Service National Hansen's Disease Center. The hospital is located on Louisiana State Highway 75, at Carville.

Plaquemine: An Indian village once stood nine miles west of Plaquemine at the junction of Bayou Gross Tete and Bayou Plaquemine. Redoubt at Indian Village was a Confederate fortification that was established in January, 1863, during the Civil War.

JEFFERSON PARISH

Metairie: Stories have persisted for years of an ancient treasure being buried within an Indian mound near Metairie. The story drove one treasure hunter to the use of dynamite. If there was anything there, it may have been blown into the next parish.

Round Lake: Petit Temple (Little Temple) was the name given to an Indian mound in the area of Round Lake. In 1884, the mound was removed for its shell content. 300,000 barrels of shell were said to have been removed from the mound.

LA SALLE PARISH

Catahoula Swamp: In an area along Cross Bayou in the Catahoula Swamp numerous Indian artifacts have been found. The site is said to have once been a large Indian campground.

Little River: Indian artifacts have been found along the Little River where Louisiana Highway 8 crosses the Grant Parish line. There are several Indian mounds located in this area.

LAFAYETTE PARISH

Lafayette: Some of the finest Indian artifacts known to exist have come from mounds in the area of Lafayette.

MADISON PARISH

Delta: Somewhere along the west bank of the Mississippi River below Vicksburg was the site of the great Indian town of Taenasa. The only reported sighting of this large Indian village was in 1682. It was said that the tribe possessed many golden treasures.

NATCHITOCHES PARISH

Cloutierville: The location of one of the few Indian battle sites known in Louisiana is along the shore of the now dry lake bed of Sang Pour Sang Lake. The battle took place in 1732 between the Indians and the French. This site is said to be rich in relics and artifacts.

ORLEANS PARISH

New Orleans: The Fort at Bayou Choupic is believed by some to have been a French post established sometime before 1718. The fort was located along Bayou Choupic near Lake Pontchartrain. There are many who believe the fort was in fact an Indian picket stockade when the French arrived. (If you have lived in New Orleans all your life, you may be scratching your head about now. Bayou Choupic is not on any of the maps I have seen, but it is believed to be Bayou Saint John.)

New Orleans: Located three-fourths of a mile west of Fort Pike, Fort Petite Coquilles (Little Shells) was built on an Indian mound composed mostly of clam shells. All signs of the fort are gone, but some of the shells can still be seen.

OUACHITA PARISH

Calhoun: The Choctaw Indians had a village near Calhoun.

Monroe: The Upper Pargoud Plantation is located on Island Drive. Approximately 400 yards north of the plantation house, between the Ouachita River and the levee, is the Pargoud Indian mound. The mound is said to be the burial site of the Indian Princess Wichita.
Around 1527, Panfilo de Narvaez (Navarez) and his men were in the process of claiming North America for Spain when they arrived at the Mississippi River. The story goes that one of de Narvaez's men, Juan Ortega (Ortego), was drowning while

trying to cross the Mississippi River. The Indian Princess Wichita saved his life. Ortega married Wichita, the daughter of Chief Ucita. In 1528 Ortega departed for Spain, leaving Wichita behind. She is said to have grieved herself to death.

NOTE: If the Spanish had managed to control the area now known as the United States, children would be reading the story of Wichita and Juan Ortega, instead of Pocahontas and John Smith.

PLAQUEMINES PARISH

Phoenix: The Fort of the Bayogoulas (Bayougoulas) was an Indian fort in the late 1600's and early 1700's. It was noted by Father Paul Du Ru in 1700 that the Bayougoula Indians had a fort on the east bank of the Mississippi River. The fort was located in the woods near Fort de la Boulaye. Fort de la Boulaye was located near Phoenix at the intersection of the Gravolet Canal and the old Mississippi River levee, and the Indian fort is believed to have been located on the old Mississippi River levee up river from the French fort. As you travel away from Louisiana State Highway 39 on the Gravolet Canal, the old levee should be the first ridge or raised ground you come to. Look for clam shells in the area.

POINTE COUPEE PARISH

Livonia: Many relics and artifacts can be found in the area north of Livonia along Louisiana Highway 78. Several Indian mounds are also located in this area.

RAPIDES PARISH

Alexandria: When La Salle explored the area of Rapides Parish in 1682, he found an Indian village on the Red River. The tribe collected pearls from fresh water oysters in the river and traded them among the other tribes.

SABINE PARISH

Converse: Twelve miles southwest of the city of Converse is an Indian burial mound. The mound is believed to have been built by a pre-Caddo tribe.

SAINT BERNARD PARISH

Indian Mound Bay: Between Lake Borgne and Chandeleur Sound lies Indian Mound Bay. At one time this entire area was covered with islands composed of prehistoric Indian mounds. Artifacts found on and in these mounds have been dated back to before the birth of Christ. Over the years the mounds were dredged up and used as fill in the construction of highways, parking lots and driveways. Only a few mounds remain and they are being eaten away by nature.

I first became aware of Indian Mound Bay through the writings of Paul Serpas. In one article he wrote of an Indian mound in the bay that resembled an alligator from the air. This I had to see for myself. From the air I could see what may be the largest Indian mound in the world. An island in the shape of an alligator. It appeared to be approximately six miles long. This Indian mound was one of dozens in what is now known as Indian Mound Bay. I could also see a three mile long sea-horse and several other smaller islands resembling animals.

Over the years several unique and unusual items have been found in various Saint Bernard Parish Indian mounds. What has been described as a prehistoric oyster shell measuring two feet by four feet was said to have been found in one mound. A pair of 2,500 year old human skulls were found in another mound. Part of a 2,000 year old dugout canoe was also found in Saint Bernard Parish. Some of the objects found have been dated at over 3,000 years old.

SAINT CHARLES PARISH

Lake Salvadore: At one time there were many Indian mounds around Lake Salvadore. A few still exist today, along with tales of pirates burying treasures in some of the mounds. The most famous Indian mound on the shores of Lake Salvadore was "The Temple." Originally the mound was a Chawasha Indian burial mound. Over the years the mound was used by Jean Lafitte as a storehouse for treasure and a slave market. In 1814, during the Battle of New Orleans, the United States erected a fort on the site. The Temple received its name because of the large quantity of human bones found on the mound. It was believed that the mound was the site of a sacrificial alter. It is now believed that the Chawasha did not bury their dead, but placed them on raised wooden platforms. This would allow the soul to leave the body at the proper time. They may have buried the bodies of their enemies to trap their souls under the ground. The Temple was located on the eastern side of Lake Joseph at the mouth of Bayou Des Allemands.

SAINT MARTIN PARISH

Saint Martinville: When the white man came to this part of Louisiana, the land was in the possession of the Attakapas (*man eater*). Neighboring tribes--the Choctaws, Alibamons, and Opelousas--formed a league to protect themselves from the viciousness of the Attakapas. A great battle was said to have been fought in the hilly area three miles west of Saint Martinville. As a result of this battle, the land of the Attakapas was divided among the three victorious tribes. The Choctaws took the Techeland, the Alibamons took the area between the Mermentau River and Vermilion Bayou, and the Opelousas received the general area of Saint Landry Parish.

SAINT MARY PARISH

Berwick: The Union Army fortification known as Battery at Berwick City was located on the west side of Berwick Bay. The battery was said to have been constructed around an Indian mound.

SAINT JAMES PARISH

Lutcher: Several Indian mounds were located near the Mississippi River along Louisiana State Highway 44, between Lutcher and Convent. Stories of buried treasure may have led some seekers to destroy these mounds. One story told of a fortune in Indian gold being buried within the mounds. A second story told of a plantation owner burying $200,000 in gold and silver coins within one of the mounds during the Civil War. Nothing has ever been reported found in this area except Indian artifacts.

SAINT TAMMANY PARISH

Abita Springs: In what has been described as one of the most unusual archaeological discoveries made in southeast Louisiana, we may find a clue to the "Lost Treasure of the Aztecs". A small Aztec Indian sculpture was found on the banks of Abita Creek--small in that it can be held within two hands. The sculpture is a delicately carved representation of an Aztec chief and has been named the "Old Man". The "Old Man" discovery coupled with the fact that several ancient mud pyramids have been found in Louisiana similar in shape and size to those constructed by the Aztecs is the basis for our next treasure story, The Lost Treasure of the Aztecs.

The Aztecs derived their name from Azatlan, believed to be their place of origin located somewhere in North America. The Aztecs dominated central and southern Mexico from the early 14th century until 1521 when the Spanish gained control of the country.

The Aztecs worshiped many gods, most notably Uitzilopochtli, the sun god. The Aztecs associated gold with their sun god. In this respect one could say that the Aztecs, like the Spanish, worshipped gold. The Aztecs acquired their lands by conquest, and by the 1520's had thirty-eight provinces paying tributes of gold, silver, emeralds, grains and other goods. Nahuatl Montezuma II, the Aztec chief, believing Hernan Cortes (Cortez) to be the god Quetzalcoatl, gave Cortes elaborate gold and silver gifts. Montezuma was later held hostage by Cortes in order to extract more treasure from the Aztecs. Montezuma, it was said, secretly ordered the vast hoards of gold, silver and jewels be taken from their storehouses near Tenochtitlan (Mexico City) and concealed somewhere in what is now North America.

Over the years people have searched for the Aztec treasure from Mexico City to Nova Scotia with the same results. The treasure has never been found, but if it were found today it would have a value of at least $1,000,000,000. The treasure of the Aztecs may not be near Abita Springs, but then again, why not?

Slidell: Several Indian villages were located in the area of Slidell. Several rather large mounds can be seen to the north of Louisiana State Highway 433, between Slidell and The Rigolets. It is believed that this site was the location of an early "Colapissa" (Acolapissa) Indian fort and village discovered by the French in 1765. It is believed that the fort was necessary because of numerous attacks made by the Chickasaw Indians. This area is fenced and posted, but other sites are not.

WEST BATON ROUGE PARISH

Maringouin: The Mound Plantation House received its name because it was built atop an Indian mound. Because human skeletons were found along with other relics during construction of the house, it is believed to have been a burial mound. The plantation is located three miles south of Maringouin on Louisiana State Highway 77.

WEST CARROLL PARISH

Epps: Poverty Point is perhaps one of the best examples of what should be done with an Indian mound. The state of Louisiana is in the process of excavating the area, but only approximately 2% of Poverty Point has been excavated to date. If you have the chance to visit the area during the summer months, there will undoubtedly be some excavation in progress. Exploration of the site began in 1913, and giving the current rate of excavation, it will still be in progress during the 40th century. The main mound at Poverty Point is a giant bird over 75 feet in height with a 640 foot wingspan, it contains 35 times the cubic volume of the Great Pyramid of Cehops and was built over 3,000 years ago. The area around Poverty Point abounds with Indian artifacts, and it is believed by many that a massive treasure is buried within the huge mound. Please notice that the concrete has been inlaid with thousands of points from the excavations done at this site. Rather then sell any of those points to the public, to help defray the cost of excavating, they apparently decided to decorate with them. Poverty Point is located approximately 5 miles east of Epps on Louisiana State Highway 134.

WEST FELICIANA PARISH

Angola: In 1706, the Tunica Indians had a large village on the east bank of the Mississippi River in an area called "Portage of the Cross." The village was located at the eastern end of Old River.

Angola: The Tunicas were considered the richest Indian tribe in North America by the French, and it was said that they "hoarded up money." On June 14, 1731, the Tunicas were attacked while they slept. The Head Chief of the Tunicas,

Cahura-Joligo, was the first person killed. The battle lasted continuously for over five days and nights. Sometime after the battle was over the new chief, Bride les Boeufs, told his people that ghosts now walk the land. He said the land was unhappy and moved the tribe to the area now known as Tunica. Legend has it that the Tunicas buried several treasure caches along both banks of the Mississippi River near the Angola Swamp. Two pots of gold have been reported found on the west bank of the Mississippi River in this area and more are suspected.

Tunica: In 1731, the Tunica Indians moved to Trudeau where they again prospered. Trudeau was excavated and the "Tunica Treasure" consisting of dozens of firearms, numerous pieces of European ceramics, and hundreds of metal kettles, pots and pans, glass beads, assorted tools, and artifacts were found and valued at $5,000,000. The "Tunica Treasure" is considered the largest collection of Indian and European artifacts from the colonial period of the Mississippi River Valley. In the late 1700's, most of the Tunica Indians moved to Marksville, where they remained, while others went on to Texas and Oklahoma.

In 1980, the United States Congress declared the Tunica-Biloxi reservation a sovereign nation. The Tunica filed suit to have the "Tunica Treasure" returned to the Tunica Indians. The court ruled that "Grave goods belong to descendants." This action laid the foundation for The Native American Graves Protection and Repatriation Act. The act declares that all objects taken from grave sites, held by museums, state and federal agencies, which are identifiable as belonging to a particular tribe, must be returned.

The Tunicas built their museum inside an Indian mound, thereby returning the bones and other artifacts to the ground, but at the same time allowing the artifacts to be seen and enjoyed by all. The museum is located on Louisiana State Highway 1 in Marksville, just next to the Grand Casino Avoyelles (owned by the Tunica-Biloxi Indians).

When the Tunica received the "Tunica Treasure," the artifacts were in need of restoration that would have cost approximately $2,000,000. The Tunica solved this problem by establishing the first artifacts conservation laboratory and training facility on an American Indian reservation. The Tunica-Biloxi tribe are now training other tribes to do their own restoration of artifacts.

THE LOST CITIES OF GOLD

Everyone has heard the stories of the "Seven Cities of Gold", but what many people may not know is that one or more of the cities may have been in Louisiana. In 1528, Alvar Nunez Cabaza de Vaca and three other men were the only survivors of four hundred Spaniards shipwrecked in a violent storm. De Vaca and the three men walked across Louisiana, Texas, New Mexico and Mexico to the Pacific coast. The journey took eight years. When he returned to Spain he told of seeing seven cities so rich that gold covered the walls. This started the Spanish exploration of the "New World" with Ponce de Leon leading the way. Ponce de Leon, of course, got involved with his own quest for youth and the fountain thereof. More and more Spanish came, but the "Seven Cities of Gold" were never found.

Today there are many who believe that one or more of the seven cities could have been in Louisiana. They do not believe that the wall and streets of the cities were paved with gold, but they do believe there was much gold to be found in these cities. The Indians used gold for decoration, other than that it had no value. Food could not be seasoned or preserved with it, nor could one use it to catch a fish or kill a deer. There were no industrial uses for gold at the time. Gold was valuable only to the "Old World" people.

The Spanish came and saw that the Indians were using the gold for decorations. The Spanish found that the Indians would trade the gold for glass beads, knives, axes and anything else the foreigners had. When the Spanish thought they had all the gold, the Indians would find more. When the Spanish had used up all their trade goods, the Indians still had more gold. The Spanish then took the gold by force and enslaved the Indians. The

Indians soon learned to hate gold and all the misery it brought. The Indians would receive word of the approaching Spanish and hide all their gold. They only gave it up as a last resort. It is because of this practice that many believe Indian mounds contain buried treasure. Because the Indians held their mounds to be sacred, an Indian mound would be the first site that a reasonable man would think to search. Although it is true that some tribes did bury their dead with all of their worldly possessions, a mound would probably be the last place the Indians would hide something.

Poverty Point was the location of one of the great trading centers of the Indian nations. Artifacts from as far away as Siberia have been found at Poverty Point. It is believed that long ago the Poverty Point Indians found they could stay in one location and trade with Indians from all over. They would trade for objects they wanted or needed, or objects they knew another tribe wanted or needed.

Suppose de Vaca heard of the Indian settlement at Poverty Point and ventured there. He would have seen all the gold trinkets being worn or traded by the natives. He would have seen a city that was rich with gold.

When the Spanish came with their greed and barbaric ways, trading Indians would have told the Poverty Point Indians of the curse the gold would bring. The Indians could very well have taken the gold far away from the settlement and hidden it.

It is quite possible that many tribes hid their gold and silver in this manner, we know that the Aztec Indians did.

NOTE: If you would like to learn more about the Indians of Louisiana, you may wish to order The Indians of Louisiana. Kniffen, Fred Bowerman. Pelican Publishing Company, Gretna: 1991. The book is in its fifth printing and has passed the test of time. This book has also passed the test of dimensions as it has a tendency to disappear. Play it safe, order two copies.

If you would like to identify your Indian artifacts you may want to order Indian Artifacts of the East and South an

<u>Identification Guide</u>. Swope, Robert Jr. Published by Robert Swope, Jr. Pennsylvania: 1982. Price $14.00, a real bargain at twice that price. I found the book to be enjoying and informative, and I am sure you will too.

If you can find a copy of <u>North American Indian Artifacts</u>. Hothem, Lar. Published by Books Americana, Incorporated, Florence, get it. The copy I have is the 1994 edition. At that time the book sold for $22.95. This book covers every aspect of Indian artifacts.

<u>Make yourself familiar with the latest ruling of the United States Archaeological Resources and Protection Act of 1978</u>.

"In the beginning, God created the heaven and the earth..."

Genesis

CHAPTER VI

PLANTATIONS

As the melting glaciers inched their way north, rivers, bayous, and creeks were formed in the great Garden of Eden we now know as Louisiana. The largest of these rivers is the Mississippi with its alluvial plain that straddles the entire length of the river. The alluvial plain was formed by the overflowing river's deposit of fertile soil. This same phenomena also occurred along the Atchafalaya, Black, Ouachita, Pearl, Red, and Sabine rivers, giving Louisiana some of the finest soil in the world. Think of it this way: As the snows melt and the rains continue to wash away the top soils of the northern states, they are deposited in Louisiana.

Louisiana has a subtropical climate that gives the state mild winters mixed with hot summers and an average of 55 inches of rain per year.

By 1780, indigo was the major crop grown in Louisiana. Tobacco was a distant second, but it required too much attention. Two new crops were soon to arrive and the South would never be the same.

In 1793, Eli Whitney invented the cotton gin, revolutionizing the cotton industry. Most of this revolution took place in northern Louisiana. Indigo and tobacco were continued as the crop of southern Louisiana, but they were not as profitable as cotton. Cotton was the perfect crop for northern Louisiana, just as sugar was to become for the southern part of the state.

From the 1740's, sugarcane of different types had been experimented with in Louisiana, but it was not until 1795, when

Jean Etienne de Bore improved the process for granulating sugar, that sugarcane became profitable.

By 1840, New Orleans had become the second largest port in North America and was about to surpass New York.

If "Cotton was King," sugar must surely have been the queen. By 1860, and the start of the Civil War, more than half of the millionaires in North America were living in Louisiana. The number of plantations had soared to 1,291. Their owners were making money in record amounts, as was anyone who had anything to do with the production of cotton or sugar.

In 1835, New Orleans had a population of about 45,000. By 1840, the population had soared to over 100,000, and it was the forth largest city in the United States. Only the ports of Liverpool, London, and New York handled more goods than New Orleans. Before the start of the Civil War, New Orleans was approaching New York in population and tonnage shipped. It seamed everyone was getting rich from sugar and cotton.

For instance, Mister Henry Clay Warmoth, a former governor of Louisiana, built the sixty-mile "Buras to New Orleans Railroad" for his wife to make trips to New Orleans. Mistress Warmoth, it seemed, disliked steamboats and found traveling by buggy took too long.

Mister Charles Duralde, the owner of the Pine Alley Plantation in Saint Martinville, had two daughters getting married at the same times. He imported spiders from China and set them loose in the alley of live oaks which lined the front of the plantation home. The spiders spun their webs until the morning of the wedding when slaves covered the webs with gold dust. Duralde's plantation carriages were embellished with gold and silver. The wedding reception lasted several days and was attended by over two thousand of the country's elite. The total cost of the wedding was said to be approximately $45,000. "A good time was had by all."

When the Civil War started Duralde buried his immense fortune and joined the war against Northern aggression. At the end of the war Duralde returned to his beautiful plantation only to find it in ruin. Duralde was crushed and removed only enough of his cache to sustain a meager existence for himself. He died a short time later a broken wisp of a man. It has been estimated that as much as $1,500,000 of Duralde's treasure may remain buried somewhere near the ruins of the Pine Alley Plantation.

The following is a list of other Louisiana plantations containing known treasures:

ASSUMPTION PARISH

Napoleonville: The Woodlawn Plantation was built in 1835 and was destroyed by fire in the 1940's. In 1933 a small cache of coins was found at the plantation, giving rise to the theory that more treasure exists.

CATAHOULA PARISH

During the time prior to the Civil War a man named Charles Durand had a well established plantation in what is now Catahoula Parish. Durand was considered the richest man in the parish. During the Civil War, Durand buried his immense wealth and went off to fight. When he returned he found that his plantation had been destroyed. Durand became deranged. When questioned as to the location of his hidden wealth, he could not remember the locations. He died a short time later, taking the secret to his grave. Several of Durand's children dug for months and found nothing.

NOTE: For more information on this story, see if you can find a copy of the book, With a Southern Accent.

CLAIBORNE PARISH

Athens: An unknown plantation owner was said to have buried his entire fortune near his plantation home with the intent of reclaiming it after the Civil War ended. The man died before the war ended, and the treasure has never been recovered.

CONCORDIA PARISH

Acme: During the Civil War, two pots of gold coins were buried near the Red River by an unknown landowner and his slave. The landowner then joined the Confederate army and went off to war, taking his slave with him. The owner was killed in action. The slave returned to the plantation and decided to keep the money, but wanted to wait until it was needed before digging it up. The slave died and the treasure has never been reported found.

EAST BATON ROUGE PARISH

Baton Rouge: In 1929, Clyde Pickett was reading some of his old family records when he learned that during the Civil War his ancestors cached the family silverware. Mr. Pickett went to the location of the plantation ruins and began to search for the silverware. What Mr. Pickett found was a cache of pre-Civil War gold and silver coins. He stopped looking for the silverware at that point. It is believed by many that the Pickett family silverware may remain buried along with other caches on the old plantation.

Baton Rouge: A treasure cache is said to be buried near an old cottage on the Conrad Plantation near Baton Rouge.

EAST FELICIANA PARISH

Saint Francisville: The Locust Grove Plantation was originally owned by Luther L. Smith who was married to Anna Eliza Davis, the sister of Jefferson Davis. Buried in the plantation cemetery is Sarah Knox Taylor Davis, the daughter of Zachary Taylor, and the first wife of Jefferson Davis. This plantation home was built prior to 1816 and was destroyed during the Civil War. The plantation has been said to be the location of several treasure caches.

The site of the Old Locust Grove Plantation is east of Saint Francisville near Louisiana State Highway 10.

IBERIA PARISH

Oliver: The owner of a plantation southwest of Oliver is said to have buried a large amount of gold coins, the family jewels and silver services before joining the Confederate Army. The plantation owner died in action, taking the knowledge of the location to his grave.

IBERVILLE PARISH

Saint Gabriel: The Houmas House Plantation was built in 1840 by Colonel John Smith Preston. In 1857, the plantation was purchased by John Burnside for $750,000 in cash.

John Burnside could have been the subject of one of Horatio Alger's stories. Burnside was a poor orphan, by the time of his death he was revered as the most successful bachelor in Louisiana.

Burnside owned several businesses in New Orleans, eleven other plantations, and had over three thousand slaves. Burnside had no heirs and was said to distrust banks. It is believed by many that Burnside buried his immense wealth near his beloved Houmas House Plantation home.

The plantation house is located at 40136 Louisiana State Highway 942, approximately two miles west of Louisiana State Highway 44.

JEFFERSON PARISH

Fairfield Plantation: In 1862, word reached the owner of Fairfield Plantation that an invasion of Union forces would soon occur. During low tide he buried his prize possessions in the battures (area of land between the river and levee) of the

Mississippi River in front of his plantation. The treasure was said to have a value of $120,000 in 1862, and should now be worth at least $1,200,000. A map to the exact location is said to exist.

LA SALLE PARISH

Little Creek: It has been said that on an unknown plantation eight miles south of Little Creek, a cache of gold and silver coins was made and never recovered.

MADISON PARISH

Tensas River National Wildlife Refuge: The ruins of a pre-civil war plantation can be found deep in the forest. A dozen handmade brick pillars are all that remain of the three story structure. Nearby can be found an old cemetery. It has been said that within the area of the old plantation home a fortune in gold, silver, and jewels awaits recovery by the right person.

NATCHITOCHES PARISH

Natchitoches: The master of the Simmons House Plantation distrusted banks as well as people in general, and upon his death only a few dollars could be found in his possession. It was deduced that his vast wealth was hidden somewhere on his property. There has never been a report of any of his wealth being found.

Natchitoches: The Melrose Plantation, also known as the Metoyer Plantation, or the Yucca Plantation, is said to be the site of a chest of gold buried by the Metoyer family. The plantation was established in 1796 by Marie Therese Coincoin (Coin-Coin), "gens de couleur libres" (free person of color). The house was recorded as being owned by Louis Metoyer, Marie's mulatto son. The plantation is located approximately sixteen miles south of Natchitoches, off Louisiana State Highway 1 at the intersection of Louisiana State Highways 119 and 493.

OUACHITA PARISH

Monroe: It has been reported that during the Civil War the owner of the Limerick Plantation buried all his valuables near his home just prior to the arrival of Union soldiers. This treasure is believed to have remained undisturbed for the last 132 years.

PLAQUEMINES PARISH

Myrtle Grove: Rumors persist of a Civil War treasure cache being made on the Myrtle Grove Plantation.

POINTE COUPEE PARISH

New Roads: Marquis Claude Vincent de Ternant built his plantation home in 1750 on False River, and it has continued to be passed down in the family. After the death of the Marquis, his wife married Colonel Charles Parlange, who also died a short time later. The plantation derives its name from the widow Parlange. Originally Indigo was grown on the plantation, later cotton, and then sugar became the cash crop. In 1842, $300,000 in cash was listed on an estate inventory.

During the Civil War all the treasures of the plantation were hidden from view by Madame Virginie de Ternant, the daughter-in-law of the Marquis Vincent de Ternant. Three chests of gold and silver coins were buried in three locations within the massive garden area. The gardens were said to be a copy of the Jardin des Fleurs at Versailles. The silverware was hidden in the walls above the windows, and the furniture was hidden in the attic. When Union Army General Nathaniel Banks arrived he was greeted, given a hot meal and generally treated with respect. The plantation was spared destruction. To counteract the treatment she gave the Yankees, Madame Parlange treated the Confederate Army General Dick Taylor in the same manor.

The plantation grounds were used by both Confederate and Union forces as a camps, and it was said that Madame Parlange's beautiful gardens were used as a mule lot.

After the Civil War the plantation returned to its previous splendor, but Madame Parlange could only remember where she had buried two of the chests. Over the past 125 years the family has conducted numerous searches, and now believe that sometime over the years the last chest may have been recovered by person or persons unknown. The plantation is located on Louisiana State Highway 1, five miles south of New Roads.

NOTE: Madame Virginie de Ternant posed for the John Singer Sargent's "Portrait of Madame X" that now hangs in the New York Metropolitan Museum of Art.

RAPIDES PARISH

Lecompte: The Old Sugar Bend Plantation is said to be the site of William Martin's treasure cache. It has been reported that Martin was one of the wealthiest plantation owners in the parish, but after his death only a few hundred dollars could be accounted for.

SAINT CHARLES PARISH

Destrehan, d'Estrehan Plantation: Jean Noel d'Estrehan was a wealthy merchant and good friend of the Lafitte brothers. Jean Lafitte is said to have buried one of his many treasures here. The d'Estrehan Plantation was built in 1787. d'Estrehan had a distrust for banks, and several sources state that when he died he left $450,000 in treasure caches near the plantation house. Other sources state that d'Estrehan buried his $450,000 treasure and mysteriously disappeared.

The plantation is also rumored to be the resting place of one of Jean Lafitte's major treasure caches. $400,000 in gold, silver and jewels, and the non-resting place of Lafitte's ghost. The plantation house is now the property of the River Road Historical Society and is open to the public. The plantation home is located at 9999 River Road, Louisiana State Highway 48, approximately four and one half miles west of the junction at Louisiana State Highway 50.

Saint Rose: $50,000 in gold coins are rumored to be hidden within an old plantation home located near Saint Rose. The treasure was placed within the residence during the Civil War and reportedly never recovered. Because of this story the Mansion has been completely destroyed by so called "treasure hunters". There is another name for people who destroy the property of others it is "CRIMINAL."

SAINT JAMES PARISH

Convent: Jefferson College was built as a gift to the Marianist Fathers by Valcour Aime in 1830. In 1831 this three story plantation house opened its doors to the young men of Louisiana as Jefferson College. In 1861, the name was changed to the Louisiana College. During the Civil War, Union Army troops were stationed in and around the house. Today the property is owned by the Jesuits and is known as the Manresa Retreat House for Laymen. The house is located on Louisiana State Highway 44, two miles south of Convent.

Vacherie: The Valcour Aime Plantation house was built in late 1799 by Don Francisco Aime. In 1861, at the beginning of the Civil War, Valcour Aime was one of the wealthiest men in America. Aime was known as the Louis XIV of Louisiana and his plantation was called "Le Petit Versailles." The plantation was also known as "The Refinery," because it was said to be the first plantation in Louisiana to refine sugar.

As the Union Army approached in 1862, Aime buried his valuables estimated at $2,000,000 somewhere near his plantation home. Among Aime's prize possessions was a solid gold table service which he displayed at his many social functions. Most people believe that Aime buried his cache in his prodigious gardens. Other stories claim that Aime may have dumped at least part of this vast wealth into the Mississippi River. Aime died in 1867 of unknown causes. There has never been any reports of his treasure being found.

The home which burned in 1920, was located just off Louisiana State Highway 18, between Oak Alley and Vacherie. The site is marked by an historical marker.

SAINT JOHN THE BAPTIST

Edgard: A large cache of gold and silver coins was reportedly made by the owner of the Bonafice Plantation during the Civil War and never recovered.

SAINT LANDRY PARISH

Grand Coteau: Gavriel Fuselier de la Claire built the Claire Plantation in the early 1790's.   Claire's grandson was a Confederate officer during the Civil War and was having a small party when word came that Union soldiers were surrounding the plantation.   The owner and his friends removed their uniforms and painted their hands and faces black.   Disguised as slaves they made good their escape.   Once the Union troops learned of this trick, the plantation was burned to the ground.

Some people believe that the owner hid his family fortune, $500,000, in several locations within and without the plantation, and that after the Civil War he never returned.   There has never been a report of treasure being found on this site.

SAINT MARTIN PARISH

Baldwin: The Darby Plantation was built in 1765 and is said to be the site of a treasure cache consisting of gold coins. When Mister and Mistress Darby died everything was left to their daughter and two sons. The daughter buried her inheritance to spite her two brothers. The cache has never been reported found.

The plantation home has been restored and is now a branch office of the Saint Mary Bank and Trust Company on Louisiana State Highway 182, at its junction with Louisiana State Highway 83.

SAINT MARY PARISH

Franklin: The Haifleigh Plantation was built in 1804 by William Haifleigh. In 1938 the plantation home was destroyed by fire. It has long been believed that a treasure was buried here and never recovered.

TENSAS PARISH

Newellton: Camp at Winter Quarters. General Ulysses Simpson Grant's forces were camped at the Winter Quarters Plantation on April 2, 1863. The plantation is located at the south end of Lake Saint Joseph on Louisiana State Highway 608 six miles east of Newellton. It is a now a Louisiana State Commemorative Area.

Newlight: Colonel Norman Frisbee, also spelled Frisby, was the owner of one of the largest plantations in Louisiana. It seems that Frisbee adopted the rank of colonel, as he was never in the service, and no one knew where his money had come from. Most people assumed that Frisbee may have been a pirate at some point in his life. What is known is that Frisbee went from working for his uncle on a Mississippi plantation to owning his own plantation in a very short time. The Frisbee

Plantation was eight miles from the Flowers Landing. There was a running feud between Frisbee and Flowers over an incident involving some of Flowers' livestock.

In July, 1861, Frisbee was in the process of building a massive 40 room plantation when he received word of the approach of Northern troops. Realizing that if and when the Union Army arrived everything he had would be seized, Frisbee devised a plan. First, he gathered up most of his slaves and took them to a market in Texas. Frisbee felt that Texas would never enter the war and, thereby, not abolish slavery. The slaves were sold at auction for a reported $270,000. Frisbee insisted on payment in gold coins. He returned to his plantation with the money and proceeded with the second step of his plan. He had two slaves load his gold and silver, valued at approximately $1,000,000, into two wagons and cart it into a swampy area near his home. Some of the items listed in the treasure were a 200 pound silver bell, an assortment of solid silver and solid gold doorknobs--at least 40 of them, gold and silver table services and at least $270,000 in gold coins. It has been written that the bell was cached in one location and the other treasures in a second location, but it is really not known how many cache sites were used. If Frisbee was in a rush as most stories state, it is most likely that only one site was used. After the treasure was buried, Frisbee killed the two slaves.

Within twenty-four hours of burying his treasure the feud between Frisbee and Flowers ended with Frisbee carrying his secret to the grave. Several sources believe that Frisbee may have written down the location of his cache in his Bible. For the last 120 years the search has focused on the Bible and not the treasure itself. Other sources state that the treasure was marked by a gun barrel lodged in a gum tree.

Most likely Frisbee's land encompassed 12,000 acres, but some reports say as much as 42,000 acres. Considering the acreage involved, it is not surprizing that the treasure has not been reported found, despite the fact that over the years thousands of searches have been conducted. With the advent of modern metal detectors, it should not be too hard to locate a treasure of this size. (For under $700 you can purchase a deep seeking metal detector that will find a treasure of that size twenty feet down in the ground.)

The ruins of the Frisbee Plantation are located just north of Louisiana State Highway 4, approximately 5.5 miles east of Newlight.

TERREBONNE PARISH

Schriever: The Ducros Plantation was constructed prior to 1845 and was used by both Confederate and Union troops during the Civil War. The plantation is located one-half mile north of Schriever on Louisiana State Highway 20, approximately one-half mile from the junction with Louisiana State Highway 24.

Schriever: The Magnolia Plantation was built in 1834 by Thomas Ellis. During the Civil War the Magnolia Plantation was used as a Union Army hospital. The plantation is located three miles south of Schriever on Louisiana State Highway 311, one and one-third miles south of its junction with Louisiana State Highway 24.

WEST FELICIANA PARISH

Saint Francisville: The Afton Villa was destroyed by fire in 1963, but the legend of treasure caches continues today.

Saint Francisville: The Cottage Plantation consists of several buildings constructed between the years 1795 and 1859. The plantation was purchased in 1812 by Thomas Butler. It is believed by many that a large treasure cache was made near the main house and never recovered. The Cottage is now open to the public and is located approximately five miles north of Saint Francisville on United States Highway 61.

Saint Francisville: The Oak Grove Plantation was destroyed by fire in 1930 and is reported to be the site of yet another buried treasure.

THINGS YOU SHOULD KNOW

Because of the fact that plantation owners were so rich, most plantations have treasure stories attached to them. Almost every legend has its beginning based in fact. One should attempt to separate the facts from the legends before spending time and money searching for any treasure.

Many subdivisions and small towns received their names from the plantations that occupied those sites. Because of the immense size of plantations, the site of a treasure cache may have been several hundred yards from the main house and could now be located in the area of modern construction.

Once you have decided to search for a treasure, every effort must be made to receive permission from the landowner in writing. An agreement should be written up between the persons looking for the treasure. "Verbal agreements are not worth the paper they are written on." Also, nothing can drive a wedge between friends and relatives like treasure.

It is true that modern metal detectors can find a quart jar of coins buried fifteen feet in the ground. It will also find old anvils and anchors. Remember this, once an object is located someone has to dig it up or forever live in doubt.

CHAPTER VII

DISASTERS

UNTIMELY DEATHS

Before 1933 and the advent of the Federal Depositors Insurance Corporation (FDIC), no bank could be trusted completely. Even after the FDIC, people continued to find it hard to trust their life savings to anyone but themselves. This was often a mistake, because of untimely deaths. It was not uncommon for the head of a wealthy family to die before he could tell his next of kin where the family fortune had been secreted. Hurricanes, floods, epidemics, and fires all caused untimely deaths. There have been very few people in this world who knew exactly when they were going to die. If a person was very old or ill for a long time, he could expect death to be near and tell a loved one where this life savings were hidden. If he knew a disaster was about to happen, he would probably just leave the area and return when it was safe. But, in many cases the death or disaster came without warning. For these reasons many family fortunes have been lost, and many a treasure hunter has been rewarded.

CALCASIEU PARISH

Vinton: Nibletts Bluff was a Confederate stronghold until an epidemic struck in May of 1863. It is believed that many individual, small caches were made in the area by soldiers assigned to that post. This site is now part of the Nibletts Bluff Park and is located 8 miles west of Vinton on Louisiana State Highway 3063.

CLAIBORNE PARISH

Old Athens: The town of Old Athens was destroyed by fire in 1849. It is believed that many small and large caches were made in this area, and never reclaimed.

EAST BATON ROUGE PARISH

Baton Rouge: Settled in 1720 by the French, Baton Rouge has had its share of disasters. In 1783 the English ran the French out of the city, nearly destroying it. Later that same year, the Spanish ran the English from the city, and it was again almost destroyed.

On August 5, 1862, the Confederates attempted to retake the city from the occupying Union forces, and the city was once again brought close to destruction. Because of these near disasters, it has been reasoned that hundreds of individual treasure caches await the right person within the Baton Rouge area.

MADISON PARISH

Tallulah: Richmond was located at the junction of Brushy and Round Away Bayous. The town was destroyed by fire in 1859 and again in 1863. It is believed that many treasure caches were made in this area and never reclaimed.

NATCHITOCHES PARISH

Grand Ecore: In 1853 the town of Grand Ecore was nearly wiped out by an epidemic of yellow fever. Treasure stories abound in this area, and it is believed that many individual caches were never recovered.

NOTE: The late Michael Paul Henson (a nationally known treasure expert), believed that there was more treasure to be found in Natchitoches Parish then in any other parish within the state.

ORLEANS PARISH

New Orleans: In 1718, New Orleans suffered the first of many recorded yellow fever epidemics. In 1832, three hundred people were reported to have died in just one month. Several thousands died that year from the yellow fever. There were twenty-three reported yellow fever epidemics between 1718 and 1860. The worst recorded epidemic in New Orleans history was in 1853 when over twelve thousand died. In 1878 more than four thousand people died. The last known epidemic of yellow fever was in 1905, when the death toll reached only four hundred and twenty-three.

If only one in one hundred left a treasure cache, there would be more then enough sites to keep a person busy for the rest of his life.

In 1722, New Orleans was destroyed by a hurricane. It was only the first of many recorded.

In 1788 New Orleans suffered its first major fire which destroyed the entire city. On December 8, 1794, the second great fire of New Orleans occurred. In 1851, New Orleans was again destroyed by fire.

NOTE: With all of these disasters it is no wonder that so much treasure was found during the construction of the Louisiana Superdome.

RED RIVER PARISH

Coushatta: It has been said that more than $30,000,000 in treasure was buried by citizens in the area of Coushatta prior to the invasion of Union troops. Before these individual caches could be retrieved, the area was inundated by a flood which washed away markers and caches.

SAINT BERNARD PARISH

Shell Beach: Proctorsville was destroyed by a sudden violent storm on August 11, 1860. Many lives were lost and whole houses were destroyed disbursing their contents throughout the area.

Delacroix Island: In Saint Bernard Parish, during the 1918 swine flu epidemic, it is believed that approximately 100 people died in the small community of Delacroix Island, approximately one third of its population. It has been said that the dead were placed in pirogues because of the shortage of coffins. Most of the people who died were the elderly who were less able to fight off the illness. This was not an isolated incident, but merely a microcosm of the times.

TERREBONNE PARISH

Isle Dernier: Prior to the Civil War, Isle Dernier was the site of a very fashionable grand resort hotel. The 1856 Hurricane destroyed everything on the island killing over 200 people. It is believed that many of the personal treasures of these victims may remain on the island today as there were no credit cards at the time and everything had to be purchased with cold hard cash. The island has been searched many times over the years, but nothing major has ever been reported found, only small amounts of coins from time to time.

WEBSTER PARISH

Minden: Overton was a small town located on Dorcheat Bayou. The town was settled in 1821 and by the 1860's the town was nearly wiped out by several epidemics. It is believed by many that dozens of individual caches remain in the area of Overton.

WEST BATON ROUGE PARISH

Baton Rouge: The town of Saint Michel was located on the west bank of the Mississippi River. The town was destroyed by flooding in the 1850's, carrying treasures and markers away.

WEST FELICIANA PARISH

Saint Francisville: The town of Bayou Sara was destroyed by flooding in 1850. It is believed that many treasure caches were made by unsuspecting residents and never reclaimed.

SHIP WRECKS

It was always easier and cheaper to build and man a ship than to build a highway. Even after the highways were built, more goods could be sent by water for less cost than by any other means. Even after the trains arrived, ships continued to be built. With the advent of air transportation very little changed except the ships continued to get bigger and bigger in order to compete. As the ships grew in size the number of rivers they could use diminished.

The Mississippi River is the largest river within the United States and has long been used as a means of transporting goods throughout the country. Ships from every nation have probably traveled much of this great North American tributary at one time or another.

Other rivers and even bayous were used to transport goods throughout the state. The first settlements had to be located on water, or the settlers could not survive in this new world. Rivers like the Red, Sabine, Tchefuncte, Amite, Atchafalaya and Pearl, bayous like the Lafourche and Teche were what made our state grow and prosper.

For over 400 years ships have transported tons of treasure along the Louisiana Gulf Coast. Most of these ships made the passage safely, but some did not. It has been said that there is just as much treasure off the coast of Louisiana as off the coast of Florida.

Boats and ships have one major drawback, they are prone to sink under certain conditions. If ships did not sink this book would be shorter. Skin divers would have one less thing to do to have fun. Lloyds of London would have gone out of business a long time ago. Nor could pirates have disposed of the evidence of their crimes so easily.

Ships sunk during World War II carried every thing under the sun, but usually the expense of a salvage operation far outweighs the profit involved. Most sunken ships of World War II are documented and their exact locations known, therefore they will not be listed unless the prize is worth the price.

During the Civil War, ships carried only items deemed as important for the war effort. Gold and silver coins, pistols, rifles, cannons, swords, knives, and ammunition are some the items carried on these ships. Some of the items are considered priceless today. Because of the value of the cargo of Civil War ships, I have listed all known ships which sank during the Civil War. Please be advised that without proper authorization from the United States government, it is illegal to remove or possess artifacts from a sunken Confederate or United States ship.

AVOYELLES PARISH

Red River: The steamboat *Creole* caught fire on February 22, 1841, and burned to the water line. At the time of the fire the *Creole* was reportedly carrying $100,000 in gold and silver coins. It is believed that this wreckage lies near the mouth of the Red River.

CADDO PARISH

Dixie: The *Monterey* was carrying $750,000 in gold bars when it sank. It is believed that the Red River has changed course and that the *Monterey* now lies under a dried up river bed.

Shreveport: In May, 1863, the *Grand Duke* and the *T. W. Roberts* were sunk by Confederate sailors to prevent their capture by Union forces. In 1864, the *Jeff Thompson* and the *Drover* were also sunk to prevent being captured. All of these ships were sunk in the Red River while carrying Confederate Army supplies.

Shreveport: The *Kentucky* sank in the Red River just south of Shreveport after striking a snag in June, 1865. The ship was loaded with a Confederate regiment with full equipment. Two-hundred soldiers were said to have went down with this ship.

CALCASIEU PARISH

Vinton: Nibletts Bluff is the reported resting place of what has been described as the largest Jean Lafitte treasure. The ship was a three masted schooner loaded with treasure. Without time to unload the treasure Jean Lafitte ordered the ship scuttled in the Old River near Nibletts Bluff. This story has been passed down from generation to generation among the long time families of the area. Nibletts Bluff is located 8 miles west of Vinton on Louisiana State Highway 3063.

CAMERON PARISH

Last Island: In 1856, the *Nautilus* was lost in a hurricane just west of Last Island. At the time the ship went down, there was a reported $30,000 in gold and silver coins locked in the ships safe.

EAST BATON ROUGE PARISH

Profit Island: The *United States Ship Mississippi* sank off the northwest tip of Profit Island during the Civil War. It has been said that the ship was loaded with Union supplies at the time of its sinking.

GRANT PARISH

Montgomery: The Union gunboat *Savannah* sank near Creola Bluff in an old branch of the Red River.   This branch of the Red River is said to now be dry.   The ship was reported to be carrying a Union payroll and loaded with munitions.

LIVINGSTON PARISH

Amite River at Bayou Manchac: In 1879 one of the ships supplying Spanish settlers was sunk where the Amite River meets Bayou Manchac.   The ship was reportedly carrying a large shipment of gold.   Its cargo, having an estimated value of $1,600,000, has never been reported found.

NOTE: At almost the same site, but across the Amite River from Old Galvez Town, one of Jean Lafitte's treasure ships was rumored to have sunk with its treasure intact.   There is no record of any treasure being removed from either of these wrecks.

Amite River and Lake Maurepas: On August 7, 1863 the Union gunboat *Barataria* sank near the mouth of the Amite River.

NATCHITOCHES PARISH

Colfax: The Union transport ship *Champion No. 9* was sunk by a Confederate gun battery just above Colfax.   The ship was said to have had 150 Union soldiers with full battle equipment on board at the time.   There were no survivors reported.

Grand Ecore: The paddle wheeler *The Roberta* struck a bridge at Grand Ecore and sank.   It is believed that the ship was carrying a large amount of gold coins at the time.   There has never been any reported salvage operation conducted on this ship.

Montgomery: To prevent capture by the Confederates, the Union gunboat *Eastport* was scuttled on April 26, 1864, near Deloach's Bluff on the Red River.

Montgomery: The *E. F. Dix* sank near Deloach's Bluff. It has been said that the ship was carrying a large gold shipment when it went down.

PLAQUEMINES PARISH

Island #82: The *Oregon* sank on March 2, 1871, near the southern tip of Island #82 in the Mississippi River. When the ship went down it was carrying $300,000 in gold coins and bullion.

Island #83: The *John Adams* sank on February 27, 1871, near Island #83 in the Mississippi River. It was reportedly carrying $500,000 in gold. A large number of gold as well as silver coins have been reported found on Island #83, most of which are believed to be from the wreck of the *John Adams*.

RAPIDES PARISH

Red River: The *Ida May* sank at an unknown location along the Red River on December 28, 1865. The ship was believed to have been carrying a Union payroll.

Red River: To restrict Union shipping along the Red River, the *City Belle* was sunk at Wilson's Landing by Confederate fire. It is believed that all the ships cargo may have been removed.

Red River: The *John Warner* sank after being shelled by Confederate artillery on May 5, 1864, on the Red River at Dunn's Bayou. The ship was carrying Union Army supplies.

Red River: The *Era No. 2* sank on the Red River in May 1864. The boat was a fully loaded tin-clad Union gunboat.

Red River: It is believed that the *Music* sank somewhere along the Red River within Rapides Parish. The cargo of this ship is unknown, but is believed by many to be valuable.

Red River: The Union Transport *Champion No. 5* was sunk at Wilson's Landing by Confederate fire on April 27, 1864. The ship was loaded with troops and equipment at the time it sank.

RED RIVER PARISH

Campti: After hitting a snag on April 17, 1861, the *Le Compte* sank in the Red River . The ship was carrying war supplies at the time.

Red River: Confederate troops sank the *New Falls City* approximately one mile above the mouth of Loggy Bayou. The ship was sunk to keep its cargo from falling into Union hands.

SAINT BERNARD PARISH

Chandeleur Islands: In 1886, the *Porlamar* sank in a storm near Chandeleur Island. At the time of the ship's sinking it was carrying $25,000,000 in cargo. The cargo was said to consist of gold, diamonds and pearls. The site of the wreckage has never been located, and the cargo is believed to be intact.

Chalmette: On December 27, 1814, during the Battle of New Orleans, the *Carolina* burned and sank in the Mississippi River.

Lake Borgne: In December of 1814, during the Naval Battle of New Orleans, several British barges were sunk in the area between Point Claire, Malheureux Island and Saint Joseph Island.

SAINT MARY PARISH

Grand Lake: On April 13, 1863, Union troops set fire to the *Queen of the West* to keep it out of Confederate hands. It burned and sank in Grand Lake. The ship is believed to have been loaded with war supplies.

SAINT TAMMANY PARISH

Covington: Three ships are said to have sunk, one on top of another, just below Covington in the Tchefuncte River. One of these ships is said to have been loaded with a Confederate paymaster's chest filled with gold coins and 100 iron cannons worth from $4,000 to $27,000 each.

TERREBONNE PARISH

Gulf of Mexico, 28.4 degrees north and 90.45 degrees west: In 1942, the United States Coast Guard sank the *U-166*, a German submarine. The boat lies in 60 feet of water and is believed by many to contain an unknown "valuable cargo." What the submarine may contain is a fortune in mercury. Mercury was used as ballast on German submarines during the Second World War.

Timbalier Island and East Timbalier Island: The Spanish galleon *Panfilo de Narvaez* was reportedly wrecked in 1527 between Timbalier Island and East Timbalier Island. This ship may have been salvaged by the Spanish and her treasure taken to Marsh Island, where it remains.

VERMILION PARISH

Marsh Island, Russell Sage Game Refuge: The Spanish kept records of all shipment of treasure leaving the New World, and, as such, many things can be learned from their archives. Spanish records indicate that Marsh Island was used as a storehouse for treasures salvaged from sunken ships along the Gulf Coast. The treasures were brought to the island for safekeeping until they could be taken to Spain. There is no record in the archives of the Spanish ever removing these treasures from Marsh Island and much of this treasure may remain on the island today.

NOTE: In 1885, a shipwrecked sailor wrote of being washed up on the shore of Marsh Island with several of his crew members. In the morning the sailors noticed "curious little spots lying on the sand." The spots turned out to be approximately 400 Spanish gold doubloons.

Pecan Island: It has been reported that one of Jean Lafitte's treasure ships sank just west of Pecan Island.

Vermilion Bay: The *San Fernando* sank during a storm on October 13, 1812. It has been said that the Captain, Guy R. Champlin, was wearing a money belt containing $7,000 in gold coins and that the weight of the coins caused his drowning.

UNKNOWN PARISHES

Gulf of Mexico: The *Fulgencia* is believed to have sunk off the coast of Louisiana in 1799, carrying a cargo of silver today worth an estimated $18,000,000.

Gulf of Mexico: The *Genovesa* is known to have sunk off the Louisiana coast carrying an estimated $1,250,000 in gold and silver.

Gulf of Mexico: The *Huerto* is known to have been wrecked somewhere off the coast of Louisiana. The ship was said to be carrying a $1,250,000 cargo of gold and silver.

Gulf of Mexico: The *Jauragia* was wrecked off the coast of Louisiana. It was reportedly carrying a $1,250,000 cargo of gold and silver.

Lake Maurepas: *United States Ship Maurepas* sank on April 7, 1863. The ship was loaded with Union Army supplies.

Bayou Teche: The *Confederate States Ship Diana* sank on April 12, 1863, carrying war supplies.

Mississippi River: The *A. W. Baker* sank on February 3, 1862, carrying war supplies.

Mississippi River: The *United States Ship Antelope* sank on September 23, 1864, carrying Union Army supplies.

Mississippi River: The *United States Ship Arkansas* sank near Baton Rouge on August 5, 1862, loaded with Union Army supplies.

Mississippi River: The *United States Ship Conestoga* sank on March 8, 1864, and was carrying Union Army supplies at the time.

Mississippi River: The *United States Ship Sallie Woods* sank on July 17, 1862. This ship was said to be carrying Union troops and supplies.

Red River: The *United States Ship Covington* loaded with Union war supplies sank on May 4, 1864.

Red River: The *United States Ship Signal* sank on May 5, 1864. The ship was reportedly carrying Union Army supplies.

GHOST TOWNS

When people hear the words <u>Ghost Towns</u> they usually think of the old gold and silver mining towns of the "Old West." Ghost towns can be found throughout the world. There are hundreds of ghost towns in Louisiana. These once prosperous communities for one reason or another simply dried up and disappeared from maps. The cause may have been an economic or natural disaster, and usually it was sudden. For this reason many treasure hunters search out these ghost towns.

Ghost town hunting can be profitable and usually requires just a little research. There are often only two reference sources required to hunt ghost towns. An old map and a current map. Should a person want to look for items from the Civil War, a map from that period is necessary. Compare the names on the old map with the names on the current one. When a name is found where none exist today that should be a ghost town. Another way to find ghost towns is to read the historic markers and monuments alongside roads and highways. It usually only takes a few minutes and may be quite rewarding.

NOTE: The known ghost towns in Louisiana could fill a book, and may one day, but if you want a good reference book on ghost towns and treasure in general, try Thomas P. Terry's, <u>United States Treasure Atlas</u>. Vol. 4. Speciality Publishing Company, La Crosse: 1985. Mister Terry's book contains over 1275 listings of possible treasure sites, including 629 ghost towns and near ghost towns. All this information on only twenty-six pages.

CHAPTER VIII

ROGUES

DOMINIQUE YOU

Alexandre Frederic Lafitte, Dominique You (Youx), was also know as Captain Alexander, General Jontelle, General Johnson and General Jossenet. Dominique You was the older of the Lafitte brothers and at one time a lieutenant in the French Artillery under Napoleon Bonaparte. You had been of such great service to France that, after fighting a duel, Napoleon allowed him to leave France rather then face "Madame Guillotine."

At the Battle of New Orleans, Jean Lafitte's men were under the command of the world's greatest cannoneer Dominique You, considered by most historians as the real hero of the Battle of New Orleans.

To demonstrate You's skill, try to imagine firing a cannon from a rolling ship moving at about twenty knots at another rolling ship moving at approximately eighteen knots. The idea is to only hit the mast with your cannon ball, well, actually two cannon balls joined together with a length of chain. Remember, if the ship is hit and sinks there is no booty. Since Dominique You did just that many times, imagine what he could do on terra firma firing at a bunch of slow marching Red Coats. At the Battle of New Orleans Dominique was credited with killing all the English officers mounted on their horses and, thereby, causing the British withdrawal and subsequent defeat.

When the Battle of New Orleans had ended, Andrew Jackson said; "I wish I had fifty such guns on this line and five hundred such devils as Dominique You." "If I was ordered to storm the gates of hell with Dominique You as my Lieutenant, I would have no misgivings of the result."

After the Battle of New Orleans, You was pardoned by President Madison, gave up piracy and remained in New

Orleans. Dominique You went from being a pirate to being a New Orleans politician, one would think an easy transition, but it was not for Dominique. Legend has it that You, the most successful of Jean Lafitte's captains, not only gave up piracy, but gave up all the booty he had accumulated over the years. You never returned to piracy and never recovered any of his ill gotten treasure caches. You lived out his life a poor but honest man, dying on November 14, 1830. He eventually befriended a young Abraham Lincoln, but that is another story.

THE LEGENDARY SITES OF DOMINIQUE YOU'S CACHES

Cameron Parish, Mallard Island: It has been alleged that Dominique You and his First Mate each buried a cache at the same location on Mallard Island. You was said to have buried his cache six feet from a fig tree. The Mate is said to have buried his six feet from the same fig tree, but on the opposite side from You. It is truly believed that on Mallard Island there are two treasure caches within twelve feet of each other. The fig tree is no longer there, and the last time the island was checked, the property was being leased by an oil company.

Saint Mary Parish, Wax Bayou: In September of 1813, Dominique You's crew captured the *Dulce Nombre* and took it to the junction of Wax Bayou and the Bayou Teche. The gold, silver, jewels, and other cargo was off loaded, and the ship was then taken out to sea and sunk. It has been said the cargo from the ship was auctioned off, and that You buried the proceeds somewhere in that area.

Plaquemines Parish, Breton Island: It is believed that Dominique You may have buried several of his treasure caches on Breton Island. Two treasure caches were reportedly made by You in 1811.

Terrebonne Parish, Cat Island: In 1813, it is believed that Dominique You and his crew captured the *Luisa Antonia*. The ship was taken to Cat Island, where her treasure was off loaded and buried. The *Luisa Antonia* was then taken into the Gulf of Mexico and scuttled.

Terrebonne Parish, Timbalier Island: It is suspected that Dominique You may have made at least one or two treasure caches on Timbalier Island.

Terrebonne Parish, East Timbalier Island: Also listed as the site of another possible Dominique You treasure cache is East Timbalier Island.

GULBERT AND MAGILBRAY

Orleans Parish, New Orleans: Between the years of 1763 and 1788, a band of river pirates under the joint command of Captains Gulbert and Magilbray operated along the Mississippi River at New Orleans. Their hideout was said to have been where Cottonwood Creek emptied into the Mississippi River. All the pirates were killed by an angry mob and their hideout searched, but no gold, silver or jewels were ever found. It is believed that their accumulate wealth is cached in this area.

NOTE: If you can determine where Cottonwood Creek once emptied into the Mississippi River, it may be a good place to look for Gulbert and Magilbray's caches, believed to be in the hundreds of thousands of dollars. One hint: Cottonwood Creek was north of the Vieux Carre, well, at least up river.

JOHN A. MURRELL (1804 to 1843)

John A. Murrell, also spelled Murrel, was known as "The Great Western Land Pirate" and often called "Reverend Devil." Murrell was a cunning, shrewd, intelligent, bold, and ruthless outlaw. It is said he was taught to steal at the age of three by his mother and was robbing drunken customers at the tavern where she worked.

Murrell traveled about as a preacher and was caught stealing horses in the Deep South. The plantation owner whipped and branded Murrell in public. Murrell claimed that this public humiliation caused him "to abandon the work of the Lord," and he vowed to inflict his revenge on all plantation owners.

Murrell was particularly fond of scams. His favorite scam would lead him deep in the south where he would find a runaway slave. If a runaway could not be found, he would talk one into running away. Murrell pretended to be an abolitionist working on the Underground Railroad. A black would have a hard time traveling alone in the South, but in the company of a white no one would ask any questions. He would tell the slave that he would lead him to the North and freedom, but along the way, just to make expenses, he had to sell the slave from time to time. After the sale Murrell would always arrange the slave's escape, and the two could continue on their journey to freedom. If any problems arose the slave would simply be shot, "dead men tell no tales." Murrell was also involved in many other forms of crime. If it was profitable he would do it.

Murrell robbed and murdered along the Natchez Trace from the Ohio Valley area to Natchez, Mississippi. Flatboats, also known as keelboats, were basically covered wooden barges. They were carried down stream by the currents and steered with a rudder. Flatboats had no sails or motors. Flatboats would make the trip down river loaded with cargo bound for southern cities. Once the boats reached their destination and the cargos were unloaded, the boats would be sold for their wood. The crew of the flatboat would then return to the north with their money, usually along the Natchez Trace, where they were easy targets for Murrell and his band of cutthroats.

At one point it is said that Murrell had more than 1,500 heavily armed members in his gang, consisting of the fiercest, strongest slaves he could find using his abolitionist scheme. Murrell called his army of men "The Mystic Confederacy" or simply "The Clan." Murrell was raising an army with the intent of capturing Natchez and New Orleans and eventually both the states of Mississippi and Louisiana. He wanted to set himself up as king of this area of North America. He had set December 25, 1835, as the starting date for his uprising, with Natchez being his first target. In 1832, Murrell's camp was raided, he was taken to Nashville where he was convicted of stealing slaves and was sent to prison. While in prison Murrell contracted tuberculosis. He was released in 1842, and disappeared from recorded history. It is believed that Murrell died in 1843 of tuberculosis and never recovered any of his caches.

POSSIBLE MURRELL TREASURE SITES

Avoyelles Parish: It is quite possible that John Murrell buried one or more caches somewhere in Avoyelles Parish. In 1930 a farmer plowed up thousands of Spanish silver coins. This treasure cache has been attributed to Murrell. In 1939 a treasure chest was found only to be lost again in quicksand. This cache was also attributed to John Murrell.

Beauregard Parish, Sabine River: It has been alleged that members of the John Murrell gang made several caches of treasure and weapons within caves located along the Sabine River.

Grant Parish, Pollock: Local citizens believe that the Murrell outlaw gang stayed from time to time at a house in the area of Pollock. It is quite possible they left some of their loot behind.

Natchitoches Parish, Clarence: John Murrell is also said to have hidden one of his treasure caches in a cave near the town of Clarence.

Natchitoches Parish, Gorum: John Murrell was reported to have made a treasure cache in the area of Gorum.

Natchitoches Parish, Kisatchie: It has been reported that John Murrell at one time had his headquarters in Kisatchie, and many people believe that Murrell buried several caches in the area.   One of the possible sites suggested is in a cave somewhere in the Kisatchie Hills.

Natchitoches Parish, Natchitoches: John Murrell was rumored to have cached $20,000 in gold in a cave along the Red River northeast of Natchitoches, near where United States Highway 84 crosses the Red River.

Natchitoches Parish, Natchitoches: Perhaps the most famous of all John Murrell's treasure caches is the one reportedly buried seven miles northeast of Natchitoches.   Murrell is said to have buried from $100,000 to $30,000,000 near the west bank of the Red River.   500 yards west of a cave Murrell had a vault constructed in the ground, and the treasure was placed in the vault.   The vault was then buried and a headstone placed over it to mark the site.   Murrell then constructed a cemetery over the area complete with other headstones.

NOTE: There is a ninety percent possibility that this treasure has been found by a "World Class" treasure hunter who shall remain anonymous.   This treasure hunter is considered world class because it is believed that over the years he and his partner have found in excess on $100,000,000 without arousing public notice.   The vault was said to have measured 4' X 4' X 6' and contained an unknown amount of gold and silver coins, weapons, and ammunition.

Other treasure caches believed to be within this same area have been attributed to pirates, Confederate guerrillas, Union troops, Spanish Conquistadors and Mexican soldiers.

The late Paul Michael Henson, who was considered by many as "The Authority on Treasure," believed that there is more treasure to be found in Natchitoches Parish then anywhere else in the state of Louisiana.

Red River Parish: Another site of a John Murrell treasure cache is near the Red River in Red River Parish.

Saint Tammany Parish, Slidell: The Honey Island, in the middle of the Honey Island Swamp, is the reported resting spot of a $45,000 John Murrell treasure cache.

Vernon Parish, Hornbeck: Caves in the area of Hornbeck have been suggested as the location of another John Murrell treasure cache.

JAMES COPELAND (1815-1857)

James Copeland, also known as John Copeland, was first arrested for theft at the age of 12. Copeland continued his unlawful career and at the age of 15 was looking at serving hard time. This he resolved by burning down the Jackson County, Mississippi courthouse. Copeland continued his life of crime and became know as the "Great Land Pirate."

By 1840, Copeland was running with a gang that operated from Florida to Texas. During a meeting of this gang Copeland killed off his competition and took control of the gang.

The Copeland gang operated along the Natchez Trace for awhile before moving into Kentucky and Ohio, but the center for Copeland's operation was in Gainsville, Hancock County, Mississippi. Copeland's ill-gotten items were fenced in Gainsville through Charles McGrath who posed as a preacher. Things went fine until a large group of the citizenry banded together and pursued the band of outlaws. They were finally cornered in Hancock County, Mississippi, in what was referred to as the Battle of Harvey on Black Creek. Copeland escaped and in the process lost a coded map indicating the site of a $30,000 gold cache. The gold is reportedly buried in the Catahoula Swamp.

Copeland next appeared in New Orleans. Fearing that his arrest was imminent, he filled three whiskey kegs with gold coins, brought them into the Honey Island Swamp and buried them.

Copeland then went to Florida where he remained until sometime in the 1850's, when he was recognized and captured. Copeland was eventually taken to Old Augustus, Mississippi where he was hung on October 30, 1857.

In the days prior to his hanging, Copeland confessed to Doctor J. R. S. Pitts, the sheriff of Perry County, Mississippi. On the day of Copeland's execution, his confession was released to the public. The confession contained the location of some of his caches. Copeland's confession started a gold rush that only resulted in a small amount of coins being found.

Some stories say that one of the treasure locations given by Copeland during his confession was that of the three whisky kegs of gold coins buried on Honey Island, near Slidell in Saint Tammany Parish. Gold coins are often found on Honey Island, but it is believed that James Copeland's treasure cache still remains where he buried it.

FRANK AND JESSE JAMES

Alexander Franklin "Buck" James, also known as Frank Colburn and Frank Vaughn, was born in 1843 and died on February 18, 1915.

Jesse Woodson "Dingus" James, also known as Thomas Howard, was born on September 5, 1847 and died on April 3, 1882. Jesse earned the dubious distinction of being known as "America's most famous outlaw."

The James brothers are believed by many to have been sort of "Robin Hoods." They were, in fact, nothing more then killers and thieves. When the Civil War began, the boys joined Quantrill's Raiders. They later joined Anderson's Raiders and quickly established a name for themselves. Because of this fame, their family was persecuted by Union troops. Their farm was the target of numerous raids. At the end of the war they were not granted amnesty because they were guerrillas and not officially part of the Confederate Army. They were considered outlaws, and rewards were posted for them dead or alive. When amnesty was offered for guerrillas, Jesse, Frank and several others were in route to surrender. A company of Union troops had other plans. The company set up an ambush for the ex-guerrillas and, when the time was right, sprang the trap. Frank and the others escaped unharmed, but Jesse was seriously wounded in the chest and almost died. Jesse managed to escape with the help of a farmer who cared for his wounds and brought him to his mother's house.

Jesse claimed that he and his men were driven to a life of crime by "Yankee bankers and railroad magnates," by "impossible farm mortgages and threaten foreclosures in underhanded land-grabbing schemes."

The first of many bank robberies occurred on February 13, 1866, in Liberty, Missouri, at the Clay County Savings Bank. This job netted the boys more then $60,000 and was the first daylight bank robbery in the United States by an organized band of outlaws.

On March 8, 1868, the James gang was in Russellville, Kentucky, and robbed the Southern Bank of Kentucky.

By June 3, 1871, the boys were operating out of Iowa and robbed the Ocobock Brothers Bank in Corydon, Iowa. This job netted the gang more then $45,000.

They continued to rob banks on a regular basis until July 21, 1873, when they boarded the Rock Island and Pacific Express at Adair, Iowa. This robbery is believed to be their first train robbery.

On January 15, 1874, it is believed that the gang pulled their first stage coach robbery. They held up the Concord Stagecoach just outside of Malvern, Arkansas. This robbery netted them a little more then $4,000.

1875 found the boys working near Dallas, Texas. On May 12, the gang robbed the San Antonio stage.

The James Gang continued their robberies on a regular basis until September 7, 1876 when they robbed the First National

Bank in Northfield, Minnesota. Most of their gang were killed or captured, but the James bothers escaped.

On October 7, 1879, after three years of hiding, the James boys held up the Alton Express, just outside of Glendale, Missouri, and took over $35,000. Nothing else was heard of the boys for a year and a half, until they robbed a stagecoach outside of Muscle Shoals, Alabama. They continued to commit robberies on a regular basis until August 7, 1881. The robbery of the Alton Express was their last. This robbery was the second train robbery at Blue Cut outside Glendale, Missouri.

On April 3, 1882, Jesse Woodson James was shot in the back of the head by Robert "Bob" Ford and died.

On October 5, 1882, Frank James surrendered to Governor Thomas Theodore Crittenden of Missouri.

On February 18, 1915, Alexander Franklin James died of natural causes.

During their sixteen years of robbing and killing the James brothers always kept the lions share of the loot with the intent of one day retiring. Also during this period, the boys would disappear from time to time.

I can find no record of the James Gang ever pulling a robbery within the State of Louisiana, nor were they ever wanted within the state. Louisiana was considered a safe place, and rumors have persisted that Frank and Jesse James had a hideout in the area of Delhi, Richland Parish, Louisiana. It is believed that they concealed some of their loot there.

As the story goes, Frank and Jesse were hiding out near the Carpenter House, near Delhi, and hid the loot from one of their bank-jobs near their campsite. When local lawman feared that the gang was about to rob the local bank, they raided the camp, and Frank and Jesse were forced to depart without their cache.

It has been reported that in the early 1900's local residents saw a man believed to be Frank James in the area of Delhi. The man was followed for several days as he roamed about the area of the Carpenter House, but was never seen retrieving anything. Because of the sightings of the man believed to be Frank James, the story of a buried treasure cache is thought by many to have begun.

To add plausibility to the story, when Frank James was pardoned by the governor of Missouri in 1902, he then moved to Louisiana. Frank James became the Betting Commissioner for the New Orleans Fair Grounds.

Perhaps the man seen roaming about the area of the "Old James Gang Hideout" in Delhi was in fact Frank James, and maybe there is a buried cache of outlaw loot in the area. With the advent of modern metal detectors and a little research this could be a good spot to check out.

Also, Jim and Cole Younger, and Frank and Jesse James are said to have once lived in the area of Floyd in West Carroll Parish. They are believed by some to have secreted some of their outlaw loot in the area.

CAPTAIN BUNCH

East Carroll Parish, Lake Providence: Between 1795 and 1809 river pirates under the command of a man known as Captain Bunch operated along the Mississippi River. Two of Captain Bunch's favorite attack sites were Devil's Elbow and Bunch's Bend, due to the fact that ships would have to slow down in order to maneuver around the sharp turns in the river. Captain Bunch had his headquarters on Stark Island, until they were raided in 1809. It has long been believed that Bunch and his pirates left several treasure caches on the island. Nothing has ever been reported found on Stark Island.

EUGENE BUNCH

Eugene Bunch, also known as Captain J. F. Gerald, was born in Mississippi and well educated. Bunch moved to Louisiana and became a school teacher. Not finding teaching rewarding, Bunch moved to Gainsville, Texas where he became the editor of a local newspaper. In the year 1888, Bunch formed a gang and began robbing trains from Texas to Mississippi.

In 1888, Bunch robbed a New Orleans and Northwestern train of more than $10,000. In 1892, Bunch robbed a train just outside of New Orleans, taking over $20,000. Bunch was pursued by Pinkerton detectives to his hideout near Varnado, in Washington Parish. On August 21, 1892, Bunch and all of his men were shot and killed. None of the loot was reported recovered.

It is believed that Bunch's headquarters was along Pushapatappe Creek west of Varnado. There is a good possibility that his ill-gotten treasure remains buried in this area.

JOHNNY GAMBI

It is believed that Johnny Gambi (Gambai) also went by the name of Vincent Gambi. It is a known fact that Gambi was one of Lafitte's captains in 1815, and some say he was still alive in 1893. Other stories state that Gambi was murdered in 1819 as he slept on a pile of stolen gold coins.

Gambi was a successful pirate in his own right, before the Lafitte's came to Louisiana. It has been said that Gambi may have cached part of his treasures within two locations near Diamond, in Plaquemines Parish. It is rumored that Doctor Hewitt L. Ballowe, of Point a la Hache, came into possession of several of Gambi's maps, receiving them from either Gambi or a member of his family. It is also said that Ballowe may have found at least one of the Diamond treasures.

POSSIBLE GAMBI TREASURE LOCATIONS

Plaquemines Parish, Homeplace: One of the locations given as the resting place for a Gambi cache is Homeplace. This cache is said to consist of $50,000 in gold coins.

Jefferson Parish, Grand Isle: Caminada Ridge at Chenier Caminada is given as the location of another Johnny Gambi treasure cache. It has been reported that at least part of this cache has been found, but more of it is believed to exist.

Chenier Caminada is a low oak covered ridge north of the bridge on Louisiana State Highway 1 where it crosses to Grand Isle.

Jefferson Parish, Isle de Gambi: According to a story printed in 1977, the Isle de Gambi near the mouth of Bayou Caillou is the resting place of several of Gambi's treasure caches.

Terrebonne Parish, Caillou Island: John Gambi is also said to have made at least one large treasure cache on Caillou Island. This cache is said to consist of $2,000,000 in gold, silver and jewels.

Plaquemines Parish, Calillan Island: Johnny Gambi is also said to have made at least one large treasure cache on Calillan Island.

Caillou or Calillan? The story goes that Johnny Gambi may have buried his treasure caches on an island that sounded like Calillan or Caillou. Some believe it is Caillou Island, others believe it is Calillan Island. If you take into account the fact that caches of $2,000 and $20,000 in Spanish gold doubloons has been reported found of Caillou Island in Terrebonne Parish, you may not want to go to Calillan Island in Plaquemines Parish.

CALICO DICK

Little is known about Calico Dick, other then he was born in Gainsville, Mississippi, and that he received his name as a child when he was caught stealing a bolt of calico. Dick began his career as an outlaw and later, after stealing a ship, turned pirate.

After raids were made on several English ships, Dick's luck ran out when a British Man of War gave pursuit. Dick headed his ship up the West Pearl River where he and his men scuttled the ship with its treasure on board and then fled into the swamp. Some stories say that he sailed the ship up a bayou south of Pearlington, Mississippi, and scuttled her. Some stories state that Dick may have buried the estimated $2,500,000 in the

Honey Island Swamp in Saint Tammany Parish. Dick was apprehended a short time later near the center of the swamp and died in an English prison.

THE KING OF HONEY ISLAND SWAMP

Pierre Rameau, also known as Kirk McCollough and Colonel Loring, held the title of "King of Honey Island." Some stories say that Rameau was once a pirate under the command of Jean Lafitte. Rameau led a band of pirates known as "Chats-Huants" (Screech Owls).

Rameau passed himself off as a wealthy Mexican businessman and was said to have had the finest home in New Orleans. It was from his residence that Rameau dispatched his pirate ships and gangs of outlaws to their assigned targets. After a falling out with Lafitte, Rameau departed Barataria with several of his followers and struck out on his own, operating from a base in the Honey Island Swamps of Saint Tammany Parish, Louisiana. Rameau and most of his men died while fighting on the side of the British during the Battle of New Orleans. Some say that Dominique You rotated his cannon shots between shooting British generals off their horses and Rameau and his men.

It has been rumored that Rameau made several caches, amounting to $450,000, in the area of the Honey Island Swamp near where United States Highway 11 crosses the Louisiana-Mississippi border.

SAMUEL MASON

Samuel Mason was an outlaw and cold blooded killer who roamed the south during the early 1800's. It is believed that he buried several caches near Delhi in Richland Parish.

Across the Mississippi River from Vicksburg, Mississippi, in Madison Parish is an area known as "Mason Hills." It is believed by many to be the location of several of Mason's treasure caches.

In October of 1803 Samuel Mason was beheaded, bringing to an end his reign of terror in Louisiana and Mississippi history. Mason was said to have had a hideout on the east side of Lake Concordia in Concordia Parish. It is believed by many that this spot is the most likely site for a Mason treasure cache.

GEORGE BROWN

George Ratti, once a member of Jean Lafitte's crew, changed his last name to Brown. George made the change from piracy to outlaw simply by jumping ship in 1818, taking with him another member of Lafitte's crew, Jose De Iuana. Brown had accompanied Lafitte on a trip up the Mermentau and Calcasieu Rivers, during which, it was said, Lafitte gave all the booty from a plundered ship to several of the residents along the two rivers. On another trip Lafitte did the same thing in the Bayou Turtle Trail area of Saint Landry Parish. A short time later Brown formed a gang and went back and stole the treasures Lafitte had given the residents.

Brown continued to rob and kill in the southwest corner of Louisiana until September 26, 1819, when he and sixteen of his men raided a plantation on Bayou Quenede Tortue in Saint Landry Parish. They stole everything they could take, including ten slaves. Brown and his men found themselves pursued by a posse and attempted to return to the safety of Galveston. Four of Brown's men were captured by the Coast Guard. Upon arrival at Galveston the rest of the gang was arrested by Jean Lafitte. Brown was hanged on November 7, 1819, after a short trial. The others were turned over to Lieutenant Commander Madison of the Unites States Navy.

In order to make good their escape, it is believed that most of the property stolen by Brown's band on this raid was cached in the area of Bayou Quenede Tortue. It is also believed that over the years Brown and his men may have made hundreds of small caches in southwest Louisiana.

HERMIT OF GRAND TERRE ISLAND

An unknown member of Jean Lafitte's crew cached all his booty at a spot somewhere on Grand Terre Island in Jefferson Parish. After the Battle of New Orleans he retired to a site near his cache. The only time the hermit was seen was when he came into the town to purchase supplies.

Time passed and several men were searching the island for runaway slaves when they came upon the hermit's old shack. Around the shack they found some gold doubloons laying about , and inside the shack they found the remains of the long-dead hermit. News of the discovery brought dozens of would-be treasure hunters to the area. A few small caches were found, but it is believed that more treasure awaits discovery.

JOHN WEST AND LAWS KIMBRELL GANG

The John West and Laws Kimbrell gang consisted of approximately 150 men. This gang of robbers and killers operated in the areas of Montgomery, Winnfield, and Atlanta, Louisiana, in the late 1860's. One of the gang's hideouts was located near Coochie Brake in Winn Parish, and it is believed that some of their caches remain in the area today.

JAYHAWKERS

Confederate troops surprised a band of Jayhawkers camped near Elizabeth in Allen Parish, Louisiana. It is believed that the Jayhawkers left behind a treasure cache believed to be $40,000.

A band of Jayhawkers are said to have used the Edgerly Campground at Vinton in Calcasieu Parish during the Civil War. It is believed that they may have made several small treasure caches at this site.

Jayhawkers are also said to have hidden $75,000 in a swamp near Vinton.

NOTE: In 1929 a work crew, digging through a dry river bed, found $75,000 in gold coins dated in the 1840's and 1850's. Some people believe this to be the Jayhawkers' treasure; others believe it to be a cache made by a wealthy plantation owner during the Civil War. If it was not one it was the other, and $75,000 still remains to be found in this area.

At one time the area between the Red and Black Rivers in La Salle Parish was infested with Jayhawkers and deserters from the Civil War. The hilly area around Catahoula Lake has been suggested as a place where several caches were made by these desperadoes.

Somewhere in the area known as Mallet Woods in Saint Landry Parish near Opelousas, a band of Jayhawkers had a hideout. It is believed by some that they left behind several treasure caches when they were run out of the area during April, 1864.

In the 1860's, a band of Jayhawkers stole a ship in northern Mississippi and sailed down the Pearl River, robbing, raping, murdering and plundering as they headed south along the Mississippi-Louisiana border. As the Jayhawkers continued south, the pursuing band of vigilantes grew. Somewhere along the east bank of Honey Island in Saint Tammany Parish the ship ran aground. The Jayhawkers were unloading their booty when the vigilantes caught up with them. The Jayhawkers grabbed all the loot they could carry and headed into the swamp. During the battle the ship was set ablaze, and, because of the lost weight of the men and their loot, the ship floated down stream. It has been said that the Jayhawkers cached their loot in the side of a bayou bank and made good their escape, but never returned to claim their spoils.

WILLIAM MITCHELL

William Mitchell was once a captain under Jean Lafitte and started where Lafitte stopped. Mitchell left Lafitte in 1816 and became the scourge of the Gulf of Mexico between Galveston,

Texas, and New Orleans. In early 1818, Mitchell and his band of pirates moved into the area of Barataria in Jefferson Parish where it is believed most of his treasure was cached. There is no official record of what became of Mitchell after 1819, but it is believed by some that his ship was lost at sea during a storm with all hands on board. Others believed that Mitchell attempted to take the wrong ship and was blown out of the water by a British man-of-war.

CAPTAIN W. GILLMAN

During the Civil War, Federal officials believed that Captain W. Gillman was operating a smuggling ring from his residence near Greensburg in Saint Helena Parish. If Gillman was operating a smuggling ring from his residence, it is almost certain that a cache or two could be near the residence.

THE CAMERON PARISH GANG

It is rumored that the Cameron Parish Gang buried $230,000 in the area of Sulphur in Calcasieu Parish.

UNKNOWN ENGLISH PIRATES

The story of the "Treasure of Skeleton Hole" is said to involve $750,000 in gold bars taken from the Spanish ship *Fatsimsa*. After an unknown band of English pirates removed the treasure from the *Fatsimsa,* the ship was burned with its crew still on board. The treasure was then taken to Breton Island in Plaquemines Parish where it was to be buried.

The English captain, the first mate and two of the crew put to shore on Breton Island in a small boat. Before the treasure could be buried a fight ensued and the captain and first mate were both killed. Two of the crew members returned to their ship for help in burying the treasure and with the hope of being named the new captain and first mate. The rest of the crew came ashore and found the treasure and the bodies of the captain and first mate. The crew then decided to divide the treasure instead. Another fight broke out over the division of the treasure. All but three of the pirates were killed. Badly wounded, the three were forced to remain on the island where they were picked up by a Spanish ship. Doomed to the gallows for being English, the three were put into irons to await their execution. An Indian slave who comforted the three was given a map to the site of the still unburied treasure and their dead comrades. The Indian did not understand the map and only knew there was some treasure somewhere with dead men around it.

CHANDELEUR ISLANDS

Numerous treasures have been reported found in the Chandeleur Islands of Saint Bernard Parish, and even more treasure caches await the right person.

One story tells of a pirate treasure consisting of $70,000 in gold coins being buried on Chandeleur Island.

A second story tells of two chests of gold being cached on the western side of Chandeleur Island.

UNKNOWN OUTLAWS

Allen Parish, Oakdale: $75,000 in gold coins was believed to have been cached in the area of Oakdale by two outlaws.

Caddo Parish, Greenwood: Rumors persist of some unknown outlaw caching $85,000 in gold and silver coins in the area of Greenwood.

Calcasieu Parish, Vinton: $55,000 in gold coins were the profits of an unknown embezzler. The money was reportedly taken from the Texas Cattleman Association and is allegedly buried somewhere between Vinton and the Texas border.

Lafayette Parish, Broussard: A band of English smugglers operated in the area of Pin Hook, and it is believed that they may have left several small caches in that area.

Madison Parish, Delta: In 1876, the Mississippi River changed course and the town of Delta was moved to its current site. Old Delta became what has been described as an "outlaw town." Old Delta, as it became known, was a haven for undesirables, and stories of treasure caches abound.

Natchitoches Parish, Bayou Pierre: In 1811 and 1812 the area around Bayou Pierre was swarming with outlaws. The unknown gang of outlaws was said to number as many as thirty men, and no one was safe traveling through the area. It is therefore believed that many treasures may remain cached in the area of Bayou Pierre.

One such cache was made in 1811. Bernardo de Laura and fifteen men departed Mexico with $30,000 in gold coins. When the outlaws attempted to rob de Laura, a battle ensued. As de Laura's men held off the outlaws, de Laura hid the gold and escaped with several of his men. When de Laura returned to the area he could not find the spot where he hid the gold.

Natchitoches Parish, Grand Ecore: In 1852, a small chest of gold coins was said to have been cached by an unknown gambler in a bluff along the Red River just north of Grand Ecore. The cache was made just hours before the gambler was murdered. The killer thought the gambler still had the money in his possession.

Sabine Parish, Many: Shawneetown, also known as Shinytown, was located along the El Camino Real and was said to have been a haven for the dregs of life. Founded in 1821 and just an unpleasant memory by 1912, it was also referred to as "Sin-town" and the "Hell Hole." It is believed by many locals that much treasure awaits discovery in Shawneetown.

One specific location to check out is the area of the Halfway House located approximately three miles east of Shawneetown along El Camino Real. The Halfway House was a notorious outlaw hangout and may be the site of many treasure caches.

NOTE: One treasure reportedly found in the Halfway House was worth an estimated $100,000.

Sabine Parish, Bellwood: Shake Hat is located approximately five miles west of Bellwood along the Nolan Trace. It was the headquarters of an outlaw gang who operated in the area, robbing travelers along the trace in the early 1800's. It is believed by some that treasure caches could be in the area of Shake Hat.

Sabine Parish, Florien: Rumor has it that after robbing several banks in the area an outlaw gang cached the majority of their loot in caves near Florien.

Saint Martin Parish, Breaux Bridge: In the early 1800's, Narcisse Thibodaux was one of the settlers of Breaux Bridge. He was known as a shrewd businessman and a miser. Thibodaux abused his slaves in order to get more production from them and in return gave them what he considered just enough food to survive.   In fact, some of then died of malnutrition.   In the early 1800's, his slaves revolted, killed Thibodaux, and stole $80,000 in gold. The slaves then tried to escape the area, but a posse was quickly formed and the slaves were captured. The posse, in the interest of swift justice, forced the slaves to dig a hole, killed them, and dumped their bodies into the hole. When the posse returned with the gold, the men realized that one of the sacks was missing. At that time, it was reasoned that the gold had to have been buried within the city limits of Breaux Bridge, and most likely on Thibodaux's plantation.

Saint Tammany Parish, Madisonville, Fairview Riverside State Park: An unknown pirate is rumored to have buried $500,000 in gold coins somewhere near the Tchefuncte River just south of Madisonville within the Fairview Riverside State Park. Gold coins have been found in this area, and it is believed that this may have started the pirate treasure story.

Tangipahoa Parish, Hammond: "The Lost Coffin Treasure" is said to be an iron casket filled with an estimated $1,000,000 in gold, silver and jewels, the profits of an unknown outlaw. In the 1880's, the coffin was buried near a "South American Tree" between Hammond and Natalbany. The story claims that the tree was removed in the 1930's.

Vermilion Parish, Abbeville: In 1866, a stage coach was robbed of $35,000 in gold coins near Abbeville. The outlaws were trailed to Abbeville and captured. The law-men searched the outlaws to no avail. Next the outlaws' horses were checked, but the gold was not there, either. The outlaws' trail was backtracked, but the gold could not be found. It has long been believed that the gold was hidden in the area of Abbeville, and that the outlaws never retrieved their loot.

Vernon Parish, Rosepine: A small band of outlaws robbed a stage north of DeRidder at Bundick Creek Crossing. The outlaws escaped with the strongbox, and a posse was soon formed. The outlaws were overtaken west of Rosepine along the east bank of Bayou Anacoco where they were camped. In the ensuing gun battle all the outlaws were killed. A search of the area was made, but the strongbox could not be found. It is believed that the strongbox was cached in the immediate area of their campsite.

Washington Parish, Bogalusa: Rumors have persisted for years that an unknown pirate treasure cache was made the area of Bogalusa.

CAMPGROUNDS

Because of numerous accounts of bandits operating along well traveled roads, it was the custom for travelers to hide their valuables before turning in at night. This held true whether they were spending the night in a comfortable inn or camped out at one of the many established campgrounds. Many personal treasures were buried in the dark and for one reason or another never retrieved. Because of this fact, a list of known campgrounds is given.

Calcasieu Parish, Vinton: The Edgerly Campgrounds was used by travelers as well as outlaws, and it is believed that many small treasure caches await daylight in this area.

Grant Parish, Montgomery: The Ebenezer Camp Meeting Grounds remained in use until the late 1920's.

Sabine Parish, Many: In the early 1800's, Fallen Springs was a popular campsite for travelers of the Nolan Trace. The campsite was the scene of many robberies and murders and is believed to be the site of many lost treasure caches.

Saint Helena Parish, Greensburg: The Methodist Campground was a popular campsite during the 1800's. This site was also used by Confederate troops going to and from Camp Moore.

INDIANS

Grant Parish, Georgetown: According to local legend, in an area five miles south of Georgetown, miners returning east with a large amount of gold dust were attacked by Indians. Fearing a second attack, the miners buried the gold, and all were killed a short time later. It has been reported that the value of the gold was as much as $5,000,000.

Winn Parish, Winnfield: In the early 1850's, approximately 50 renegade Indians robbed a bank in Natchez, Mississippi. It has been estimated that the Indians made off with between $1,000,000 and $3,000,000 in gold and silver coins and headed for the safety of a familiar area. The Indians broke into two groups. One group headed to Possum Neck, the site of an old Indian village located north of Winnfield. The second group headed to Berdo Springs, southwest of Louisville.

A large posse was formed and the Indians were trailed to the two different locations. The Indians were caught, and in the interest of swift justice all were killed. None of the stolen coins were ever reported found, and it is believed that the money was hidden at one or both locations.

CHAPTER IX

THINGS THAT GO BUMP IN THE NIGHT

I do not wish to debate the issue of whether or not ghosts exist. For one thing there could be no rebuttal, thus no debate. Some people swear ghost stories are true and that ghosts do exist. Having always had an analytical mind I think there is a reason for the stories. I have had several experiences which cannot be explained with any certainty, except to say I saw what I thought I saw, and I believe there is a logical explanation for what happened. The explanation, so far, has alluded me, but there has to be one.

It is my belief that some stories were created to scare away would-be treasure hunters, thereby eliminating the competition. Other stories may have started as jokes. Some stories may even have a scientific explanation such as swamp gas, ionized particles in the atmosphere, condensation or, my personal all time favorite; "Gee I don't know. What do you think it was?" Grandma "Dinkey" would have explained at least one of my experiences as being caused by eating tuna fish and drinking milk or eating bananas before going to sleep.

Ghosts are said to be the aberration of the disembodied sole of a person who has died an untimely death. Whether you do or do not believe in the spirits, I think you will enjoy the stories.

GHOST STORIES

Ghosts have long been associated with buried treasures. There are however a few "Treasure Hunting Rules," that everyone should know:

1. Pirates would always ask for volunteers to help them bury their treasures. The greedy men would always volunteer so they can learn the location of the treasure and return to steal it. After the treasure was in the ground the volunteers would be killed,

buried with the treasure, and their ghosts left to guard the treasure.

2. Never utter a sound while digging for treasure or the ghosts who guard the it will cause the treasure to slip further into the ground. This rule usually comes into play when you reach the bones from rule number one.

3. A poltergeist appearing in the form of a chicken, snake or other animal wearing a piece of human clothing, usually signifies a voodoo treasure. It could be a large blue chicken wearing a top hat or a large purple snake wearing a bow tie. One condition to this rule is the person seeing the aberration must not be intoxicated. Apparently this rule applies only in south Louisiana. I have not heard of it anywhere else.

4. The treasure must be retrieved during the full moon or in the daylight hours. If you try to retrieve a treasure in the dark the bogeyman will get you.

5. Before most treasures can be retrieved, a varying number of people must lose their lives in the quest. This is to appease the spirits who guard the treasure.

6. Under the right atmospheric conditions a ball of fire will appear above a treasure. This ball of fire is known as "feux follet" (false fire). If the treasure is meant for you the feux follet will disappear when you are at the location. If the treasure is meant for someone else, the feux follet will lead you around until you are lost or attack as you draw near.

7. When finding a treasure, take as much of it as you can carry. If you happen to find your way back to the site, nine times out of ten the treasure will be gone. The spirits will move the treasures in order to make you look like a fool, thereby, lessening the chance of anyone else looking for it.

8. When a treasure is guarded by a spirit, the spirit may become tired and want to move on to the next level of existence, call it heaven, hell or purgatory. When this occurs the spirit must give the treasure to someone living close by. The spirit will often speak to that person in his or her dreams, giving instructions to the whereabouts of the treasure. Once this is done, no one else but that person can have the treasure. If someone else attempts to retrieve it, the spirit will move the treasure or harm the intruder. If after some period of time has passed and the treasure is not claimed, it will be given to another.

Often this gift of a treasure is accompanied by a set of rules that must be followed. Usually the treasure can only be used to help others, and you may not spend any portion of it on yourself. If you violate the rules, you will guard the treasure for the next hundred and fifty years.

I am sure that there are a lot more rules, but those are only the ones I can remember.

VOODOO

In the early 1700's slaves from Africa began arriving in the "New World." The slaves brought with them their religious beliefs. The God of the African slave was "Vodu." Over the years the name underwent changes in spelling from Vodu to Voodoo, Voudou, Vaudau, Voudoux, Vaudaux and sometimes Hoodoo. The word eventually came to mean everything from the African slave sect-rites, priest and priestesses, spells, and anything else that could not be explained in usual Christian terms.

Because of the general population's fear of Voodoo, in 1782, the governor of Louisiana prohibited the import of slaves from Martinique. Slaves from Santo Domingo were later bared entry into Louisiana for the same reason.

Almost from the time the slaves arrived in New Orleans, they began to conduct Voodoo rituals in what became known as

Congo Square. One of the rituals was called a "sangre." This rite was a curse and consisted of writing nine times on a piece of paper the name of the person to be cursed. The paper was rapped around three nickels or half-dimes and placed into the hollow of the large tree which once stood within the square. The person making the curse would then dance around the tree until dawn. The tree was located somewhere within an area enclosed by North Villere, Saint Philip, North Rampart and Saint Louis Streets. This practice was known to continue until the 1950's. The first tree used has long since vanished, but over the years they used several other trees. Some of the coins may have remained in that area. Keep in mind that from 1794 half dimes were used and, after 1866, nickel five-cent pieces were used. The value of each coin would range from as little as $1 to as much as $2,200.

MARIE LAVEAU

Marie Laveau I, was born a free mulatto in 1789, in New Orleans. Marie II was the daughter of Marie Laveau and Louis Christrophe Duminy de Glapion. Over the years the stories of the two Maries have become so intertwine that it would take a complete book or two to separate the women. For the sake of this story they will be treated as one.

Marie had a well established career as a hairdresser for the New Orleans' elite. Woman love to talk and they love to be pampered. As Marie did their hair the ladies would tell her intimate details of their love life. Marie soon learned where all the skeletons were, and who was doing what to whom as well as where and when. It was not uncommon for Marie to attend to the wives and the mistresses of many of New Orleans' leading citizens within the same day. Marie had a vast memory for details, and all the gossip she heard was stored until the time when she could profit most. As a sideline to her hairdressing business, Marie sold potions and amulets. As Marie's business grew so did her voodoo knowledge and powers. In 1830, Marie became the official Voodoo Queen of New Orleans.

Marie's hairdressing business continued to grow as more of the ladies of New Orleans sought her help with their personal problems. One of the ladies came to Marie with a special problem. It seemed that her son had committed a crime and was sure to go to prison. Marie assured the lady that the problem would be resolved. The son was later acquitted of the crime, and as payment Marie was given a modest little cottage at 1020 Saint Ann Street. This house was used by Marie as her residence within the City of New Orleans. The original cottage was destroyed around 1903 and was later replaced by the shotgun double that now bares that address.

Marie also had a house built near Lake Pontchartrain which she called Maison Blanche. Marie used Maison Blanche to hold voodoo rituals until 1869 when she was replaced as the Voodoo Queen. Mason Blanche was located near an area referred to as the Milne Swamp and may have been located in the area of the University of New Orleans campus.

Marie lived out the remainder of her life at the cottage on Saint Ann Street. In 1881, at the time of her death, it was estimated that she may have accumulated as much as $3,000,000. It is believed that Marie Laveau's treasure was buried at either Mason Blanche or 1020 Saint Ann Street. Some people believe that parts of her treasure may have been buried at both locations.

DOCTOR JOHN (1803-1885)

Doctor John, also known as Voodoo John, Bayou John, Jean Bayou, Jean Montaigne, Jean Montanet and John Fecelle, was born a Senegalese prince and bore the tattooed face in keeping with the tradition of his regal forefathers. He has been described as a huge black man who liked to dress all in black except for his ruffled white silk shirt. Taken from his native land at a young age by Spanish slavers, John was eventually sold to a man in Cuba. In Cuba, John grew to manhood and was considered by most to be a great cook. He eventually obtained his freedom from his master and began to travel the world as a cook on various ships. One day he found himself in New Orleans and liked what he saw.

John worked for awhile on the docks of New Orleans and, due to his size and the marks on his face, was feared by the other workers. Because of this fear, John was made an overseer. An intelligent man, he began to learn little Voodoo tricks and soon realized that people would pay for his services. With the money he made, he was able to purchase a small house on Bayou Road. John purchased many female slaves and eventually took fourteen as his wives. He later married a white woman. Among his fifteen wives they produced fifty offspring.

One of the services preformed by John was to rid a house of evil spirits. For no apparent reason, someone's house was suddenly rained upon by rocks and bricks in the middle of the night. The objects came from nowhere, and John always had an ironclad alibi. He would then be summoned to the residence to do his magic act, and the haunting would stop. After one such service John was sued, and the court ordered the money returned. After the money was refunded, the showers continued until a larger sum was paid for John's services.

As John's family grew so did his Voodoo practice. Thousands of the cities finest people came to Doctor John for advise, potions, spells, cures and charms. He charged the wealthy as much money as he thought they would pay, and pay they did. John had a different charge for the slaves and servants. Usually they paid with information concerning their masters and employers. John would then use the information to his advantage, either for blackmail or to trick someone into thinking he knew all and saw all.

At the time of John's death, it was believed he had hidden as much as $150,000 near his Bayou Road home. It was never found. Legend has it that an alligator appears in the area of Bayou Road and North Galvez Street. They say it is black as the ace of spades, walks upright and is wearing a lacey white shirtfront.

THE OVERSEER'S HOUSE

New Orleans: There is a house in the 1200 block of Ursuline Street that is said to have been the residence of the Treme Plantation overseers. The overseers were usually white and were the equivalent of the plantation foreman. This two-story, brick building is large enough to have housed the overseer and several slaves. Marie Laveau is believed to have been a frequent visitor to the house. The fact that spirits have been seen suggest to some that a treasure may have been secreted within the residence. The treasure is not believed to be one of Marie's caches, but possibly that of one of the overseers.

One of the spirits who was known to inhabit the residence was a Poltergeist in the form of a large purple rooster wearing a black top hat. This spirit has been seen dancing near the fireplace in one of the bedrooms on the first floor.

Another ghost appeared to be wearing an African Mask. This aberration was seen with only its head protruding from one of the walls in a downstairs bathroom.

Yet another spirit has been seen as just a misty, glowing image who roams the house between the hours of 11:00 p.m. and 4:00 a.m..

The most common occurrence at the house has been described as a spirit coming into the residence via the rear double doors, usually after sunset. This could be the ghost of the overseer who would have returned to his residence about that time each day. For some unknown reason, the double French style doors were often seen flying open. With the addition of a bathroom at the rear of the residence, these doors became interior doors, but they continued to open on their own, only slower and quieter.

THE CURSE OF MISERY MANSION

Saint Charles Parish, Destrehan: The Ormond Plantation was built by Pierre Trepagnier, a Frenchman of nobility. Trepagnier distinguished himself honorably in the fight against the British in 1789. Louisiana was under the control of the Spanish at that time, and as a reward for his heroism, Governor Bernado de Galvez gave Trepagnier the plantation site which extended from the Mississippi River to Lake Pontchartrain. By 1796, Trepagnier had completed construction of the plantation, and slaves from Santo Domingo were purchased for the day-to-day operations of the plantation.

It is believed by some that during the early part of 1798 one of Trepagnier's slaves was whipped for attempting to "cause an uprising." The slave or someone acting in his interest had a "crossing gris-gris" (a spell cast to inflict harm and/or bad luck) created against Trepagnier and his beloved plantation.

One evening as Trepagnier was holding a formal dinner, a stranger on horseback approached the big house. Trepagnier excused himself and went to talk to the man. Trepagnier returned to the house and informed his wife that he had to leave, but would return shortly. Trepagnier mounted his horse and departed with the stranger. Trepagnier was never seen again.

Trepagnier buried his money in a secret location known only to himself. Without her husband's wealth, his wife was forced to leave the plantation within that same year.

In 1812, the plantation was purchased by Richard Butler. The plantation was a success, and he soon married. Butler named the plantation Ormond, after the Earl of Ormond, a distant relative. Within a few years Butler's fortunes grew. He kept his wealth buried on the grounds of the plantation. In 1814, both Butler and his wife died within days of each other of yellow fever.

Samuel McCutchon was the next owner of the plantation. McCutchon soon married and over time had nine children. The plantation was a success, and the money was rolling in. No one knows what happened to the McCutchon family. All that is known is that by the time of the Civil War, the plantation was already in ruin.

In 1897, the plantation was purchased by Louisiana State Senator Basile LaPlace and was restored to its former grandeur. Once again the plantation and its owner prospered, but it was short lived. One night, as Mister LaPlace was seated at the dinner table, a strange noise was heard outside. He excused himself and went outside to learn the source of the disturbance. LaPlace did not return that night, and his body was found the following morning hanging from a large oak tree which still stands in the front yard of the big house. LaPlace's body was riddled with bullets. As with the previous owners, LaPlace also hid his wealth about the plantation, and another wife was forced to leave in poverty.

Some claim that the soul of the slave who cast the spell returns as a "feux follet" to wander the Ormond Plantation. A "feux follet" is a night light (ball of fire) which causes one to get lost during a journey.

The plantation house now has new owners. Another chapter of the Ormond Plantation yet to be written? Ormond is located at 8407 River Road (Louisiana State Highway 48) in Destrehan. The plantation is open to the public and offers bed-and-breakfast accommodations.

GHOST IN THE WALL

New Orleans: If you ever stroll along Barracks Street on a moonlit night, pay close attention to the reddish brick walls that line the street. The faces of ghosts have been seen with just their heads protruding from the walls like sadistic holograms.

One story says they are the ghosts of Spanish soldiers who were billeted in the barracks there in the 1760's. The soldiers refused to take part in the robbery of the paymaster, who's ghost is also said to haunt the same building. The soldiers were hung on a wall, tortured to death and bricked into the wall. The stolen payroll is also said to be encased within this same wall.

This story does not jibe with the facts. A check of maps from that period does not show any military being housed in that area of the city. One may ask, where did the name Barracks Street come from? On May 15, 1819, the land at the end of Barracks Street between Rue de la Levee (Decatur Street) and

Rue de Conde' (Chartres Street) was sold to the United States for the construction of military barracks and a hospital.

Further research revealed that in 1760, when the Spanish Lieutenant General Alexandre O'Reilly arrived in New Orleans he reported to Major General Arrigo that the only building material available was wood which rotted too fast in the tropical, humid climate. In 1788, fire destroyed the city of New Orleans, and it was not until 1792 that plans were approved to build any brick military structures within the city. This would mean that during the 1760's (the time of the supposed hangings) there were no brick structures in New Orleans.

The building may have, at one time been the residence of Pierre Lafitte's son, also named Pierre.

Although the ghosts have been seen by many in the area of Barracks and Burgundy Streets, the treasure may have been created to justify the ghosts.

THE DEVIL'S TREASURE

Our next story has its beginnings in pre-Civil War Calcasieu Parish. Two slaves decided to run away on the night of a full moon. With the moon was so big and bright, the two thought they would have no trouble finding their way to freedom. Once every year the moon is seen larger than on any other night of the year, but this particular night the moon also had an orange tint to it.

The slaves thought they could be half-way to Texas before they were missed. However, their escape did not go unnoticed. The overseer was awakened. Within minutes he was putting together a search party, and the hounds were summoned. The escaping slaves continued their leisurely pace until they heard the baying of the hounds. They knew they were in big trouble. They picked up their pace, but the dogs kept getting closer and closer. All of a sudden they noticed a far off glow in the woods. The two ran in the direction of the glow, hoping it would lead them to safety. As they approached the light, they saw what appeared to be a large cauldron, like the ones used to cook down sugar cane. The cauldron was glowing with a greenish-yellow light emanating from within and was filled to the top with gold and silver coins. The coins appeared to be boiling over the top of the cauldron and flowing onto the ground. The two thought of nothing but the coins spilling from the big green cauldron and no longer heard the fast approaching search party. One of the slaves reached down, picked up a coin, and scalded his hand. He immediately dropped the boiling hot coin and let out a scream. Within a few seconds the two slaves were captured. They were returning to the plantation and an appointment with the "Cat" (cat-o'-nine-tails). They were somehow glad to be going home.

All the way back to the plantation the two were speechless, but once safely home they could not stop talking about the cauldron full of gold and silver coins. As proof of what they saw the slave showed the palm of his hand, in the middle of which was a blister in the shape of a Spanish doubloon. Members of the search party returned to the spot, but could find no sign of the Cauldron or the spilled coins.

It is believed that this tale was told to the slaves to keep them from running off, and to keep them from touching any of the master's coins. However, the story could be true.

KENILWORTH PLANTATION

Saint Bernard Parish, Kenilworth: The Kenilworth Plantation, also known as Bienvenue House, was built by Pierre Antoine Bienvenue.   Said to be the richest man in 1700's Louisiana, Bienvenue is rumored to have buried a large treasure at the Kenilworth Plantation.

Originally constructed as a one-story French blockhouse for Bienvenue in 1759, the plantation is said to be haunted by several ghosts.

The ghosts have made their presence known to several people who have resided within this stately, Louisiana, colonial home.   A headless man has been seen roaming the second floor during the full moon. The house was originally one story until the early 1800's when the second floor was added, and it is possible that the ghost resided within the residence after that time. It has been suggested that the "headless ghost" is that of an overseer beheaded during a slave uprising in the 1850's.

On your treasure hunt, you may come across a second ghost roaming the grounds of the plantation. This ghost, known as the "maiden in white," is believed to be the young bride of General Pierre Gustave Toutant Beauregard. P. G. T. Beauregard was born a short distance from the Kenilworth Plantation at the neighboring Contreras Plantation. It is said that Beauregard and his first wife Marie Antoinette Laure Villere spent their honeymoon at the plantation. Marie Beauregard died a short time after their honeymoon and is buried nearby.

The Kenilworth Plantation is located on Louisiana State Highway 46 (Bayou Road), approximately four and one-half miles east of the Poydras junction on Louisiana State Highway 39.

UNION OFFICERS OF CONSTANCE STREET

New Orleans: An impressive three-story, 1820's mansion stands at 1447 Constance Street. At one time it served as a perfume factory, then as a lamp factory, and later as a mattress factory. During the Civil War the building was occupied be Union officers. After stealing an army payroll, two of the officers, identified as Captain Hugh Devers and Major Charles Crowley, cached the stolen gold within the mansion. A short time later the two officers, fearing they were about to be accused of the crime, committed suicide.

There have been numerous reports of ghostly activity involving the spirits of the two Yankees. From time to time the ghosts have been seen looking out from a second floor window. There have been reports of doors opening accompanied by the sound of boots walking across the floor. The whistling of the "Battle Hymn of the Republic" and the singing of "John Brown's Body" have been heard emanating from deep within the bowels of the building.

If you are brave enough and have permission to spend the night, you may see two spirits reenact their death. One of the ghosts is seated near a window on the third floor as the second enters the room and approaches. The two talk for a few moments and approach the window where they stare into the darkness. They draw their service revolvers and step away from the window. Both aim their revolvers at each other and fire. As their forms fall to the floor a thud can be heard. They then melt into the floor not to be seen again until their next performance.

As for the stolen gold coins, they have never been reported found. Some people believe the coins will remain where they are hidden until the ghosts are no more. Others believe that the ghosts will remain until the coins are found.

FELICITE NEDA CHRETIEN

Saint Landry Parish, Sunset, Chretien Point Plantation House: Hippolyte I, Jules and Dazincourt Chretien each received a Spanish land grant in the Louisiana Territory and each established a plantation.

After his marriage to the much younger Felicite Neda, Hippolyte II was given the Chretien Point Plantation, among other gifts, and eventually inherited everything from the estate of his father and two uncles. Not trusting banks, Hippolyte II put all of his accumulated wealth into several iron chests and buried them in various locations about the plantation. The only two people who knew the location of the chests were Hippolyte and a trusted slave.

Felicite was said to be a cigar smoking, gun toting, card playing, hard drinking, strong-willed woman. She was only 4'10" tall and barely weighed 90 pounds, soaking wet, but Felicite ran every aspect of Hippolyte's life, except when it came to money. Although Felicite asked Hippolyte time and time again, he refused to divulge the location of his caches.

The Civil War came and found Hippolyte old and nearly paralyzed. With the war at his door, Hippolyte had neither the strength nor the will power to leave or fight. It has been said that as Major General Nathaniel P. Banks and his troops approached the Chretien Point Plantation, Hippolyte struggled to his feet and moved slowly to the porch railing. The only thing that Hippolyte could do was give the sign of a Master Mason and hope for the best. General Banks returned the sign, and he and his men departed, sparing the plantation.

Shortly after the Civil War, and during one of the yellow-fever epidemics, both Hippolyte II and the slave died. It has been estimated that as much as $650,000 was cached by Hippolyte before his death. Felicite began a search for the chests that lasted several years, with slaves digging everywhere on the plantation where Hippolyte was seen spending any time.

Finally, Felicite gave up and decided to get on with her life. With young Hippolyte III to think of, she went on running the plantation. A woman could not borrow money in those years: so, in order to raise much needed capital, Felicite held small parties for the gentlemen of the community. At these parties the alcohol flowed like water, and the food was as good as it could be, but, mostly, the men came for the card games. Having loosened up the gentlemen with liquor, Felicite would fleece them at the card tables.

Felicite ran the plantation as well as any man could have and eventually doubled the size of the plantation. This-new found wealth led to new problems. One night, Felicite was awaken by a noise. She arose, armed herself, and started down the stairway to see what had caused the noise. As she descended, she observed a shadowy figure on the stairs. Felicite demanded to know who it was. There was no reply, but the figure continued to approach. Felicite commanded the person to stop, but the figure continued to draw closer. Felicite fired her pistol, striking the man in the head. It was then learned that the man was a pirate, and only one of several who surrounded the house with plains to sack it.

Felicite reloaded her pistol and walked out of the house to challenge the remaining pirates. As she spoke to their leader, Felicite's servants armed themselves and took up positions in the windows and doorways behind her. Refusing to yield her ground, Felicite drove off the other pirates.   The body was removed and the blood was washed from the stairs, but the stain continued to return.   The stairs were painted time and time again, and even to this day the stain can be seen on the stairs.

For awhile everything was great, but Felicite could never get ahead. Droughts, floods, weevils. Every time Felicite saw the light at the end of the tunnel it turned out to be the 603 bound for Opelousas, and it was always running twenty minutes ahead of schedule.   Over the years Felicite continued to operate the plantation, but with her inability to find Hippolyte's immense fortune she never prospered.   Felicite eventually succumbed to the pressures of life and died.

It has been said that the plantation continued to deteriorate and was eventually sold to satisfy creditors.   Over the years many searches have been conducted, but as far as it is known, not one of the chests has ever been found.

It has been rumored that the plantation is haunted by the ghost of the pirate killed as he neared the top of the stairs. This ghost is said to climb the stairway, forced to reenact his death time and time again.

There is a second ghost who roams the plantation grounds and house, it is that of Felicite Neda Chretien. Felicite is said to roam the grounds of the old plantation looking for Hippolyte's buried treasures.   With pistol in hand, Felicite can be seen usually on foggy nights along Louisiana State Highway 93 just southwest of Sunset. If you are ever in the neighborhood around midnight stop and say hello. I have been told that if you bring a deck of cards you could win a really big pot. If, that is, she is playing with Hippolyte's money.

By the way, cars have been found abandoned along that stretch of road from time to time. The owners, however, have never returned to claim their vehicles.

The plantation home has been restored and is now open to the public between 10:00 A.M. and 5:00 P.M., except on major holidays. Bed-and-breakfast accommodations are also available, if you care to spend the night.   Do not forget to bring your playing cards. The plantation is located three miles southwest of

Sunset. From Sunset drive west on Louisiana State Highway 93, go to Louisiana State Highway 356 (Bristol-Bosco Road) and turn right. After approximately 200 yards, turn right again onto Chretien Point Road. The plantation is located approximately one mile down this road, on the left.

LALAURIE HOUSE

New Orleans, 1140 Royal Street: In the 1830's Madame Delphine LaLaurie was considered a one of the pillars of New Orleans society. LaLaurie was extremely wealthy and said to be most generous when it came to charities.

On April 10, 1834, as Madame LaLaurie enjoyed an evening out, a fire started at her residence. The firemen had to break down the front door in order to extinguish the fire. While checking the residence the firemen found a gruesome sight. In the kitchen was an old slave, chained to the stove, almost dead from starvation. In a bedroom were several female slaves chained to beds. These, too, were almost dead from starvation and showed signs of being tortured. In the attic were several male slaves chained to the walls in several cells. Many of these were dead, and all had been mutilated. The walls were lined with glass jars that contained numerous body parts. Also in the attic were tables stained with blood and a display of assorted instruments of torture. In all, seven dead slaves were found in the house.

The fire drew a crowd, as fires tend to do, and when word of the atrocities reached the crowd it became a mob. It was about this time when Madame LaLaurie returned to her residence, and realizing that her secret was now public, quickly departed for Mobile, Alabama. She later returned to the safety of France.

Madame LaLaurie was an extremely wealthy person, and it is known that she never returned to her residence after the discovery of the tortured slaves. It is believed that Madame LaLaurie, like most other people of that time, kept a large supply of cash within and without her residence. The mob looted the residence and many objects were taken, but it has been said that only a few gold and silver coins were found. It is believed that as much as $50,000 in gold and silver remains somewhere in or around the LaLaurie House.

Several years later the house was purchased, and the owner had the place renovated. During this renovation, workman found "a pile of human Skeletons" in an area under the house.

The screams and groans of the tormented souls who died in the LaLaurie House may still be heard piercing the still of the night, and ghostly apparitions continue to be reported seen within this building.

At one time it was occupied by a furniture store. The owner opened the store one day to find that it had been vandalized. Everything in the store had been covered with a putrid fluid and had to be thrown out. The owner replaced his stock and waited for the vandals to return. When employees entered the store the next morning, they found the entire stock had again been ruined. The owner was alive, but quite insane. It has been said that these tormented spirits are awaiting the return of Madame LaLaurie. They know she will return one day for the treasure she left behind.

JEAN LAFITTE (FIRST SIGHTING)

Saint Charles Parish, Destrehan, d'Estrehan Plantation: Jean Noel d'Estrehan was a wealthy merchant and good friend of the Lafitte brothers. The d'Estrehan Plantation is often referred to as the only site of a documented Jean Lafitte treasure, $40,000 in gold, silver, and jewels. Try as I may I can not find the documents referred to, other then its first listing in a W. P. A. work, (Federal Writers' Program. Louisiana, A guide to the State. New York. Hastings House: 1941.)

The shadowy ghost of Jean Lafitte is said to haunt the first floor of the d'Estrehan Plantation. Only seen at night and then usually during stormy weather, the ghost of Lafitte enters the room through a wall. It floats across the floor and stops in front of the western most fireplace. Here the beclouded spirit raises his right arm and points its eerie finger at the base of the fireplace.

The plantation home is located at 9999 River Road, Louisiana State Highway 48, approximately four and one half miles west of its junction with Louisiana State Highway 50. In 1972, the plantation was donated to the River Road Historical Society. The plantation is open to the public, but leave your picks and shovels at home.

JEAN LAFITTE (SECOND SIGHTING)

Lafourche Parish, Mathews: At an old camp ground near the junction of United States Highway 90 and Louisiana Highway 1 there is a legendary ghost. It is the ghost of none other than Jean Lafitte. Lafitte's ghost, it is said, will awaken travelers and offer to lead them to his treasure. There is a catch, the person must take an oath to use the treasure for only good and not spend any of the money on themselves. No one has ever taken Lafitte up on his offer.

JEAN LAFITTE III (THIRD SIGHTING)

Jefferson Parish, Jean Lafitte National Historic Park: In the Barataria area of the Jean Lafitte National Park there is said to be a very large, very old oak tree. Jean Lafitte is rumored to have buried a large treasure under the tree. The treasure is said to be protected by Lafitte's ghost, and anyone who digs for the treasure is found dead hanging from the tree.

One story tells of a young couple who parked under the tree in the 1970's. The couple began to cuddle in the front seat. After about a half an hour, the young man felt the need to answer the call of nature and stepped out of his car. He walked around to the other side of Lafitte's tree. The young lady sat patiently waiting for what seemed an eternity, then started calling out the boy's name. There was no reply to the calls, so she too exited the vehicle and walked to the other side of the tree. There she found the young man dead, hanging from the tree.

The tree is within the confines of a national park, and, as such, any excavation would require prior approval. No record could be found to confirm the deaths described in the story.

PIRATES OF IBERIA PARISH

The ghosts of five pirates are said to roam an Iberia Parish residence. Often heard but seldom seen, the ghosts continue to make their presence known to the occupants of this residence. During the building of the house in 1980, the ghosts made themselves known as they observed every phase of its construction. Not long after the house was first occupied, the owner awoke to find the five pirates standing around the dining room table. The next day he opened his eyes to see the same five standing around his bed. On the third morning when the owner awoke, he saw the five ghosts again. This time they appeared to be talking to each other, but not a sound could be heard. Upon talking with a neighbor, the owner learned that his was not an isolated incident. Others had witnessed similar occurrences. The neighbor thought that the five ghosts were tied to the legend of a Jean Lafitte treasure that is said to be buried somewhere in the area.

Over the years, the five ghosts continue to make their presence known, but the owners, at last report, are determined to stay.

GRAND COTEAU

Saint Landry Parish, Grand Coteau: Near Louisiana State Highway 182 in a stretch of road known as "Dead Man's Curve" sits an old plantation home. It has been said that the house is the center of many supernatural occurrences within the area. The main spirit appears to be a black slave described as a large female who is full of mischief.

During the Civil War, the owner may have used the slave to help hide the family fortune. After the cache was made, it is believed that the slave was killed to insure that no one else would learn her master's secret. The owner died before the war ended and is said to haunt the plantation house where he keeps vigil over the treasure from a second story window. The slave, also trapped in time, guards the exact location where the treasure was buried--across the road from the plantation house.

NEW IBERIA

Iberia Parish, New Iberia: Nestled atop a large Indian burial mound is a quaint colonial style home of new construction. From the outside the house appears picture perfect, but inside the spirits are restless. The spirits have never been seen by the owners, but have made their presence known in other ways. Doors open and close, lights go on and off, and the furniture moves about the house as if under its own power. Several people have reported seeing an unknown figure peering from a second story window, but this has never been seen by the owners. Most people believe that the activity is due to the spirits of the mound, but some believe that a treasure is buried under the house.

UNKNOWN SPIRITS

Vermilion Parish, Gueydan: According to the Reed Family in Abbeville, several ghosts guard one of Lafitte's treasures on a reservoir south of town and near the Lake Arthur Hunting Club. William Reed has searched for the treasure since his father gave him a map in 1967, and during that time he has seen many visions. The site is reported to be near an Indian burial ground.

The story goes something like this. In the winter of 1930, William's brother Sallas went on a hunting trip alone. After shooting a duck, he waded out, retrieved the game. He was wading back to his pirogue when the ghost of a soldier arose from the water. The soldier was full of what appeared to be gunshot wounds and his heart could be seen pumping. The ghost asked; "What are you looking for? Are you looking for what is here?"

Sallas was terrified but managed to reply, "Yes."

The ghost stated that he would show Sallas where Lafitte's treasure was buried. As Sallas followed, first in his pirogue and then on foot, the ghost led him to the Indian burial ground and pointed to a bricked area. The ghost stated that Lafitte's treasure was buried there.

Sallas left and never returned to the area, but the ghost continued to visit Sallas every year and ask why he would not take the treasure.

In 1935, while Sallas lay dying, he gave the directions to the treasure to his father. However, the ghost of the soldier has not been seen by anyone since Sallas' death.

In 1967, Reed followed the directions and dug for the treasure. He found only ancient human remains which he brought home.

The next time Reed visited the area, he saw the ghost of a slave. The ghostly vision was accompanied by howling sounds. Reed watched as the ghost drowned a white woman.

The next vision occurred in Reed's home and appeared to his wife. This ghost had a limp. Mrs. Reed persuaded her husband to return the ancient remains to their original resting place. Reed replaced the remains, but continued to see the slave as he would pass the area along the Intercostal Canal. Reed now feels that the treasure may have been removed, but that the ghosts still haunt the area to discourage anyone else from digging in the area.

OLD CAMP PLACE

Ouachita Parish, Monroe: Built in 1855 and located ten miles west of Monroe on Old Wire Road, Old Camp Place was once a beautiful two story inn that serviced the Monroe, Shreveport Stage Line.   Old Camp Place also served as a campground and rest area for travelers. During the Civil War a reported $20,000 to $180,000 in gold, silver and jewels were buried by refugees fleeing Union Army troops. Little remains of the original Old Home Place except the treasure and an uneasy spirit who is said to haunt the one story home that now occupies the site.

HONEY ISLAND SWAMP

Saint Tammany Parish: It is estimated that as much as $4,000,000 is hidden within the Honey Island Swamp. With a treasure that big you have to have a few ghosts and maybe something really big to guard it. Well, folks, I am here to tell you that I have just what you would expect a treasure of that proportion to have. The biggest, meanest creature we could find lives in the Honey Island Swamp. We are talking about the one and maybe not the only Bigfoot or "Wookie" as he is sometimes called by locals. Bigfoot is also known as "paume faix" in other areas of Louisiana.

The legend of Bigfoot began with the Indians in the Honey Island Swamp (as in most areas of North America where he has been reported.) As you drive around the area you will see many signs of Bigfoot, usually 4' x 8', with large lettering stating "Honey Island Swamp Monster tours ahead."

There have been hundreds of sightings of Bigfoot in this area over the years and even more reports of the blood curdling sounds made by the creature. At most of the souvenir shops in the swamp area you can see plaster casts of the footprints left by the creature and hear tales of narrow escapes from certain death at the hands of Bigfoot.

The story of one Chalmette man goes something like this: "We were on a fishing trip, in the middle of the swamp, when the motor on our boat quit. We paddled to shore and decided to spend the night and work on the motor in the daylight. It was just about 10:30 p.m. when we heard a disturbance in the woods behind us. We all moved around to the other side of the fire, to try and see what it was. The noise kept getting closer and closer. I grabbed a big stick that we were going to use for the fire and waited. Then all of a sudden there it was--about 8 to 9 feet tall, all covered with hair, and it smelled worst then my cousin Joe-Joe's feet. Well, I threw the stick and hit him right on the nose. He let out a scream like I have never heard before and went running back the way he came. We all jumped into the boat and paddled back to Slidell non-stop. I do not want to be caught in the Honey Island Swamp at night ever again."

Having grown up in Louisiana I find it hard to believe in Bigfoot. In Louisiana we are known for what we eat. I am sure that if Bigfoot did exist I would have heard Justin Wilson say, "Bigfoot, oh yea, it taste just like chicken, I guar-an-tee."

If Bigfoot were not enough, the Honey Island Swamp also has its own unique monster. The Honey Island Monster. The monster has been described as a shorter, webfooted version of Bigfoot. Other stories describe the monster as closer to the "Creature From the Black Lagoon." Standing only four to five feet tall and brown in color, the monster has been spotted exiting the Pearl River and running into a wooded area. It was said that the monster is covered with hair. It has also been said that the monster is covered with scales. Yet other reports claim that the monster is of a hairless and scaleless variety with his skin a dark brown color. Some claim the Bigfoot and the Honey Island Swamp Monster are one in the same.

GHOST OF RED RIVER BEND

War really is hell, and it always changes a person, sometimes for the good and sometimes for the worse. So it was with the Civil War, where brother fought brother and nothing and no one would ever be the same. War makes a person do things they would not normally do, and, thereby, sets into motion a chain of events from that point on to the grave. Sometimes that chain extends beyond the grave.

This story has to do with one Johnny Reb who grew up with good family values. Johnny knew right from wrong, good from evil and moral from immoral. He worked the land as his father and his father's father had done. He went to church every

Sunday. Johnny had plans for the future that included a wife and children.

Then the Civil War came, and the nation was in turmoil. What was right was now wrong and what was wrong became right. Things that Johnny would never have thought of doing became the norm. The taking of a human life, stealing, drinking and consorting with loose women. Johnny would never be the same.

After the war ended, Johnny, like many others, found it hard to return to the farm. Instead he joined a renegade band of Confederate soldiers operating from the Red River Bend area. Johnny was trusted by everyone and as such placed in charge of the booty from the raids. After one of these raids, Johnny left the camp and hid the gang's loot. While Johnny was away an argument erupted over the split of the booty. Johnny heard the shouting and returned to camp. Tempers flared and guns were drawn. When the smoke had cleared, Johnny was dead. The other renegades searched for the booty, but it could not be found. Eventually they went their separate ways.

Twenty years later two men found a small cave near the bend and entered. Once inside, the two found they were not alone. A hellish creature dressed in what appeared to be an old Confederate uniform came from the rear of the cave and pursued the duo to the entrance of the cave. The creature then dissipated like smoke.

Stories of the Confederate ghost have continued well into the twentieth century. Johnny Reb, it is said, still guards the treasure put into his charge one hundred twenty-eight years ago.

THE LOVERS OF FORT PROCTOR

Saint Bernard Parish, Shell Beach: Fort Proctor, also known as Fort Beauregard, was build in 1856, under the supervision of General P. G. T. Beauregard as a defense of Lake Borgne at Proctorsville (Shell Beach). Shortly after Beauregard's attack on Fort Sumter, the levees around Fort Proctor were dynamited, flooding the fort and limiting its use by the invading Union Army.

Local legend has it that during the civil war the fort was used as a hideout by a group of deserters and that one of the deserters was murdered by the others.

This story of spirits appears to have its origin in the late 1930's when mysterious lights (feux follet) were seen rising from the water just to the south of Fort Proctor. The lights would hover in the Spanish moss of the nearby trees or dance along the walls of the fort. The lights are usually accompanied by strange sounds and are said to occur only on nights of a "DEAD CALM." The mysterious lights are said to be the souls of a one-armed soldier and his lover who dance the nights away.

One hunter was in a pirogue when he saw a light hovering about three feet above the water. The light first appeared to be orange in color and then changed to a pale green and then blue. As the hunter approached the light, it continued to move away at the same speed. The hunter followed the light and, after approximately one hour, found himself near the old fort where the light grew into a massive white glow that lit up the midnight sky. It was at this point that the hunter decided he had seen enough and departed the area. As the hunter departed, the white glow rose above the tree line and continued to be seen by the hunter all the way to the camp where he was to stay the night. The light was joined by a second one, and it was as if two blue eyes were watching him all the way to the camp. The hunter stood and watched as this huge white glow with two piercing blue eyes continued to scrutinize his every move. The hunter packed up and went home.

A scientist might say that the light was nothing more than a collection of swamp gases. That same scientist could say that treasure is just a collection of elements put into an equation: Au (gold) + Ag (silver) = T (treasure).

Having friends in the area who knew of my interest in treasure hunting, I was told of the treasure part of the story. It seems that it was the practice of a few of the residents of Shell Beach to go to the area where the mysterious light had been seen. During the daylight hours, and at low tide they would "scoop for coins." Using a pirogue they would paddle out to the fort and use a scoop net to sift through the sandy bottom for old Spanish coins. As further proof, I was shown dozens of specimens of Spanish milled dollars (pieces of eight), all with dates in the 1750's. I was also told that several people had found Spanish gold doubloons.

To my knowledge there has never been an explanation given for the treasure being in that location. The finders were content with the unexplained treasure. Perhaps if they had made up a story people would have come to look for the treasure. Maybe it was better to have a ghost story to keep people away from the area and not mention the treasure at all.

If you decide to go to this area be advised that there are several large alligators residing nearby, and try to be gone by dark if you believe in ghosts

THE GHOSTS THAT GO TO COLLEGE

Natchitoches Parish, Natchitoches: During the early 1800's a band of Red River pirates looted and burned a riverboat near Natchitoches killing all of the passengers. It is believed the booty from this venture was buried where Northwestern State University is located today. This story was said to have been passed to the family of one of the pirates. The pirates family made several attempts to locate the treasure, but were unsuccessful. The story was passed on to following generations, but nothing has ever been reported found.

On the campus of Northwestern State University one can hear many ghosts stories. The ghosts are said to be those of some the passengers of that ill-fated riverboat who roam the halls of the university in search of their lost valuables.

PIRATES OF ISLE DE GAMBI

Jefferson Parish, Isle de Gambi (Gombi): According to a story printed in 1977, the Isle de Gambi, near the mouth of

Bayou Caillou is the resting place of several of Gambi's treasure caches. It also said to be the haunting grounds of Johnny Gambi and his ghostly crew.

According to stories, a young, local fisherman was having a hard time making the payments on his new boat. To alleviate the problem, he decided to go to the Isle de Gambi, and dig up some of the reported treasure that is rumored to be buried there.

During a night of the full moon, the man went to the island alone and beached his boat. After a few minutes he found a likely spot to dig between three old oak trees. The man looked in the direction of where he had beached his boat, but it was not there. Returning to the water, he found the boat had dislodged itself and was now adrift. The man swam out, secured his boat, and returned to the island. This time the man tied the bow line to a tree, returned to the site between the three oak trees and started to dig.

After several shovelfuls of dirt, the man struck something solid, at the same time a noise came from behind him. As the man turned, he saw several pirates approaching with swords drawn. Each sword was said to be dripping with blood.

The man threw himself to his knees and began to pray. The man swore that if he lived, he would never return to Isle de Gambi. When the man had finished his prayer, he looked up and the pirates were gone.

The man jumped to his feet and ran to his boat. When the man arrived at his boat, he found Captain Gambi sitting in it waiting for him. Gambi ordered him into the boat. The man complied. Next Gambi ordered him to head out to sea. Again, he complied. After several minutes the man was ordered to stop, and when he did, Captain Gambi slipped over the side and into the deep blue water.

The man returned to his home, and to this day has never gone within a mile of Isle de Gambi, and vows to never venture there again.

CHAPTER X

CIVIL WAR TREASURE

As this is being written, 130 years has passed since the last official shot was fired in the war that tore apart this great nation of ours. In conversations with ladies from the South it is not uncommon to hear the Civil War referred to as the "Recent Unpleasantness" or the "War of Northern Aggression." "War is hell" and it has left many an unpleasant memory in the hearts of Southerners.

Stories of the splendor that <u>was</u> the South have been passed on from generation to generation. The magnificent balls and garden parties. Some plantations enjoyed indoor plumbing, silver and gold doorknobs, yes, and even central heat. Money flowed as freely as the Mississippi River.

The men pampered their ladies, afforded them the respect one would give royalty, spoiling them beyond belief. Some were arrogant, aristocratic snobs. Even today, true Southern ladies are not usually given to the use of profanity. However, you may hear the word Yankee still used as an expletive.

As if "The War" was not enough, there was Reconstruction. What a misnomer. Most of the plantation owners who managed to survive the Civil War with their holdings intact lost just about everything during the reconstruction period. Many plantations were taken away, divided and given to the slaves. Some plantations were sold for little money or given outright to the Carpetbaggers who were in charge of the reconstruction. Very few of the plantations remained in the hands of the original families. Those that did were just a shadow of their former splendor.

Before the Civil War, many plantation owners maintained large sums of money at their plantation. Many plantation owners distrusted banks and kept all their money hidden about the plantation. Those who did trust banks withdrew their money when the war started. When the stories of Yankees stealing everything that was not nailed down began to circulate throughout the South, money, jewels, and other valuables were usually buried to keep them from falling into the hands of those "Damn Yankees."

By the time the Civil War and Reconstruction had ended, the land was changed, many people had died, and most of the plantations were in the hands of new owners. Many of the fortunes that were buried or somehow concealed before the coming of the Yankees remain in their location, lost forever--or at least until that stroke of luck occurs and they are again brought into the light of day.

Some of the sites of treasures listed in this chapter are obvious because of their dollar value. Other sites are listed because of their not-so-obvious treasure values. The value of a discovered object from one of these treasure sites may be difficult to realize at first. Often it requires some research to find out exactly what it is you have found. Collectors of military paraphernalia are many, and the prices paid for Civil War artifacts can be very high. I have therefore listed the general going rates for Civil War items that may be found at some of these sites. These prices are for items that are excavated. If you have any of these items which were not buried for one hundred thirty years, they would be worth a lot more.

U. S. plates, belt, breast, cartridge, etc..: $75 to $4,750.
Confederate plates: $850 to $9,000.
Miscellaneous plain buckles: $60 to $900.
Iron cannons: $4,000 to $27,000.
Bronze cannons: $6,000 to $50,000.
Artillery equipment: $2 and $3,000.
Artillery fuses: $10 to $500.
Artillery rockets and grenades: $300 to $1,500.
Artillery shells: $45 to $1,200.
Angular or socket bayonets: $60 to $2,400.
Sword-sabre bayonets: $125 to $2,000.
Civil War bottles, jars and inkwells: $10 to $150.

The basic prices for dropped bullets (not fired): $1 to $300.

NOTE: Bullets with bite marks in them seem to command the highest prices, followed by bullets that are lodged in objects, as well bullets that have been carved into chess pieces or other objects.

Iron Bullet molds: $60 to $325.
Brass bullet molds: $30 to $475.
Buttons with state seals: $5 to $2,800.
Confederate buttons: $25 up, with most worth over $100.
Union buttons: $1 to $325.
Military school buttons: $70 to $600.
Camp gear: One collapsible brass candlestick, $75. (This is the lowest price listed for any piece of camp gear.)
Canteens: $30 to $4,500.
Cartridges: $3 to $250.
Confederate Cavalry spurs: $50 to $1,000 each.
Union spurs: $40 to $600 each.
Confederate stirrups: $25 to $200 each.
Federal stirrups: $75 to $150 each.
Confederate bits: $25 to $650.
Federal bits: $75 to $300.
Picket pins: $50 to $125.
Corps badges: $300 to $550.
Pocket knives: $100 to $6,000.
Pikes: $100 to $2,000.
Federal swords: $275 to $4,100.
Confederate swords: $700 to $17,000.
Saddle shields: $15 to $250.
Rosettes: $15 to $350.
Martingales: $200 to $500.
One brass lieutenant insignia: $30.
One brass general insignia: $200.
Brass hat pins: $85 to $475.
Medical items: $30 to $150.
Tools: $5 to $30.

Heel plates: $1 to $10.
An iron jew's harp: $3.
A brass candle holder: $30.
A knife, fork, or spoon, with some wood on the handle: $5.
Firearms: $200 to $450.
A brass bayonet scabbard tip: $4.
A brass Bormann fuse wrench: $160.
Regimental numbers: $20 and up.
Personal identification discs (Dog tags): $300 to $950.
A Louisiana hat plate: $550.

ASCENSION PARISH

L'Hermitage Plantation: Post at L'Hermitage Landing was the name of a Union Army post that was established in 1864 on the L'Hermitage Plantation. The plantation is located on Louisiana State Highway 942, just east of the junction with Louisiana State Highway 22.

AVOYELLES PARISH

Marksville: Many Civil War battles were fought in the area of Marksville. Relics and artifacts are said to be abundant in this area.

Marksville: Several unnamed Confederate camps were located near Marksville. One was on the railroad line south of town, and the second was near Little Lake. Both of these camps were established in 1864.

BIENVILLE PARISH

Friendship: It is believed that the Confederates operated a salt mine in the area between Friendship and Lucky. It is also believed that weapons may have been cached in the mine along with other Civil War treasures.

CADDO PARISH

Shreveport: The Land's End Plantation was built in 1857 by Colonel Henry Marshall. In April of 1864, the plantation was used as quarters for several Confederate generals. After the Battle of Mansfield, the plantation home was used as a Confederate field hospital. The plantation is located approximately sixteen miles south of Shreveport on Red Bluff Road, one-quarter mile east of the Linwood Avenue Extension.

CALCASIEU PARISH

Vinton: The Post at Nibletts Bluff was a Confederate stronghold established in May of 1863. This area is now within the Nibletts Bluff Park.

Nibletts Bluff is also reported to be the location of what has been described as the largest of Jean Lafitte treasures, $1,000,000. Nibletts Bluff is located eight miles west of Vinton on Louisiana State Highway 3063.

CAMERON PARISH

Johnson's Bayou: Post on Sabine Lake was a United States Army post established in 1838. It is believed that the post was located on the shore of Sabine Lake, just north of Louisiana State Highway 82. Little is known about this post, but it appears to have been in operation after 1845. It appears on Confederate maps as a "U. S. Garrison."

CONCORDIA PARISH

Vidalia: In July, 1863, Federal troops captured the town of Vidalia. Several treasure caches are rumored to have been made and never recovered after the war ended. The area around Vidalia is said to abound with relics of the Civil War.

DESOTO PARISH

Keatchie: The Fairview Plantation was built in 1840. During April of 1864, the plantation was used as a Confederate Army camp for troops going to and from the Battle of Mansfield. The plantation is located approximately four miles west of Louisiana State Highway 5 on Louisiana State Highway 172.

Mansfield: During April of 1864, several battles were fought around Mansfield. Today the Mansfield Battlefield State Park is situated on only a part of the massive area covered by this battle site.

EAST BATON ROUGE PARISH

Baker: Post at Springfield Landing was the name of a Union Army supply post. It was considered a major supply point of the Union Army during the siege of Port Hudson. A number of Union troops were kept at the landing to protect the supplies. On July 2, 1863, the post was attacked and a large quantity of the supplies was destroyed. This post was located on the Springfield Plantation at the Mississippi River. The plantation was located in the area of Irene Road, and the landing was across from Profit Island Chute.

Baton Rouge: The Magnolia Cemetery is the reported resting place of a treasure of gold, silver and jewels. A plantation owner fleeing the Battle of Baton Rouge was trying to leave the city with his valuables. Realizing that if he were stopped and his wagon searched, his valuables would be taken from him, he buried them in the Cemetery. Because this site is within a cemetery, it is not likely that if the treasure were ever found it would be reported.
Other treasure caches were reportedly made within the Magnolia Cemetery.   One story states that a wealthy

businessman secreted an immense treasure in several locations about the cemetery, but died before the end of the Civil War.

Baton Rouge: During the Civil War several hundred individual treasure caches were believed to have been made within the area of Baton Rouge. One group of Southerners made three caches of weapons, gold, silver and jewels. One of the caches was located within an old cemetery. This cache consisted of guns, swords, gold silver and jewels. Of the remaining two, one is believed to contain approximately $500,000 in gold and silver coins. It is believed that these and many other caches remain buried today as they have been for the past one hundred thirty-five years.

Baton Rouge: Camp Banks was the name of a Union Army camp established in December of 1862. This camp was located near the present day intersection of Government and eighteenth Streets, at the site of an old race track. Race tracks were often used as army camps, and usually thousands of soldiers were stationed at these sites. Also several battles were fought in this same area.

Baton Rouge: Camp at Bayou Sara and Clinton Roads was the name of a Union Army camp established in 1862. The camp was located at the intersection of Bayou Sara (Scenic Highway) and Clinton (Plank) Roads. It is believed that the site of this camp is now located close to the present day intersection of North and 19th Streets. (The camp did not move, but the roads did.) This site was the scene of a battle on August 5, 1862, when the position was overrun by Confederate troops.

Baton Rouge: Camp Bird was the name of a Confederate Army camp established in 1862. The camp was located on the Bird Plantation at the present day intersection of North Foster Drive and Greenwell Springs Road.

Baton Rouge: Camp Breckinridge was also known as Camp on Comite River. This was a Confederate Army camp used from August 10, 1862 to May 6, 1863. The camp was located on the Comite River near Louisiana State Highway 408 (the Baton Rouge, Greenwell Springs Road).

Baton Rouge: Camp Clark was the name of a Union Army camp established in early 1862. This camp was located at the present day junctions of Government Street and Seventeenth or Eighteenth Street.

Baton Rouge: Camp Indiana was the name of a Union Army camp that was established in 1862. This camp was located in the area of the present intersection of Laurel and 19th Streets.

Baton Rouge: Camp at Magnolia Grove was the name of a Union Army camp used during the Baton Rouge Campaign. This camp was located on the Magnolia Mound Plantation. The plantation home was built in 1871 and was once the home of Prince Achille Murat. It is located at 2161 Nicholson Drive.

Baton Rouge: Highland Road Cavalry Camp was a Union Army camp. The camp was located where the Woodstone subdivision is today.

Baton Rouge: Mount Hope Plantation was built in 1790 by Joseph Sharp. During the Civil War the plantation was used as a Confederates Army camp. The plantation is located at 8181 Highland Road.

Baton Rouge: Stewart-Dougherty House was built in the 1840's, for Nathan Knox. During 1862 and 1863, the plantation was used as a United States Army General Hospital. The Stewart-Dougherty House is located at 714 North Street.

NOTE: At one time I owned a current city map of Baton Rouge that showed the locations of all the fortifications and battle sites of the Civil War. The battle sites were shown in red over the current street map, but it, too, grew feet and walked off under its own power. If you live in the Baton Rouge area, you may be able to find your own copy of this map.

EAST CARROLL PARISH

Lake Providence: The Arlington Plantation was built in 1841 for Mistress T. R. Patten. During the Civil War the plantation house was used as headquarters for several Union Army officers, including General Ulysses Simpson Grant. In 1863, the plantation was the site of much activity as General Grant's troops attempted to dig a canal across DeSoto Point in order to allow Union gunboats safe passage during the siege of Vicksburg. The plantation is located just off United States Highway 65, east of Lake Providence on Schneider Lane.

Lake Providence: Camp Neal was a Union Army camp, first established at the site of Lake Providence High School and later at the lake shore along the northern edge of town. It has been reported that Camp Neal had the largest concentration of Union troops in northeast Louisiana.

Lake Providence: An unnamed Union post was established in 1863 at the Mounds Plantation near Lake Providence.

EAST FELICIANA PARISH

Clinton: The story goes that when word of approaching Union troops reached one Clinton man, he loaded three packhorses with gold and entered a nearby wooded area. After the cache was safely in the ground, he marked the spot with two very old dueling pistols. With his task complete, the man returned to his home to await the outcome of the Civil War, safe in the knowledge that whichever way the war went he and his family would be comfortable for the rest of their lives. Upon his arrival at home the man explained what he had done, but did not give explicate directions to the burial site. The man believed that there would be time for minor details at a later date. Not feeling very well after the strenuous ordeal, the man decided to take a nap. He laid down and died in his sleep.

One of the pistols was supposedly found by a man putting up a fence near Clinton. The other pistol and the buried gold has never been reported found.

Clinton: Camp Beal was the name of a Confederate Cavalry camp. The camp was located near Plank Road, ten miles south of Clinton. This camp was established in January of 1863.

Jackson: The Milbank Plantation was built in 1825, and over the years has served as a hotel, pharmacy, and during the Civil War as an army barracks and camp. The plantation is located at 102 Bank Street in Jackson.

Lindsay: The Linwood Plantation was built in the 1830's by Albert G. Carter. During the Civil War the plantation house was used as a Union Army hospital. The plantation is located south of Saint Francisville. Take Louisiana State Highway 61 to Louisiana State Highway 964 and turn east. At the junction of Louisiana State Highway 995 turn right.

IBERIA PARISH

Avery Island: Confederate soldiers operated a salt mine on Avery Island until April of 1863, when Union troops assaulted the island. The Union Army continued to operate the salt mine for the remainder of the Civil War.

Jeanerette: The Albania Plantation House was constructed in 1837. After the Battle of Berwick Bay, the house was occupied by General Nathaniel Banks. His troops were encamped about the grounds of the plantation. The plantation is located on Louisiana State Highway 182, one-quarter mile east of Jeanerette.

New Iberia: Camp Qui Vive was the name of a Confederate Army training camp established in 1862. The camp was located at Fausse Pointe on the Bayou Teche.

New Iberia: The Dulcito Plantation was constructed in 1788 and was used as a Confederate Army hospital during the Civil War. The plantation is located seven miles northwest of New Iberia on Louisiana State Highway 182, approximately two miles west of the junction with Louisiana State Highway 677.

JEFFERSON PARISH

Harvey: During the Civil War Union soldiers stole an estimated $30,000 from the Magnolia Lane Plantation. Approximately $27,000 of the money stolen was in gold coins, the rest in silver coins. The plantation was built in 1784, and was the first to grow strawberries in Louisiana. The plantation is approximately one and one-half miles down river from the Huey P. Long Bridge on Louisiana State Highway 18, at Nine Mile Point. It is quite possible that the treasure was buried where a grove of pecan trees once stood one-half mile up river from the Harvey Canal.

As far as is known, no one has ever searched this area for the treasure. The original story was based on fact, but there were a number of inadequacies. Most people who attempted to locate the treasure site ran into several problems and had to give up.

The story that was passed on had the treasure being placed on the east side of the Mississippi River. Even though the city named in the story was New Orleans, one clue fit Baton Rouge. The key was finding the right Magnolia Plantation. In my research I found six of them. Only one of the plantations fit New Orleans and none fit Baton Rouge. If the soldiers were 20 miles up river from New Orleans then the Magnolia Lane Plantation, near Bridge City, would have to be the one in the story. That would put the treasure on the west bank of the Mississippi not the east bank. If you reverse all of the other points in the original story everything fits except for one point--the small town that was named in the story as being across the river from the treasure site. Baton Rouge had the small town, but it is not on the Mississippi River as the story stated.

It may have been that the person who buried the treasure was confused about which side of the river he was on--he was a Yankee. In some areas of New Orleans the west bank is to the south and the east bank is to the north. In other areas of the city the west bank is east and the east is west. After all New Orleans is the "Crescent City."

Jefferson: Post at Whitehall was a Union Army post established in 1864. The post was located on the Whitehall Plantation at River Road and Central Avenue. The plantation house was constructed in 1762 by Francois Pascalis Labarre, and over the years has served as an army post, casino, Jesuit retreat. Today it is The Magnolia School.

LAFAYETTE PARISH

Broussard: During the Civil War, a small battle was fought in the area of Pin Hook. It is said that relics and artifacts abound.

LAFOURCHE PARISH

Thibodaux: Post at Lafourche Crossing was a Union Army post and the site of a battle on June 21, 1864. It was maintained by the Union Army until the end of the Civil War. The post was located approximately four miles southeast of Thibodaux at the Opelousas and Great Southern Railroad crossing on the east bank of Bayou Lafourche.

Thibodaux: Post at Bayou Du Ashland was a Union Army post established in 1865. It was located near the Post at Lafourche Crossing.

LIVINGSTON PARISH

Abrian's (O'Briens) Island: Post at Carthage was the name of a Confederate Army post established in 1864. This post was located on the east side of the Amite River on the first rise of land below O'Briens Island. It was once known as Carthage Bluff Landing.

Amite River: Camp at Benton's Ferry was a Confederate Army camp established in June of 1862 along the Amite River at Benton's Ferry.

MADISON PARISH

Delta: Post at Milliken's Bend was a Union Army post from June 1863 until November 1865. This camp was the scene of heavy fighting on June 6th and 7th in 1863.

Delta: Post at Young's Point was the Headquarters of Major General Ulysses Simpson Grant's Army of Tennessee in January and February of 1863. On June 7th of that same year, Confederate forces attempted to capture the Union troops camped there, but failed when Federal gunboats arrived in support of the troops. This camp was used until January of 1868.

NATCHITOCHES PARISH

Campti: During the Civil War many of the residents of Campti hid their valuables when word of the approaching Union Army came. Campti was destroyed during the ensuing battle, and it is believed that many caches remain buried there today.

Grand Ecore: Samuel Davenport, with land holdings of 50,000 acres in Louisiana and Texas, was undoubtedly the richest man in Natchitoches Parish. As the Union Army approached Grand Ecore, Davenport buried his entire fortune and awaited the outcome of the war. When Davenport died all that could be accounted for was $5,000. It was believed that Davenport may have made as many as 15 separate treasure caches. In the 1930's, one of Davenport's caches of $6,000 was reported found, but many more remain.

Grand Ecore: The Union Army plundered the city of Grand Ecore in 1863, but before the Yankees arrived most of the townspeople managed to bury their valuables. Stories of several businessmen and other citizens in Grand Ecore burying their money between Grand Ecore and Natchitoches, along the west bank of the Red River, and never recovering these caches have been reported.

Some of these caches were not recovered because of the Great Flood of 1863, which removed treasure markers as well as treasure caches.

ORLEANS PARISH

New Orleans: From 1838 until 1861 and again from 1879 until 1909, the United States operated a mint in New Orleans. At the start of the Civil War, the Confederacy seized control of the New Orleans Mint and produced coins using existing dies and the gold, silver and copper on hand. The ultimate goal was to produce Confederate coins. Just prior to New Orleans falling to the Union, the coins, along with the un-minted gold and silver, with an estimated value of $500,000, were removed from the mint and spirited away.

17,741 twenty-dollar Double Eagles were produced by the United States at the New Orleans Mint. They were locked in the mint vaults, but could not be removed before Louisiana seceded from the Union. Several Confederate States of America twenty-dollar dies were designed, but there are no known coins in existence. It is believed by most people that the Confederates never produced any twenty dollar gold pieces.

330,000 Liberty Seated silver half-dollars were produced just prior to Louisiana joining the Confederacy. The half-dollar presses were sabotaged. An additional 1,240,000 silver half-dollars were minted by the State of Louisiana, using an old hand-operated press, and 962,633 silver half-dollars were struck under the Confederate States' control of the mint. Between March 9, 1861, and May 14, 1861, Confederate States of America silver half-dollars were struck, but only four of these are known to exist. One was stolen from President Jefferson Davis' wife by an unknown Union Officer. It was taken while she was imprisoned aboard a Federal prison ship. The second coin was in the possession of J. L. Riddell, a professor at the University of Louisiana. The third was in the possession of a New Orleans physician, Doctor E. Ames, and the fourth coin was in the hands of a New Orleans physician, Doctor B. F. Taylor.

After May 3, 1861, all the copper at the New Orleans Mint was used to make percussion caps for use in the weapons of the Louisiana State Militia.

By May 1, 1862, the City of New Orleans was in the hands of the Union Army, and the New Orleans Mint was empty. Some stories state that the treasure of gold and silver was concealed somewhere within the mint or the surrounding area.

The New Orleans Mint is still at the corner of Esplanade Avenue and Decatur Streets. The treasure is still missing. Or is it?

Based on fact and a little conjecture, this is probably what happened to the New Orleans Mint Treasure.

On or about April 25, 1862, word reached the Confederate officers stationed at the New Orleans Mint that the capture of New Orleans was imminent. The coins and bullion were put into ammunition boxes, loaded first on to wagons and later transferred to a ship that was standing by in Lake Pontchartrain. Lake Pontchartrain would have offered the only egress from the city because Union forces were attacking from the mouth of the Mississippi River. The ship departed New Orleans in the direction on Mobile, Alabama. However, they could not travel the Gulf Coast because--the Union Navy had set up a base on Cat Island, Mississippi, and had boats patrolling the Mississippi

Sound. The Confederate officers also figured that if the Yankees were moving on New Orleans from the south, they could also be attacking from the north and east. If Forts Pike and Macomb had fallen, the ship and its treasure would be trapped in Lake Pontchartrain. They reasoned that the treasure would be better hidden in the lake until a larger force could be sent to retrieve it. The depth of the lake at its deepest point was only 14 feet, making recovery of the boxes at a later date an easy task. The officers chose a prominent point. As the ship passed the "Point" near Irish Bayou, the boxes containing the coins and bullion were tossed overboard. The ship continued on through The Rigolets and Fort Pike and into Lake Borgne.

New Orleans fell to the Union, as did all the fortifications in the area of the lake, making recovery of the treasure during the war difficult at best. The information would have been undoubtedly passed on to higher authorities, but the war did not go well for the South. No record was ever found of the disposition of the New Orleans Mint treasure. It is, also, possible that the ship could have been sunk by one of the Union boats in the Mississippi Sound.

During the time the mint was in the hands of the Confederacy, several sets of dies were known to have been made and only a few sample coins struck. These dies were made using existing 1861 United States dies from the New Orleans Mint. A set of one cent dies was ordered from an engraver in Philadelphia. The engraver, afraid of being arrested by the United States government as a traitor, hid the dies and twelve specimens. There were no Confederate States of America coins ever circulated. The four known half dollars are priceless. The twelve known cents have a value in the range of $5,000 each. If other coins could be found, their value would be hard to phantom.

At the time word arrived of the impending Union take over of New Orleans, the mint was in the process of mass producing coins. A lot of the bullion had already been converted into planchets ('plan-chet; a metal disk to be stamped into a coin).

During the late 1950's and early 1960's some of these dollar and half-dollar size planchets were found along the shore of Lake Pontchartrain between Irish Bayou and the railroad bridge to the west. It is believed that one of the boxes containing silver planchets may have been disturbed during the construction or repair of the train trestle in that area. Numerous dives were made in the area, usually after storms, and hundreds of silver half-dollar and dollar size planchets were found. Remember there is no such thing as a hunted out location, and as far as it is known no one has ever checked this area with a metal detector. With the advent of modern underwater metal detectors thousands more of these gold and silver wafers could be found and, perhaps, an unknown Confederate States of America coin or two.

The people who found the planchets had no idea what the were, other than half-dollar and dollar size silver disks. The disks had the value of silver only because they had no markings on them. Due to the fact that no one knew what they were, it was assumed that they were part of a Spanish treasure. Before long the tale evolved that they were part of a Lafitte treasure. The story began to circulate that one of Lafitte's treasure barges had sunk during a storm spilling its precious contents into the lake. After storms people would comb the beach, and divers would scour the floor of the lake in that area.

If anyone has ever made the recovery of this treasure it is not known. This version of the New Orleans Mint Treasure has never appeared in print anywhere else and should be investigated by divers with good underwater metal detectors. The gold and silver alone would have a value of at least $2,500,000 today. If any Confederate States of America coins were found, they would authenticate the treasure as being that of the New Orleans Mint and bring the value to at least $5,000,000.

New Orleans: Camp at Orleans Cotton Press was a Confederate Army camp established in 1861. After New Orleans fell in 1862, the site was used by the Union Army. The Orleans Cotton Press was built in 1834. It was 308 feet wide and 632 feet long and could be compared to a modern day Mississippi River Wharf warehouse. Bales of cotton were placed in presses and reduced to approximately one-half their regular size. This made it easier to ship more cotton at a time. While in the presses, the cotton was out of the weather and was classified, reweighed, and marked for shipping. The size of these buildings made them perfect for housing soldiers. The buildings gave the soldiers not only sleeping quarters, but also a place where they could march and drill out of the rain. This press was located at South Front Street and the Greater New Orleans Mississippi River Bridge.

The Alabama Cotton Press was also used as a barracks by both Confederate and Union troops. The press was located on Race Street, between Saint Thomas and Tchoupitoulas Streets.

The Freret's Cotton Press was another press used during the Civil War to quarter both Confederate and Union soldiers. It is believed that this press was located at the west end of Freret Street and the Mississippi River.

The Louisiana Cotton Press was used by both the Union and Confederate Armies from April 1861 through reconstruction. The press was located on Robin Street near Saint Thomas Street. The building and streets are now gone, but the location would have been within a box formed by Annunciation, Thalia, Terpsichore, and Tchoupitoulas Streets.

The Louisiana Steam Press on Old Levee Street was the site of Camp Dudley, a Union Army camp established in December of 1863.

The Lower Cotton Press was used as quarters by the United States Army during the Mexican-American War in 1845 and by the Confederate Army at the beginning of the Civil War. After New Orleans fell in May of 1862, Union troops occupied the press. During 1865 the press was used to house prisoners of war. It was located on North Peters Street between Montegut and Saint Ferdinand Streets.

The Southern Cotton Press was located at the corner of Poydras Street and Claiborne Avenue. This press was used to house troops beginning in 1861 with the Confederates, until

November of 1869 with United States troops during Reconstruction.

The Union Cotton Press was used as Union Army quarters from May of 1862 until after the Civil War had ended. The press was located on Henderson Street, between Tchoupitoulas and South Front Streets.

Algiers: Two Union Army posts were established at Algiers during the Civil War. One of these posts was located at the Bellville Iron Works. The second post was located at the New Orleans, Opelousas and Great Western Railroad Terminal.

New Orleans: Camp Annunciation Square was established on March 25, 1862, as a Confederate Army camp. After May 1, 1862, the Square was used by Union troops until well after the Civil War had ended. This camp was located at Annunciation Square.

New Orleans: Camp Benjamin was a Confederate Army camp established in 1861. The camp was located east of the Pontchartrain Railroad (Elysian Fields Avenue) near Gentilly Road.

New Orleans: Camp Caroline was a Confederate Army camp established in 1862. The camp was located on the Hopkins Plantation east of Elysian Fields Avenue on Gentilly Road.

New Orleans: Camp Corbin, Camp Foster, and Camp Gladden located at the New Orleans Fair Grounds were a few of the many Confederate and United States Army camps of the Civil War and the Spanish-American War. At times several thousand troops were stationed at the Fair Grounds. Many Civil War artifacts have been found there.

New Orleans: Camp Lafayette was the name of a Confederate Army camp established in 1861, and later used by

Union troops until the end of the Civil War. This camp was located in Lafayette Square.

New Orleans: Camp Louis was a Confederate Army training camp established in 1861. After the fall of New Orleans on May 1, 1862, the site was used as a Federal Army camp and had the names of Camp Kearney, Camp Williams, and Camp Mansfield. All of these camps were established in 1862. It is believed that these camps were all located in what is now Audubon Park near Saint Charles Avenue.

New Orleans: Camp at Metairie Race Track, Camp Metairie, Camp Walker, and Camp Smith were the names of Confederate Army camps established in April of 1861 at the Metairie Race Track. After the fall of New Orleans on May 1, 1862, the camp site continued to be used by Union troops. At one time there was a reported population of 7,000 troops at the site. Unfortunately it is now the Metairie Cemetery.

New Orleans: Post at Greenville was a United States Army post established in 1864 and continued to be manned through 1874. The post was rather large and contained enough barracks to house over thirty companies on soldiers, a cavalry training camp with eight large stables, two railroad spurs and a large general hospital. The post was located on land that was once part of the Foucher Plantation. This site is now part of Uptown New Orleans in the area of Lower Line Street.

New Orleans: Post at Lakeport was a Union Army Post established in 1863. The post was located at the end of Elysian Fields Avenue and Lakeshore Drive.

PLAQUEMINES PARISH

Quarantine Station: Camp Lovell was a Confederate camp established in 1861. Approximately 500 men were dispatched to the Quarantine Station in April of 1862. The unit established

Camp Lovell across the Mississippi River from the Quarantine Station on the west bank. On April 24, 1862, Federal ships attack this position causing thirty casualties.

POINTE COUPEE PARISH

New Roads: The Riche Plantation home was constructed in 1825 by Fannie Riche, a free black. During the Civil War, the plantation was used as a Union Army Hospital. The plantation is located on Louisiana State Highway 420, approximately two and one-quarter miles south of Louisiana State Highway 10.

RAPIDES PARISH

Alexandria: Camp at Clear Creek was a Confederate Army camp established in 1863. The camp was located twelve miles from Alexandria on both sides of Clear Creek just above the junction of Wise's Creek. This site would have to have been rather large as it has been reported that as many as four Confederate Armies were there during the Red River Campaign.

Alexandria: Camp Canby was a Federal Army camp established in 1865. Federal troops were stationed here during reconstruction. The camp was abandoned on May 23, 1877. The camp was located at the current site of the United States Veterans Hospital at Alexandria.

Alexandria: Camp Crow was a Confederate post established in 1863. Camp Crow was located approximately 2 miles north of Alexandria. Rumors have persisted since the Civil War that small treasure cashes were made by the soldiers stationed at the camp. The rumors may be true. Camp Crow served as a payroll camp where troops from the surrounding areas would come to be paid.

Pineville: Camp Buckner was a Confederate Army camp established on July 20, 1864. This camp was occupied until after February of 1865. The camp was located two and a half miles north of Alexandria near what was the Pineville Alexandria Road.

Pineville: Camp DeSoto was a Confederate Army training camp established in April of 1863. The camp was located approximately two and one half miles northeast of Pineville along both sides of Holloway Prairie Road and on the west side of Bayou Marais.

Pineville: Post at Pineville was a United States Army post established in 1873. This post was maintained until 1875, and was located at the present site of the Veteran's Administration Hospital, in Pineville.

RED RIVER PARISH

Coushatta: On April 12, 1864, the entire town of Coushatta was burned to the ground by Union troops. The troops burned the town after being fired upon by an unknown person believed to be residing in Coushatta. At the start of the Civil War many of the townspeople cached their valuables, and it is believed that several of these caches were never recovered.

RICHLAND PARISH

Delhi: During the Civil War, a man named Jesse Bullen is said to have hidden his valuables in one of several wells on his land. The well was then filled in and covered over so no one could tell where the hole was dug. Bullen died a few days later. After the war ended his children searched for the cache, but the exact location of the well could not be determined. The site of Bullen's farm is said to now be the McLaurin Farm on Endora Road.

SABINE PARISH

Pleasant Hill: Old Pleasant Hill was the site of a Civil War battle.

SAINT BERNARD PARISH

Lake Borgne: In 1878 a group of young boys found what is believed to be the first iron-clan submarine. That submarine, the "*Pioneer*," is now on display at the Louisiana State Museum at New Orleans (the Calbildo). Built in 1861 by the Confederates in New Orleans, the submarine, had it ever been used, might have changed the outcome of the Civil War. The Confederates tested the submarine in Lake Pontchartrain just before New Orleans was captured by the Union forces. To keep the submarine from falling into the hands of the Yankees it was taken into Lake Pontchartrain and scuttled.

Many people have trouble believing that the "*Pioneer*" which now sits at the Cabildo is the real one. The submarine at the Cabildo is nineteen feet four inches long and shaped like a fish. The original documents for the *Pioneer* describe it as being thirty-four feet long and cylindrical in shape. Some of those who believe the real *Pioneer* is not at the Cabildo think it still remains at the bottom of Lake Pontchartrain.

The story around Shell Beach is that the *Pioneer* is at the bottom of Lake Borgne. There are several shrimpers living in the area who will swear they have lost time and money because of that submarine getting caught up in their nets.

Chalmette: Camp Carondelet was a Confederate Army camp established in 1861, as was Camp Benjamine. These and many other camps of the Civil War, both Confederate and Union Army, were located on the Chalmette Plantation. It encompassed the area from the Mississippi River running north of Saint Bernard Highway almost to Patricia Street and along the east side of the canal that runs behind Norton Avenue and

Cougar Drive. Most of the artifacts found in this area were found lying on top of the ground.

SAINT CHARLES PARISH

Des Allemands: Federal Army troops stationed in the area of Des Allemands established a headquarters along Bayou Des Allemands. From this point they raided the surrounding area, stealing everything that was not nailed down. Confederate troops attacked the garrison, and, when the smoke had cleared, one hundred thirty-six Union soldiers were marched off to a Confederate stockade. It is believed that much of the treasure taken in those raids remain in the area of that Union encampment.

Des Allemands: Post at Bayou Des Allemands was a Union Army post established in 1864. This post was located on the New Orleans, Opelousas & Great Western Railroad crossing at Bayou Des Allemands.

Hahnville: Camp Pane was a Confederate Army camp established in 1862. This camp was located in the area around Pane's Sugar Mill.

SAINT HELENA PARISH

Beaver Creek: Camp Beaver Creek was a Confederate Cavalry camp established in January, 1863. The camp was probably located near Beaver Creek.

Grangeville: Camp at Williams Bridge was a Confederate Army camp established in 1861. The camp was attacked on June 28, 1862 by Union forces. The camp was located on the east bank of the Amite River, just south of Lilley Creek near Louisiana State Highway 37. The original bridge was destroyed during the Civil War. The State of Louisiana has placed a historical marker near this site.

Greensburg: The Methodist Campground was used during the Civil War as a campsite for Confederate troops going to and from Camp Moore.

SAINT JOHN THE BAPTIST PARISH

LaPlace: Post at Bonnet Carre was a Union Army post from December, 1862, to May 22, 1865. This post was located on the east side of the Mississippi River near Bonnet Carre at the bend in the river.

SAINT LANDRY PARISH

Bayou Maria Croquant and Bayou Teche: Camp Barri Croquant was a Union Army camp established in October, 1863. This camp was located on the north side of Bayou Maria Croquant at Bayou Teche.

Plaisance: The Poiret House was built in 1791 and is one of the oldest occupied residences in Louisiana. During the Civil War, the Poiret House was used as a Confederate Army field hospital. Poiret House is located off Louisiana State Highway 167 on Parish Road 5-70.

Sunset: Carencro House was built in the 1830's by David Guidry. During the Civil War, the house was occupied by four different Union Army generals. The house was also used as a Union Army hospital during the war. The Battle of Bayou Bourbeaux was fought near the house, and it is said to be haunted by the ghosts of soldiers who died there.

Washington: The Magnolia Ridge Plantation, also known as the Old Prescott Home and the Oakland Plantation, was built in 1830 by Judge John Moore. During the Civil War, the plantation was used as headquarters for both Confederate and Union forces and the grounds as an Army camp. The plantation is located six miles north of Opelousas on Louisiana State Highway 103 near Louisiana State Highway 10.

Washington: During the Civil War the Starvation Point Plantation house was used as quarters for both Confederate and Union officers, and the grounds as a camp by their troops. Many skirmishes are said to have taken place on the grounds. The plantation is located on Louisiana State Highway 746, approximately two and one-half miles northwest of Washington.

SAINT MARTIN PARISH

Cade: Camp Pratt was a Confederate Army training and prisoner-of-war camp. It was established in February of 1862. The camp was the site of several small battles during October and November of 1863 and was held for a short time by the Federals. The camp is believed to have been located along the entire western shores of Spanish Lake.

Saint Martinville: Camp Bayou Portage was a Confederate Army camp which was attacked and overrun by Union troops on November 23, 1863. This camp was located east of Bayou Portage and north of Lake Dauterive.

SAINT MARY PARISH

Adeline: Camp Hunter was a Confederate Army training camp established in 1863. The camp was located at the northeast corner of the junction of United States Highway 90 and the road that leads to Charenton.

Morgan City: Morgan City was the scene of much activity during the Civil War. During the war, Morgan City was known as Brashear City and was considered of major importance to the Confederacy. Confederate troops took possession of Brashear City on June 23, 1863. During this battle, three Confederate soldiers were killed and eighteen wounded. The Union loses were forty-six killed, forty wounded, and one thousand three hundred prisoners.

Patterson: The Fairfax House was used as headquarters by both Confederate and Union forces during and after the Battle of Bisland. Several small battles are said to have taken place around the area of Fairfax House.

Patterson: Part of the Battle of Bisland was fought on what is now Wally Post Airport.

SAINT TAMMANY PARISH

Mandeville: During the Civil War, several bankers had all the money removed from the banks in New Orleans, an estimated $6,000,000 in gold bars and coins, just before the city fell to the Yankees. The Original story goes like this.

The money was put into three large chests. The chests were given to several Confederate officers with instructions to bury the money in three different locations on the Walter C. Flowers Plantation in Mandeville. The orders were carried out to the letter. After the war ended only two of the chests could be located, touching off a gold rush of sorts. Over the years when the story was told and retold, it usually stated that the treasure was at the Flowers Plantation in Covington. Other stories indicate that the plantation was between Covington and Madisonville. However, research has shown that the Walter C. Flowers' Plantation involving the chests was probably in the area of what is now the Greenleaves, Cherry Creek, Wisteria, and Pac Du Lac subdivisions. Flowers also had a home in Mandeville, and as far as it is known this area has never been searched. Rumor has it that the Flowers home in Mandeville was purchased by a New Orleans chef who turned the home into a restaurant. The key to locating this site seems to be a portrait of Walter C. Flowers that is said to hang in the restaurant.

The treasure cache had a value of approximately $2,000,000 one hundred and thirty years age. Today this cache would have a value of about $30,000,000.

Madisonville: The city of Madisonville was burned to the ground during the Civil War by invading Union forces. It is believed that many individual treasure caches were made and never recovered after the war ended.

TANGIPAHOA PARISH

Amite: Camp Pulaski was a Confederate Army training camp established in June of 1861. The camp was located south of Amite on the Simpson Plantation. The land was later sold to Benjamine D. Gullett.

Pass Manchac: Camp Manchac was a Confederate Army camp established in 1861. This camp was located on the south side of Pass Manchac at the New Orleans, Jackson and Great Southern Railroad bridge.

Tangipahoa: Camp Moore, established on May 13, 1861, was a very large Confederate Army training post and prisoner-of-war camp. The camp was attacked in 1863 and again on October 7, 1864, by Federal Cavalry troops, destroying most of the camp. On November 30, 1864, the camp was once again attacked by Union troops marking the end of Camp Moore. At times more then 8,000 soldiers were in residence at Camp Moore. The camp was described as being located approximately one-half mile north of Tangipahoa Station bounded by the New Orleans, Jackson, and Great Western Railroad line on the west side, Beaver Creek on the south side, and the Tangipahoa River on the east side. The north side of the camp was believed to be bordered by Camp Tracy, another Confederate Army camp. Little is known about Camp Tracy, except for its location. It may have been considered as part of Camp Moore.

TENSAS PARISH

Saint Joseph: Camp Bruin, also known as Camp Brown, was a Confederate Army camp established in August of 1861 and was in use until after January of 1863. This camp was located six miles north of Saint Joseph on the shore of Lake Bruin.

Saint Joseph: Stories have been told of numerous plantation treasure caches being made during the Civil War in the area of Lake Bruin. These stories claim that most of the caches were never recovered after the war ended.

Waterproof: During the Civil War, several small battles took place in the area of Waterproof. Many relics and artifacts have been found in this area.

TERREBONNE PARISH

Gibson: Post at Tigerville was a Union Army post established in 1864. This post was located at the New Orleans, Opelousas, and Great Western Railroad Station in Tigerville, now Gibson.

WEBSTER PARISH

Minden: Post at Minden was the name of a post established by the Federal forces of occupation in Minden. The post was established after the Civil War and used during the Reconstruction period. The location of this post was in the residence and about the property of J. W. Berry, which is said to have been on the north side of the first two blocks of United States Highway 79 North from Minden.

WEST FELICIANA PARISH

Old Port Hudson: There is one story that tells of hundreds of weapons being buried in one spot somewhere within the city limits of Old Port Hudson. The cache was made by the town's people just prior to the Confederate surrender and never recovered.

Port Hudson: Camp Beauregard was only one of several Confederate Army camps named after General Pierre Gustave Toutant Beauregard. This Camp Beauregard was established in December, 1862, and is believed to have been located in West Feliciana Parish along Thompson Creek and very near Port Hudson.

Port Hudson: Sandy Creek Camp, established in 1863, was a United States Army camp in use well after the Civil War ended. The camp is believed to have been located near Louisiana State Highway 68 and Sandy Creek.

CHAPTER XI

FORTIFICATIONS

As with the previous chapter, aside from the listed treasure caches, priceless artifacts may be the prizes that await the treasure hunter at many of these fortification sites. The prices listed in the previous chapter will still apply to most of these sites, but some sites are much older and the values of the artifacts much higher.

Today, as it has always been, soldiers of most countries are usually paid in cash (paper Money). In the past, before paper money was considered acceptable, they were paid in "cold hard cash," silver and gold coins. Many coins have been found with small holes drilled through them. During the Civil War it was the practice of some soldiers to tie their coins together with a string and wear them as necklaces. When a coin was needed they would pull one off their necklace. Often these necklaces were lost and never recovered. It was also the custom of some soldiers to bury their money until it was needed. The practice of burying one's money or valuables probably goes back to the beginning of time. It may be instinct, like dogs burying their bones or squirrels hiding their nuts. Soldiers cached their valuables near their camp or fort before going into battle. The Romans did it; the Huns did it; the French did it; the Spanish did it; the English did it, and probably every army in history has done it, including the Americans. Today when most people leave home for a long period of time, they hide their valuables within their house. A good burglar will always look in cookie jars, refrigerators, cabinets and drawers. If a person shared an area with dozens of people whom he could not trust, he would most likely hide his valuables outside.

The following is a list, by parish, of Louisiana fortifications.

ASCENSION PARISH

Saint Gabriel: Fort Butte was a British fort established in 1765. The fort was situated at the northeast junction of the Mississippi River and Bayou Manchac.

Donaldsonville: Fort Butler, also known as Fort Barrow, was a Union Army fort established in January of 1863. The fort was located on the north side of Bayou Lafourche across from Donaldsonville at the Mississippi River. This was the site of several small battles. On June 28, 1863, Confederate forces attacked the fort, suffering over 250 casualties before withdrawing. The Union troops suffered only twenty-five casualties. Union gunboats then shelled the withdrawing Confederate troops who were exposed along the Mississippi River levee.

Port Vincent: Fort at Galveztown was a Spanish fort established in 1778. The fort was located in Ascension Parish at the junction of East Baton Rouge and Livingston Parishes. During the Battle of New Orleans this fort was used by United States troops.

AVOYELLES PARISH

Marksville: Fort De Russy was a Confederate fortification established on November 1, 1862. The fort is located on the south side of an old bed of the Red River three miles north of Marksville. The fort was in the hands of Union forces from May 1, 1863, until they destroyed it around May 10, 1863. By May 14, 1863, the Confederates had improved the fort and were back in place. Union forces attacked the fort in a battle that lasted two and one half hours. The Confederates surrendered with five men killed and four wounded. Twenty-five officers and two hundred ninety-two enlisted men were captured. The Union troops listed three killed and thirty-five wounded.

Simmesport: Fort Scurry, Fort Humbug, Yellow Bayou Redoubt, Old Oaks Fort, and Norwood Plantation Fort were names for this Confederate fortification established in 1862. The fort was attacked and captured in April, 1864. The last battle of the Red River Campaign was fought in this area. The fort was located on the north side of Yellow Bayou and on the east side of Bayou de Glaise (Glaize). The location is now within the State of Louisiana Pomme de Terre Wildlife Area.

BOSSIER PARISH

Bossier City: The Fortifications at Bossier City began with Fort Smith and the Red River. Fort Smith was a Confederate fortification established in 1862. This fort was located on the Cane Plantation in what is now Bossier City. Also on this plantation were Batteries: Ewell, Price and Walker. Fort Smith was located on the south side of Coleman Street, between Ruston and Monroe Streets. Battery Ewell was located in the area of Central Park Elementary School. Battery Price is believed to have been located in the area of Broadway Street, running from the Red River to Benton Street on to west of Minden Street. Battery Walker is believed to have been within an area bounded by Bacon Street on the north, Leindecker Street on the south, 2nd Street West on the east, and the Red River on the west.

CADDO PARISH

Shreveport: The Arsenal at Shreveport was a Confederate arsenal established prior to 1864. It was located on seventy-three acres. The arsenal was captured and maintained by the United States Army until 1873, when the land reverted back to its owner. The arsenal was located on the "Old Logan Place" in the area of Arsenal Hill.

Shreveport: The Fortifications at Shreveport consisted of the Confederate fortified line beginning at Fort Turnbull, also known as Fort Humbug. Fort Turnbull was a Confederate fort established in 1862 and located at Confederate Memorial Park. The fortification line ran through Greenwood Cemetery, crossed Centenary Boulevard, then ran along the alley between Wall and Vine Streets, and continued to Egan and Nutt streets. From this point the line went onto Jordan Street and then to Murphy Street and Charity Hospital; continued through Allendale to Arsenal Hill, and ended at Clay and Webster Streets. Battery #1 was located in front of Fort Humbug. Battery #2 was located near Royal Street and Stoner Hill. Battery #3 was located in the Greenwood Cemetery, as was Battery #4. Battery #5 was on the hill to the rear of Highland Sanitarium. Battery #6 was at the corner of Egan and Nutt Streets. Two unnumbered batteries were located on Jordan Street; one in front of the Herold Home, the other on the northeast corner of the intersection of Fairfield Avenue. Battery #7 was on the grounds of Charity Hospital. Batteries #8, #9, #10, and #11 were spaced in a line between Charity Hospital and where Battery #12 stood on Arsenal Hill.

Fort Jenkins was a Confederate fort established in 1862. It was located on a hill at the Schumpert Sanitarium. Fort Albert Johnston was established in 1862 and was located near the intersection of Webster Avenue and Clay Street and west of Pierre Avenue.

A large unnamed camp serviced the area. It was located on twelve acres east of Louisiana Avenue, from Buckely Street to Jordan Street. This area may also have been the site of Camp Boggs, a Confederate prisoner-of-war camp established in 1863.

CALCASIEU PARISH

Lake Charles: Cantonment Atkinson was a United States Army fortification established prior to 1822, and abandoned in 1832. This fortification was located on the Calcasieu River and is believed to be in the area of the Old Bilbo Cemetery.

CARROLL PARISH

Goodrich's Landing: Fort Mound was a Union Army fortification established in 1863. The fort was located on an Indian mound near Goodrich's Landing on the Mississippi River.

CATAHOULA PARISH

Harrisonburg: Fort Beauregard was one of several Confederate Army fortifications named after General P. G. T. Beauregard. This fort was established in 1862 on a hill overlooking the Ouachita River near Harrisonburg. The fort was attacked on May 10th and 11th of 1863. On September 4, 1863, the fort was destroyed.

Jonesville: Fortification at Trinity was a Confederate Army fortification established in 1863. The fortification was raided by Union troops in November of that year. After the raid the fortification was reoccupied by the Confederates. Three cannons were brought to the site, but before they could be mounted, a fleet of Union ships approached and the cannons were hidden. It is believed that these cannons remain hidden at the site. The fortification was on an Indian mound at the southwest junction of the Little, Ouachita, and Tensas Rivers.

Sicily Island: Fort Natchez was the name giving to a Natchez Indian fort established in 1730 on Sicily Island. In 1729, after the Massacre at Fort Rosalie by the Natchez Indians, the French declared war on most of the Indian tribes. The war lasted until 1740. After the attack at Fort Rosalie, the Natchez Indians reportedly buried the Fort Rosalie treasures at Cash Knob. On January 20, 1731, in retaliation for the earlier Indian massacre the French attacked and burned the Indian settlement known as Fort Natchez. This fort is believed to have been located on the Battle Ground Plantation at the eastern edge of Sicily Island, one-half mile north of the town of Sicily Island and east of Louisiana State Highway 15. This is also believed to be the site of an unnamed Confederate camp established in 1864.

EAST BATON ROUGE PARISH

Baton Rouge: Fort New Richmond was a British fortification established in 1765. The fort was located south of the Pentagon Barracks in the area of Boyd Avenue, Spanish Town Road, and Lafayette Street. The fort was the site of a 1779 battle with the Spanish. It was occupied by the Spanish until September 23, 1810, and was referred to as Fort San Carlos.

Baton Rouge: Campo De Baton Rouge was established by the Spanish in 1779 and used during the battle with the British at Fort New Richmond. The Spanish camp was located in the area of the British fort.

Baton Rouge: Fort Williams was a Union Army fortification. The fort was started by the Confederates. When Baton Rouge fell in May of 1862, Union soldiers occupied the unfinished fort. After the Confederates attacked on August 5, 1862, the Federals were forced back to the Mississippi River. After the Federals regained possession of the fort they began improving their position. The Union Army departed Baton Rouge on August 21 and returned on December 17, 1862, where they remained until the Civil War ended. The Fortifications ran from the Mississippi River levee west of Capital Lake along the southern end of the lake around the powder magazine (Arsenal Museum), southwesterly along North 6th Street, west along University to North 4th Street, and then southwest to Riverside and North Streets, ending at the foot of North Street.

NOTE: If you take a map of Baton Rouge and a compass. Place the pointed end of the compass at Laurel Street and the Mississippi River; the pencil end at Florida Boulevard and South Acadian Thruway. Make a semicircle back to the river in both directions. Within this area there should be a virtual gold mine of Civil War relics.

Baton Rouge: Highland Stockade was a Union Army stockade established in 1864. The stockade was located on Highland Road near Benton Drive. The Highland Road School is believed to be the location of the center of the stockade.

Baton Rouge: Post at Thompson Creek was a British Army post established in 1776. The post was located on the Mississippi River at its junction with Thompson Creek.

Bayou Manchac: Fort at Manchac was a French Army fortification established in 1729. Also established in this same area was the British Fort Bute. It was also known as Manchac Fort and Fort at the Iberville. The British began construction of their fortification in October of 1764 and completed it in 1766. The fort was located approximately 400 yards north of Bayou Manchac at its junction with the Mississippi River. It was approximately 100 yards from the Mississippi River across Bayou Manchac from the Spanish Fort Saint Gabriel. The British may have built several forts in this same general area. In 1765, the British repelled an attack by Indians. In September, 1768, the fort was abandoned by the British. In January of 1774, the site was again occupied by British troops. On March 22, 1778, United States Army troops seized the fort. The British attacked and regained the fort, killing three, wounding five, and capturing thirteen American prisoners . On September 7, 1779, the Spanish attacked the fort with 1400 men, only to find that most of the British had pulled out several days before. The Spanish captured two officers and twenty-four enlisted men. One British officer and twenty enlisted men escaped just prior to the Spanish attack. On November 24, 1794, the Spanish abandoned both Fort Bute and Fort Saint Gabriel. (See Iberville Parish.)

Greenwell Springs: Camp Cobb was a United States Army camp established in 1855. The camp was located near Greenwell Springs at the junction of the Comite and Amite Rivers. The camp continued to be used throughout the Civil

War by Confederate forces. This site is believed to have been the location of an 1822 army camp named "Camp at Sandy Creek Springs."

FRANKLIN PARISH

Montgomery: Fort Bon Dieu Falls was a French Army fortification located on the Red River near Montgomery. This fort was established by the French in 1712.

IBERVILLE PARISH

Plaquemine: Fort at Plaquemine was a Union Army fortification established in November, 1863, and abandoned in 1865. The fort was located at the junction of the Mississippi River and Bayou Plaquemine.

Plaquemine: Redoubt at Indian Village was a Confederate fortification established in January, 1863. The fort was located nine miles west of Plaquemine at the junction of Bayou Gross Tete and Bayou Plaquemine.

Saint Gabriel: Saint Gabriel De Manhack (San Gabriel De Manchac), also known as Fort at Manchac and Fort at Iberville, were the names for a Spanish fortification established in 1767. The fort was located just south of Bayou Manchac at the Mississippi River.

JEFFERSON PARISH

Barataria Bay: Fort Blanc is believed to have been a French Army fortification. Little is known except its location. The fort was situated on the north side of Caminada Island, where Fort Blanc Bayou intersects with Bay Saint Honore.

Bridge City: Fort Banks was a Confederate fortification established in 1861 and was later occupied by Union troops.

The fort was located in the area where the Huey P. Long Bridge crosses over the Mississippi River levee in Bridge City, approximately 600 yards north of the Magnolia Lane Plantation.

Caminada Island: Cantonment Caminada was a United States Army fortification established in 1813. This fortification was located on Caminada Island.

Causeway Boulevard: Fort John M. Morgan, also known as "The Parapet," was a Confederate fortification established in 1861. The fortification ran along the general route of Causeway Boulevard for approximately one mile, with a large fort-like construction in an area bounded by Harlem Avenue, Avalon Drive, Airline Highway, and Santa Rosa Drive. After the Federals captured New Orleans, the fortification was renamed "The Parapet" and maintained until February, 1866.

Grand Terre Island: Fort Livingston was a United States Army fortification. It was first established in 1813, during the War of 1812, as Fort at Barataria Pass. The actual fort was not built until 1835 and was destroyed by a Hurricane in 1893. During the Civil War, the fort was occupied by both Union and Confederate forces. Numerous relics and artifacts from the Civil War have been found in the area of the old fort.

The Temple: An unnamed United States Army fort was established at The Temple in 1814 during the Battle of New Orleans. The Temple is located at the junction of Bayou Perot and Bayou Rigolets.
During the Civil war, the Confederates had a fort at the "Little Temple." This fortification was established in 1861 and was abandoned on April 27, 1862. This fort is believed to have been located at The Temple.
The Temple was used as a storehouse for treasure by Jean Lafitte. It is believed that many treasure caches were made on this island by Lafitte and his band of pirates. The island

received its name because it was believed to be the site of an Indian Temple mound. (See Chapter III, Jean Lafitte.)

Westwego: The Fortification at Barataria Canal was also known as the Company Canal Defense Line. It was a Confedcrate States Army fortification line established in 1863. This position was later refortified by the Union Army. This fortification appears to have been in the area of Sala Avenue, Laroussini Street, and Avenue A, and ran from the Mississippi River to the Bayou Segnette.

LAFAYETTE PARISH

Lafayette: Fortification at Lafayette was a Confederate fortification line established in 1863 and lost to the Union troops midway through that year. This fortification line was located on the north side of the Vermilion River, between Pinhook Road and the river. It was approximately two miles long.

LIVINGSTON PARISH

Port Vincent: Fort Graham was a British fortified settlement consisting of a fort, two barracks, and two storehouses. The fort was established in 1779 and was captured by the Spanish in September of that same year. The fort was located near the banks of the Amite River at the junction of Bayou Manchac. This site is believed by some to be within a park today. Records indicate that several sites were developed in the area, but no trace of this sites has ever been made known.

NATCHITOCHES PARISH

Galbraith: The Fortification at Monett's Bluff was a Confederate fortification that was attacked by Union forces on

April 23, 1864. The fort was located on Monett's Bluff overlooking the Cane River.

Grand Ecore: Fort Seldon was a United States Army fortification established in 1816 and abandoned in 1822. The fort was used by the Confederate Army in 1863 and was located on a high hill a mile and three-quarters north of Grand Ecore where Bayou Pierre joins the Red River. Union troops manned the fortification after the Civil War. In 1820, Lieutenant Colonel Zachary Taylor was stationed at Fort Seldon.

Natchitoches: Fort Charles was constructed by the French in the 1760's. Around 1790, the Beau Fort Plantation was built on the site of Fort Charles. The plantation is located approximately ten miles south of Natchitoches on Louisiana State Highway 119 near its junction with Louisiana State Highway 1.

Natchitoches: Fort Saint Jean Baptiste de Natchitoches is the site of the oldest permanent European settlement within the Louisiana Purchase Territory. Established by Louis Juchereau de Saint Denis in 1714, the city of Natchitoches grew around the fort. When Saint Denis arrived the area was inhabited by the Natchitoches Indian Tribe, members of the Caddo Indian Nation. The site of the first fort was located between Jefferson Street and the Cane River, and between Sibley and College Avenues. The Spanish occupied the fort and then later the Americans, who on April 26, 1804, changed the name to Fort Claiborne. The fort was abandoned by the Americans in 1820.
The second fort was believed to be at the site of the American Cemetery.

Robeline: Presidio de Nuestra Senora del Pilar de Adais was a Spanish post established on August 29, 1721. The post was located one and a quarter miles northeast of Robeline. This site is also believed to be the location of Camp Addais, a United States Army camp established October 24, 1806.

New Orleans: Artillery Park was first used by the Spanish and later by the French as a sort of parking lot for artillery pieces. The park was located in the block bounded by Dumaine, Chartres, Saint Philip, and Decatur Streets. Also used as an artillery park was the block bounded by Barracks, Governor Nicholls, Decatur, and Old Gallatin Streets.

New Orleans: Bois Gervais Line was a United States fortification line constructed during the Battle of New Orleans. It was a mud rampart that was formed on the west bank of the Mississippi River in the area of the Unites States Quarantine Station in Algiers. The line ran from the river into the swamp. There were several of these lines on both sides of the river. A copy of Major Lacarriere Latour's 1815 map of the "British Campaign for New Orleans" may be obtained from the National Park Service office in Chalmette.

NOTE: I know people who have hunted this site. The finds were beautiful--old French coins, antique jewelry, and War of 1812 relics.

New Orleans: Camp Bertonniere was a United States Army fortification established in December, 1814. The camp was located on the Bertonniere Plantation near Chef Menteur Road.

New Orleans: Fort Macomb (McComb), Fort at Chef Menteur, Fort Woods, and Battery at Chef Menteur, were all names for United States Army fortifications at this same location. It was first established in 1814 as a simple breastworks. Construction on the fort was begun on December 1, 1818, and completed three years later. The fort was captured by Confederate forces at the start of the Civil War. When New Orleans fell on April 25, 1862, the fort was abandoned by the Confederates. It was then occupied by Union troops and was maintained by the United States until it was abandoned after 1899.

On August 24, 1927, the United States Government attempted to transfer title of the fort to the State of Louisiana, but it was learned that the land was never purchased from the original owner. On March 27, 1939, the owner of the land donated the site to the State Parks Commission of Louisiana.

For the longest time the site was left unattended. Over the years thousands of searches were conducted with innumerable Civil War artifacts being removed from this site. At the same time the action of dredging in the area and the wakes of boats and storms caused the destruction of other parts of the fort.

In 1966, the Parks and Recreation Commission of the State of Louisiana granted a long term lease of the property to a private corporation. In 1981, after a long battle waged by several historical preservation groups, the State of Louisiana was forced to pay a large sum of money to regain possession of the fort.

Fort Macomb is said to contain what has been described as a large treasure within its walls. It is now protected by the state. It is supposedly being made into a museum. For years Fort Macomb was one of the most hunted locations within the state of Louisiana. During that time several attempts had been made to find the treasure, some ending in near death. No one knows the real story behind the hidden treasure or the amount involved, but the theory has been sustained for well over fifty years.

The fort is located at Chef Menteur Highway (United States Highway 90) and the south side of Chef Menteur Pass.

New Orleans: Fort Petite Coquilles (Little Shells) was originally a French fortification established in 1793. By 1810, the entire French fort had been destroyed, and in December of 1812, construction was begun on an American fort at the same location. This fort was completed on May 17, 1813 and was abandoned in November, 1827.

During the Battle of New Orleans, Fort Petite Coquilles was under the command of Captain Francis Newman. Not one shot was fired from the fort during the war, but its presence forced the British to attempt to enter New Orleans via Villere's Canal and Chalmette. This route greatly slowed the British plan of attack on New Orleans. The fort was located on Pass Rigolets (The Rigolets) three-fourths of a mile west of Fort Pike. The site can only be seen as a small shell mound during very low tides.

In 1815, a wounded British soldier escaped from the hospital at Fort Petite Coquilles, taking with him $20,000 in gold coins. The soldier was captured at the approximate site of where Fort Pike stands today, but he did not have the coins in his possession. It is believed that the cache had to have been made in this immediate area. A search was conducted for the coins, but nothing was found.

A 1977 version of this story states that it was a British paymaster in charge of $275,000. Prior to being captured he hid the British gold coins in this area.

Over the years several searches of the area have been made using older metal detectors, but it is doubtful that modern ones have ever been used.

New Orleans: Fort Pike was a United States Army fortification established in 1818. In January of 1861, the fort was captured and held by the Confederates until April 30, 1862, when New Orleans fell. The Union regained control of the fort and abandoned it around 1870. The fort is now a State Commemorative Area. It is located near United States Highway 90 and The Rigolets.

New Orleans: Fort Saint Charles was a French fortification established in 1760. The fort was used by the Spanish and called Fort San Carlos from 1792 until the United States took control of the area in 1803. The fort was demolished in 1821. It was located at the foot of Esplanade Avenue, the site of the New Orleans Mint.

New Orleans: Fort Saint Ferdinand was a Spanish fortification established in 1794. When Louisiana became a United States Territory the fort was used by the United States Army. The fort was located at what is now the North Rampart Street entrance of the Municipal Auditorium.

New Orleans: Fort Saint John, Fort Saint Jean, Fort on Bayou Saint John, Fort of the Lake, Fort San Juan, Spanish Fort, and Fort at Bayou Choupic were all names for what was first a French fortification established in 1716. Later the site was occupied by the Spanish, and then by the Americans on December 20, 1803. The fort was located along Bayou Choupic, now Bayou Saint John, near Lake Pontchartrain. The current location is south and east of the corner of Beauregard Avenue and Jay Street, north of Robert E. Lee Boulevard, and on the west side of Bayou Saint John. The site is now a part of New Orleans City Park. The fort was near Lake Pontchartrain, but the shore line of the lake in that area was moved north approximately 600 yards. The areas of Lake Terrace, Lake Vista, West End, Lakeshore West, and Lakeshore East were created using land fill.

The fort was abandoned in 1825 by the United States Army, and a hotel was erected on the fort's foundation. In 1911, restoration of the fort was begun. It was completed during the 1930's by the Works Progress Administration.

New Orleans: The Batteries on Bayou Saint John were two American fortifications which were established in December of 1814 during the Battle of New Orleans. These fortifications were located near Lake Pontchartrain, on the east side of Bayou Saint John. The batteries were across the bayou from Fort Saint John, between the bayou and Saint Bernard Avenue and at the junction of Frankford and New York Streets. This site is now also part of New Orleans City Park.

New Orleans: Fort Saint John (San Juan) was a Spanish fortification established in 1794. This fort was located at the corner of North Rampart and Barracks Streets.

New Orleans: Jackson Barracks, originally known as New Orleans Barracks, was a United States Army post. Construction on the post was completed on December 31, 1835. During the Civil War, the post was captured and held by the Confederates for approximately one year. On May 1, 1862, the post was returned to the control of the United States Army. Famous people who have served at Jackson Barracks include General Zachary Taylor and Lieutenant Ulysses Simpson Grant. On October 31, 1909, President William Howard Taft attended a luncheon given by the Louisiana Historical Society at Jackson Barracks. It is located at the Orleans-Saint Bernard Parish Line, between the Mississippi River and North Tonti Street. The post is now the property of the Louisiana National Guard.

New Orleans: The Line Dupre was a United States Army fortification line established in 1814 during the Battle of New Orleans. The line was on the Dupre Plantation just up river from Jackson's Line at the Chalmette Plantation. This fortification ran from the Mississippi River north for approximately one and one half miles. The approximate location of this fortification would have been in the area of Forstall Street.

This was also the location of Camp Dupre, established during the War of 1812.

New Orleans: The McCarty-Montreuil Line was also a United States Army fortification of the Battle of New Orleans. This line was similar to the Jackson Line at Chalmette, but was located close to New Orleans as a backup defense line. The line ran from the Mississippi River into the swamp. It is believed that the current location would be between Congress and Independence Streets, and between the Mississippi River and North Claiborne Avenue.

New Orleans: The McGehee Fortification, also known as Fort McGee, was a Confederate fortification established in 1862. This fortified line was located on the McGehee Plantation. The fortification line was in the area of Aurora Gardens and ran from the Mississippi River, at approximately Simpson Place to Eton Street and Berkley Drive. This fortification was shelled by the approaching Union fleet on April 25, 1862.

New Orleans: The Redoubt on Bayou Saint John was a Confederate fortification established in 1861. The redoubt was located in the area of Demourelles Island and Island Drive. This fortification was manned by the Union Artillery after New Orleans fell in May of 1862 and was abandoned in May of 1865.

New Orleans: The Redoubt at Pass Chef Menteur was a United States Army fortification of the Battle of New Orleans. This redoubt was located on the south side of Chef Menteur Pass from Lake Pontchartrain to Lake Borgne.

New Orleans: The Jefferson and Lake Pontchartrain Railroad Battery was the name of a Confederate Army fortification established on December 5, 1861. This fortification was located on both sides of what is now the Outfall Canal, at approximately Hedwich Street on the east and Narcissus Street on the west.

OUACHITA PARISH

Monroe: Fort Miro was a Spanish fortification established in 1790. The fort was located at 520 South Grand Street. On April 1, 1804, units of the American Army were sent to the fort to assume command, but for some reason they could not find it.

Monroe: The Post at Ouachita was an American Army post established on January 31, 1804. This post was located 400 yards down river from Fort Miro.

PLAQUEMINES PARISH

Belle Chasse: In the 1950's, Cuban Revolutionaries were training in the New Orleans area.   It has been written that Che Guevara buried $1,500,000 at the old military base in Algiers before he returned to Cuba. Most people have assumed that this site is at the old 8th Naval District in Algiers. As this site is on government property, people have been reluctant to search for the treasure.   However the old military base referred to in the stories might be in Plaquemines Parish.   This property now contains the United States Coast Guard Station, Fort Saint Leon, The Belle Chasse Special School, the Tulane Animal Research Center and numerous parks and recreation areas.   It is possible to gain permission to search some of these areas.

English Turn: Fort Saint Marie was a French fortification established in 1756 on the east bank of the Mississippi River at English turn. This site is not located on government land.
Fort Saint Leon was the French fortification established in 1748 on the west side of the Mississippi River at English Turn. It is now on the property of the United States Coast Guard Base at Belle Chase. Forts Saint Leon and Saint Marie were only two of many fortifications located at English Turn.
Upon seeing this particular stretch of the Mississippi River Sieur Jean Baptiste Lomoyne de Bienville realized its importance as a defense.   Because of the bend in the river, sailing ships going up river could not negotiate the turn. Before a ship could proceed up river it had to be anchor part of the way into the turn and await a change in the wind's direction. This point in the river was perfect for a fort.
Upon spotting an English ship in September, 1699, Bienville met with the ships officers and convinced them that the French had already established a settlement there.   The English immediately turned around and headed back the way they came. The French named the area Detour de L'Anglais (English Turn).
Construction of the first of two forts began in 1747. The fort on the west side was called "Batterie de l'ance," and the one on the east bank of the river was called "Batterie do la pointe." By

1757, the names were changed to Fort Saint Leon on the west bank and Fort Saint Marie on the east bank. The French later added a fortification line that ran from the Mississippi River into the swamps on each side of the river. Two other batteries were added down stream at what was the narrow part of the river. In 1762, the Spanish acquired control of Louisiana and the two forts. Nothing more was done to the forts at that time. In 1803, the United states Army constructed a barracks at the southwest corner of Fort Saint Marie. A fort was built on the west side of the river next to the French Fort Saint Leon. The new fort was also named Fort Saint Leon. The new fort was completed on March 18, 1810. In 1812, the United States Army constructed another set of barracks on the east bank of the river near Fort Saint Marie. It was said that the barracks could house three thousand troops. Both of these forts were abandoned in 1817. During the Civil War, the Union Army reestablished a post at the site of Fort Saint Marie.

Garden Island Bay: Fort of La Balize was a French fortification established in 1722. The French abandoned the fort in 1803. The fort was occupied by United States troops in December, 1803. It was in use until 1865. During the Civil War, the fort was occupied by both Confederate and Union Armies.

Garden Island Bay: Fort Real Catolica San Carlos was a Spanish fortification established in 1767. It is believed the fort was abandoned in 1768. In 1795, the French raided the fort and threw three cannons into the water near the fort.

Head of Passes: Battery at Head of the Passes was a United States Navy fortification established in 1861. The fort was located at the junction of South and Southwest Passes of the Mississippi River. On October 15, 1861, Confederate forces landed and destroyed the fortification. It was never rebuilt.

Phoenix: Fort Iberville, also known as Fort de la Boulaye, Fort on the Mississippi, Louisiana Fort, Vieux Fort, Old French Settlement and Old Fort, was the site of the first French settlement in Louisiana. The fort was occupied between the years 1700 and 1709. The French had a treasury of $160,000 in gold coins. The treasury was intended to be used to pay Indians for various services and to purchase the necessities for establishing this first colony on the Mississippi River. The French were forced to leave the area on foot. Since the gold would have been an added burden, causing them to sink further into the swampy terrain, they buried it. Later attempts to retrieve the treasure failed as the fort was reclaimed by the swamps.

The fort was lost until 1932 when workers digging the Gravolet Canal discovered the remains of the old fort's walls. Some of the gold coins have been found, which leaves many to believe that the cache may have been scattered as a result of the combination of wave action and dredging in the area. The fort was surrounded by a moat, and the dredging cut the fort in half, leaving the remainder of the fort's site resembling two half moons. If the dredge cut through the treasure cache, a large portion of the coins may have been deposited with the dirt that made up the canal banks.

The actual location of the old fort is at the intersection of the Gravolet Canal and the old Mississippi levee and can only be reached by boat from Phoenix. As you travel away from Louisiana State Highway 39, the old levee should be the first ridge or raised ground that you come to.

NOTE: Do not attempt to go into this area during times when the temperature reaches over 70 degrees. You would not believe the number of snakes that try to sun themselves on anything that lies out of the water.

Plaquemines Bend: Fort Jackson was a United States Army fortification established in 1814 during the Battle of New Orleans, although construction on the actual fort did not begin until sometime later. The fort was completed by December 2,

1837. Prior to the Civil War, external batteries were added north and south of the fort. At the beginning of the Civil War the fort was captured and held by Confederate forces. During the Union attack of April 15, through April 25, 1862, sections of the fort were heavily damaged. Nine men were killed and thirty-five wounded during this siege. A large portion of this fort was located outside the walls, the barracks, hospital, officer quarters, supply warehouse, as well as other minor buildings.

During World War I, the fort was used as an anti-aircraft warning installation and training post. Fort Jackson was abandoned in February of 1922. The land was purchased from the government and donated to Plaquemines Parish. It is now classified as a national historic monument.

Plaquemines Bend: Fort Saint Philip, Feurte San Felipe de Placamines, Fort Plaquemines and the Fort at Plaquemine Bend were names of a Spanish fortification established in 1795. The French acquired the fort in 1803 and then turned it over the Americans on December 20, 1803.

The Americans constructed a new fort at this same site. During the Battle of New Orleans, between noon on January 9 and early morning on January 18, 1815, over 1,000 mortar rounds were fired into the fort by British ships. Because of a lack of ammunition for their long range guns, the Americans could not return fire until the ammunition arrived on January 17. Once the Americans began to fire back, the British withdrew.

The fort was seized by the Confederates at the beginning of the Civil War. As the Union Navy approached for their assault on New Orleans, a battle began on April 24, 1862. The Confederates eventually withdrew, as the fort was being bombarded by the Union ships. The fort was manned by Union troops on April 28, 1863. Both Fort Saint Philip and Fort Jackson were abandoned by the United States in February of 1922. The fort is located across the Mississippi River from Fort Jackson.

During the 1920s and 1930s, smugglers used the abandoned fort as a warehouse. Rumors abound of buried treasure caches in this area.

POINTE COUPEE PARISH

Morganza: Fort Morganza was a Union Army fortification established in May of 1864. The fort was abandoned at the end of the Civil War. Reports state that at times more than 20,000 troops were stationed in and around Fort Morganza. The fortification extended from the Mississippi River over the levee and would have had to have been very large to accommodate over 20,000 troops.

New Roads: Two unnamed French forts were reportedly located in the area of New Roads. The fortifications were established in 1722 and in 1760. One of these forts was called Fort de la Pointe Coupee and was located on the northern part of False River on the east side of the island, opposite Bayou Sara. The site of the second fort is unknown, but may have been at Bayou Sara in East Feliciana Parish. Both forts were maintained until 1769. The Spanish may also have occupied this site as "Punta Cortada" after 1769.

RAPIDES PARISH

Alexandria: Post at Alexandria was established in 1864 by Union troops. The post was located two thirds of a mile from the Red River and extended from the railroad tracks to Bayou Rapides. In 1866, troops at this post were under the command of General George Armstrong Custer. This site is believed to extend from Saint Francis Xavier Cathedral to the Red River.

Alexandria: Fort Buhlow was a Confederate Army fortification established in 1864. The fort was located on the east bank of the Red River and on the north side of United States

Highway 71. The fort was located approximately 600 yards north of Fort Randolph.

Alexandria: Fort Randolph was also a Confederate Army fortification established in 1864. Fort Randolph was located south of United States Highway 71 and on the north side of the Red River. This site is on the grounds of The Central Louisiana State Hospital. No battles were fought at either Fort Randolph or Fort Buhlow. After the Civil War ended, United States Army troops manned the forts for approximately one year. Historical markers mark the site of the two forts.

RED RIVER PARISH

Grand Bayou: Post on Bayou Pierre was a Spanish post established in June of 1805. This post was on Bayou Pierre near its junction with Grand Bayou. The post was abandoned in September of 1806. At the time the Spanish withdrew there were three companies of soldiers stationed at this post.

SABINE PARISH

Many: Camp Sabine was a United States Army camp established in 1836. The camp was established because of the Texas Revolution and was maintained until August, 1838. The camp held approximately 400 soldiers at one time. It is believed that this camp was located at what is now known as the Beulah Baptist Church, thirteen miles west of Many and two-tenths of a mile south of Louisiana State Highway 6.

Many: Fort Jesup was a United States Army fortification established in May of 1822. The fort was abandoned in January, 1846. The fort was located approximately six miles northeast of Many on Louisiana state Highway 6. Part of this site is now within the Fort Jesup State Commemorative Park. This fort was at one time under the command of Lieutenant Colonel Zachary Taylor. During the Civil War, the fort was used for a short time by the Confederate Army. During 1868, the 4th United States Cavalry was stationed there.

SAINT BERNARD PARISH

Chalmette: The American Fortification at Chalmette was the United States Army Fortification known as Jackson's Line. The main location is within the Chalmette National Historic Park, but extends out to the east and north off government land.

Chalmette: The American Redoubt on Bayou Bienvenue was established by the United States Army in 1815 during the Battle of New Orleans. This fortification was located south of Bayou Bienvenue and west of Bayou Mazant. This redoubt was also known as Fort Villere.

Chalmette: Battery Bienvenue was a United States Army fortification. Construction on this fort was begun in December of 1826. The fort is located at the junction of Bayou Bienvenue and Bayou Villere. The fort was occupied by Confederate soldiers at the beginning of the Civil War and was abandoned in late April, 1862. In early May of 1862, the fort was again occupied by Unites States Army troops. In May, 1865, the fort was abandoned for good.

Chalmette: The British Redoubts on Bayou Bienvenue were constructed during the Battle of New Orleans. The British established three redoubts in the area along Bayou Bienvenue. One redoubt was located at the junction of Bayou Bienvenue and Bayou Mazant, across Bayou Bienvenue from Fort Villere. A second, larger redoubt was located on the east bank of Bayou Bienvenue, approximately three miles from Lake Borgne. The third redoubt was located at Bayou Mazant and Villere's Canal. Perhaps because of its remoteness these sites have continued to offer fine artifacts of the War of 1812.

Chalmette: Camp at Chalmette Battleground was a United States Army camp established in 1846 and used throughout the Mexican-American War. The camp was located on the Chalmette Plantation in the area of the Battle of New Orleans' fortification known as Jackson's Line.

Chalmette: The Civil War Fortification at Chalmette was a Confederate fortification line established in 1861. This fortification line ran from the Mississippi River almost to Saint Bernard Highway. The location of this site was just east of the Chalmette National Cemetery, in the area of the old Kaiser Aluminum Plant. This site is now part of the Saint Bernard Port Authority.

Delacroix Island: Fort Darby was a United States Army fortification established on February 8, 1815. This site is actually in Plaquemines Parish and is located on the west bank of Bayou Terre Aux Boeufs and on the north side of the Lake Lery outlet, but it is easier to reach from Saint Bernard Parish.

Kenilworth: Blockhouse at Kenilworth was a French fortification established in 1759 on the grounds of the Kenilworth Plantation. It is believed that the blockhouse was incorporated into the original plantation house. The Kenilworth Plantation is located on Louisiana State Highway 46 (Bayou Road), approximately four and one-half miles east of the Poydras junction on Louisiana State Highway 39.

Meraux: An unnamed Union Army camp was established in 1863 on the Villere Plantation. The camp site probably was located along both sides of the Villere Canal, both sides of the Twenty Arpent Canal, and extended to the Forty Arpent Canal. This site is now the property of an oil refining company.

Meraux: The American Redoubt at Bayou Ducros, the British Redoubt at Bayou Jumonville (Bayou Ducros), and the British Redoubt on Bayou Mazant (Maxent)--also known as

Bayou Villere--were all located at the Junctions of Bayou Mazant and Bayou Jumonville. These posts and fortifications were all established in 1814 and 1815 during the Battle of New Orleans.

Poydras: Camp Terre-Aux-Boeufs was a United States Army camp established in May, 1809. This site was also used during the Battle of New Orleans, and it is believed that as many as 1,609 men were at the camp at one time. Also in this area was a camp cemetery with approximately 126 graves. The camp was located near the Mississippi River where Bayou Terre-Aux-Boeufs would have entered the river. It was due east of the junction of Louisiana State Highway 46 (Saint Bernard Highway), and Louisiana State Highway 39 (Pointe A La Hache Highway) and Bayou Road.

Poydras: The Redoubt on Bayou Dupre was an American fortification of the Battle of New Orleans. This fort was established in 1815 and was located along Bayou Dupre (Philippon), approximately 7,680 feet (forty arpents) from the Mississippi River.

Shell Beach: The Tower at Proctor's Landing, also known as Fort Beauregard, was a United States Army fortification. The fort was being constructed at the start of the Civil War and was only used as a lookout station. The fort was never completed and was abandoned in 1870. In 1915, there was a report that a "large gun" was found outside the fort. It is not known whether the cannon was removed or not, but it is believed that it remains somewhere near the old fort.

Violet: Fort Dupre Tower, also known as Bayou Philippon Tower and Martello Castle, was a United States Army fortification established in July of 1830.   Confederate forces occupied the fort after the Civil War began, but when the city of New Orleans fell the Confederate troops abandoned the fort. On May 6, 1862, Union soldiers occupied the fort, and it remained a

United States fort until 1883. The fort is located in Lake Borgne at the mouth of the Violet Canal.

Yscloskey: Battery at Proctorsville was a Confederate Army fortification constructed in 1861. The Battery at Proctorsville ran across the tracks of the Mexican Gulf Railroad one mile south of the dock at Proctorsville. It is believed that this battery was located in the area of Yscloskey. In June of 1861, several units of Confederate infantry were camped between the battery and Proctorsville. After the fall of New Orleans in April, 1862, Union troops were stationed at this same area. The Union troops were removed on May 27, 1865.

SAINT CHARLES PARISH

Narco: Fort Tigouyou was a French fortification established in 1750 and later occupied by the Spanish. The fort was destroyed by a hurricane on October 9, 1778, and was located at the mouth of Bayou Tigouyou and Lake Pontchartrain. Bayou Tigouyou is now Bayou Trepagnier, but where Lake Pontchartrain was is now Bayou Labranche. This site is now near the northeast edge of the Bonnet Carre Spillway.

SAINT JOHN THE BAPTIST PARISH

Pass Manchac: Fort Stevens, also known as Battery at South Pass Manchac, was a Union Army fortification erected in April, 1863. This fortification was located on the southwest end of South Pass Manchac east of the New Orleans, Jackson and Great Northern Railroad track.

Ruddock, Frenier: The Redoubt on Bayou De Sair was a Confederate Army fortification established in 1862. The small fortification was located below Pass Manchac, about six miles from Frenier. In 1864, Union soldiers occupied this site and further fortified the location.

SAINT LANDRY PARISH

Opelousas: Camp Hamilton was a United States Army post established in January, 1804, and used by Confederate and Union troops during the Civil War. It was located east of town and north of where a railroad track crosses United States Highway 190.

SAINT MARTIN PARISH

Butte la Rose: Fort Butte-A-La Rose, also known as Fort Burton, was a Confederate fortification established in November, 1862. The fort was located at the west end of Cow Island at the junction of the Atchafalaya River, Cow Island Bayou, and Bayou La Rose. On April 20, 1863, the Union gunboats *Arizona*, *Calhoun*, *Clifton*, and the *Estella*, along with several companies of infantry captured the fort.

SAINT MARY PARISH

Amelia: Fort Weitzel was a Union Army fortification established in 1862. The fort was located on the south side of the New Orleans and Opelousas Railroad tracks and on the east bank of Bayou Teche.

Calumet: The Embankments of Madame Mead's Plantation was a Confederate fortification line established in 1861. This fortified line was a part of the Battle of Fort Bisland and was located on the Mead Plantation.

Mossy Point: Fort Chene was a Confederate Army fortification established in May, 1861. The fort was located at the junction of Bayou Chene and Bayou Shafer and east of the Lower Atchafalaya River. When New Orleans fell on May 1, 1862, the Confederate troops moved out and the Union troops moved in. The Federals abandoned the fort on June 10, 1863, and in late June of that same year the Confederates returned. In late July, 1863, the Confederates again abandoned the fort.

Morgan City: The Battery at Berwick City was a Union Army fortification established in May of 1862. This fortification was located on the west side of Berwick Bay and was constructed around an Indian mound.

Morgan City: Fort Berwick was a Confederate Army fort established in 1861. The fort was located on the north side of the junction of Wax Bayou and the Lower Atchafalaya River. The fort was abandoned in April of 1862.

Morgan City: Fort Brashear, also known as Fort Star, was a Confederate fortification established in December, 1861. The fort was occupied by the Union Army in 1862. Fort Brashear was located south of the New Orleans, Opelousas and Great Western Railroad line approximately one mile south of Fort Buchanan.

Morgan City: Fort Buchanan was a Union Army fortification established in 1862. This fort was located opposite the entrance to Bayou Teche, approximately one mile north of Fort Brashear.

Morgan City: Fort Shafer was a Confederate Army fortification established in 1861. The fort was located south of Morgan City at the junction of Bayou Shafer and Bayou Boeuf.

Morgan City: The Redoubt at Brashear City was a Federal fortification erected in 1864. This redoubt was located north of the New Orleans, Opelousas and Great Western Railroad line approximately three blocks from Berwick Bay.

Patterson: The Fortifications at Bisland were Confederate fortifications located along United States Highway 90 between Patterson and Centerville. These fortifications extended across

Bayou Teche and into the swamp. There were three fortified positions located approximately eight miles west of Patterson and east of the Bisland Plantation near the Bethel Church. The Union Army began shelling these positions on April 12, 1863, with the Confederates returning fire from their fortifications and from the *Confederate States Ship Diana*. On April 14, 1983, the Confederate forces withdrew. Forty Union soldiers were killed and 284 were wounded. The Confederate losses are unknown. The Fortifications were then occupied by the Union Army until May, 1865.

SAINT TAMMANY PARISH

Covington: Camp Caffery was a United States Army, Spanish-American War camp, established on May 18, 1898. The camp was located on the Tchefuncte River approximately one mile north of Covington.

Madisonville: The Tchefuncte Navy Yard was a United States Navy shipyard established prior to 1813. The Navy yard was located in an old brick yard two miles up the east side of the Tchefuncte River from Madisonville at Gates Landing.

TANGIPAHOA PARISH

Pass Manchac: Pass Manchac Batteries were three Confederate Army fortifications placed in the area of Pass Manchac along the New Orleans, Jackson and Great Southern Railroad tracks. These fortifications were erected in January, 1862 and were located on both sides of South Pass Manchac and on the south side of North Pass Manchac. The batteries were captured by Union troops in June, 1862 and held until May, 1865.

WEST FELICIANA PARISH

Port Hudson: On Civil War maps, the Port Hudson Fortification appears to be the size of Rhode Island and may have had a larger population. Construction on this Confederate fortification began in 1861. The fort continued to grow even after it was captured by the Union Army. While under the control of the Confederates, the fortification was growing so fast there was a shortage of cannons. To solve this problem, at night the Confederates would replace some of the cannons that had been used during the day with wooden cannons and then move the real ones to the new positions.

Note: I have four Civil War Maps of this area, and it appears that between Union and Confederate defenses the area ran from north of Bayou Sara to several miles into East Baton Rouge Parish and inland as much as a mile and one-half. The perimeter of the Confederate line of defense was approximately four and one-half miles long. The Union line around the Confederates was over six miles long.

In January, 1863, there were approximately 15,000 (Confederate) fighting men at Port Hudson. A few months later there may have been as many as 17,800 men in the post. At the time of the final assault of Port Hudson in July of 1863, there were 7,893 Confederate soldiers assigned. 6,340 were taken as prisoners, approximately 400 died and 1,153 were not accounted for. The Union forces were said to consist of 25,000 men. 4,363 were wounded, 708 were killed, and 3,336 were listed as missing in action. The Federals held Port Hudson until July, 1866 when it was abandoned.

Port Hudson: Fort Babcock was a Union Army fortification constructed on a small hill on the west side of Sandy Creek.

Saint Francisville: The Post at Bayou Sara was established by Union Army troops in 1864 and abandoned after the Civil

War ended. From March 1, to November 11, 1876, the United States Army again stationed troops at this post. The post was located on the Mississippi River two miles southwest of Saint Francisville.

Saint Francisville: Thompson Barracks was a British Army outpost established in 1763. The post was captured by the Spanish in September, 1779. This post was located at Thompson's Creek near Murdock's Ford.

WINN PARISH

Winnfield: Fort Coochie was a Spanish fortification established in the early 1700s. Fort Coutier was also a Spanish fortification established in the early 1700s.

During the 1700's, pirates roamed the Gulf of Mexico attacking treasure laden Spanish ships almost at will. A plan was devised by the Spanish to bypass the pirates. The gold and silver from the Spanish mines in the Americas were transported overland to Natchez where they stored it until a flotilla arrived via the Mississippi River. The treasure would then be transported by mule train to the ships which would then continue on their journey to Spain.

The Spanish constructed Fort Coutier on the top of Rock Mountain twelve miles southwest of Winnfield. The popular belief is that the Spanish tunneled into Rock Mountain and placed the treasure in the tunnels. Things went fine until 1803 when the French took possession of Louisiana and the fort had to be quickly abandoned. The Spanish had to leave the fort, but did not have time to remove all the treasure. It is believed that they covered the entrance with stones in the hope of some day returning.

This same story is told of Fort Coochie, which is said to have been located nine miles west of Winnfield. This story is a lesser known version, and people may be looking in the wrong area for this treasure site. However, there might be a treasure at both locations.

From time to time over the past one hundred ninety-two years, individuals of Spanish decent have been reported in the area searching around Rock Mountain for certain signs that, so far, have never been found. The Spanish were known for their treasure signs, usually carved into rocks. These signs could lead a knowledgeable person directly to a treasure or mine.

NOTE: If one day you are in the area of Rock Mountain and turn over a rock with funny looking signs on it, you will need one of these books: Treasure Signs and Symbols, by Carson ($6.95), or Treasure Signs, Symbols, Shadows, and Sun Signs, Kenworth ($19.95). These are just two of the many books on Spanish treasure signs readily available at this time.

Anyone who is interested in locating military sites within the state of Louisiana should acquire a copy of Powell A. Casey's Encyclopedia of Forts, Post, Named Camps and Other Military Installations in Louisiana, 1700-1981, Claitor's: 1983. This book lists over one thousand locations.

Before going treasure hunting, make yourself familiar with the latest ruling of the United States Archaeological Resources and Protection Act of 1978.

CHAPTER XII

BITS AND PIECES

"Pieces of eight" were Spanish milled dollars (pillar dollars). They had a value of 8 reales and were the equivalent of one dollar. It was the coin the United States of America used as the model for its silver dollar. When our country was in its infancy there was a shortage of coins, especially those of lesser value. So, one simply took the 8 real and cut it in two, making each piece equal to one-half of a dollar or 4 real. If a quarter dollar was needed, a 4 real was cut in half making two, 2-real pieces. For three quarters of a dollar, one 4-real and one 2-real piece were used. This brought about the expressions of "2 bits, 4 bits, 6 bits, a dollar."

This brings us to the last chapter and my last 2-bits. It is a collection of stories and treasure leads that did not fit anywhere else in the book.

Fix yourself a cup of coffee, sit back, relax and enjoy this *bonne bouche* (something saved for that last delicious bite).

THE EVANS' TREASURE

Franklin Parish, Baskin: In 1900, a widower named Evans was known as a hard working man who saved every penny he could. He distrusted banks and was determined to leave his two sons better off than his father left him. Over the years Evans had managed to accumulate two gallon jars full of gold coins. The coins were ten and twenty dollar gold pieces. One day Evens called his two sons into the house and showed them the jars. He told them the coins would be divided between them when they were older. Evans left the house with the two jars and returned approximately thirty minutes later without the jars. After a year had passed, Evans became ill, and the two boys were sent into Baskin for the doctor. When they returned they found the house ablaze with Evans inside. Over the years the two boys searched for the jars in vain. The Evans Farm was located approximately three miles east of 1900's Baskin.

MADAME JOHN'S LEGACY

New Orleans: At 632 Dumaine Street is the structure known as Madame John's Legacy, a name derived from "Tite Poulette," a story by George Washington Cable. The house was built in 1788, and the basement is said to have been used to store pirate treasures during the seventeen hundreds. For this reason it is believed that pirate treasure is still located in the area of the basement. In 1947 the house was donated to the Louisiana State Museum and is now open to the public.

THE SELMA GOLD MINER

Grant Parish, Georgetown: Legend has it that a man from Selma, Louisiana traveled to Arizona and did a little prospecting. Upon his return it was said that he brought with him $250,000 (some stories say as much as $750,000) in gold dust which he buried near his residence. The old prospector was the talk of the town and everyone's friend. When the prospector was absent from town for a while, a few of his friends went to his cabin to check on him. They found the prospector dead of natural causes. The entire area was searched, but nothing was ever found. It is not known if a modern deep seeking metal detector has ever been used to search the area.

LOST MINERS' GOLD

East Baton Rouge Parish: Somewhere south of Baton Rouge, in a swampy area near the east bank of the Mississippi River, lies a mystery. The remains of what may have been an ancient stone fort or a prehistoric Indian structure have been found and lost as many times. The site was constructed from gold-bearing ore laid out in crossing parallel lines averaging two to three feet in height. Where did the gold ore come from?

Who built the structure? It is possible that this next story was contrived to explain these ancient walls.

Three miners from Alabama went out west to seek their fame and fortune. They found what they considered to be enough gold to last their lifetimes and were returning to their homes in Alabama. The three men each had two pack mules loaded with gold-rich ore. Sometime after leaving Baton Rouge, the three became hopelessly lost in a swamp. Finally they made it to the Mississippi River where they constructed a stone fence to keep in the mules. Due to a lack of building materials, the fence was said to have been erected using their gold ore. One of the miners remained with the mules, while the other two departed for New Orleans with some of the gold ore. They arrived in New Orleans two or three months later. They obtained a boat and barge and returned for the third member of their party. Upon their return to the area, the miners could find no trace of their partner, mules, or gold ore. It was believed that the miner and mules had perished and that the gold ore fence had been covered by the swamp's fast growing vegetation.

Several times over the past one hundred forty years, hunters have come across a stone-fenced area in the swamps south of Baton Rouge. Upon hearing the story of the "Lost Miners' Gold," they usually return to the area, but can never find the exact spot again.

LOST BRASS CANNON OF CHALMETTE

Saint Bernard Parish, Chalmette: Approximately one mile west of Paris Road (Louisiana State Highway 47, Unites States Interstate Highway 510) along the levee of the Forty Arpent Canal, a bronze cannon was found during a hunting trip in 1972. The person who found the cannon had every intention of returning to remove the cannon. The days turned into months, and before he knew it years had passed.

When he decided to returned to the site, he thought he could find the cannon in short order and brought the necessary equipment to remove it. He looked and looked, but could not find the cannon.

Believing that if he had a deep-seeking metal detector he could surely find the cannon, he called me and related the story. I offered to lend him the detector. Then, to my surprise, he asked me to come along to operate the detector. I told him I would be ready whenever he was. Weeks and months passed until finally I called him. He still wanted to go and retrieve the cannon, but he did not have the time. Years passed, and every time I saw my friend I asked him the same question, "Are you ready to go and get that cannon?" His answer was always the same, "I am much to busy now, maybe in a couple of days I'll call you."

It has been 17 years since the cannon was first mentioned, and, alas, the cannon is wherever he saw it. It would be impossible to retrieve an object of that size and importance without word leaking out. The value of the cannon would have to be between $6,000 and $50,000, and it may have been used during the Battle of New Orleans.

COUNT PAULO FAENZO'S BUTTONS

Orleans Parish, New Orleans: The Italian Count Paulo Faenzo came to visit New Orleans in 1873. While in the crescent city the count did something most visitors do in New Orleans, he got intoxicated. The count and five other gentlemen decided to go for a canoe ride in Lake Pontchartrain. After paddling out approximately 100 yards, the canoe capsized. The count and four others drowned.

At the time of Count Faenzo's death he was wearing his Ambassador-to-the-Court finery, which included a coat with twenty-five, sixteenth-century buttons. The buttons were crafted by Cellini. Each button had a large ruby set in the center of a swirled mound of gold, with six diamonds arranged about each ruby. The value of the buttons at the time was $10,000 each. Today each button is valued at over $100,000.

The Count's body was never reported found nor were any of the buttons. It is believed by some that the count drowned near the end of Elysian Fields Avenue. Others believe that the count drowned near Bayou Saint John. The night the count died he was attending a party at the residence of Anthony Ridger. If you can locate the site of the Ridger home, it would be a good starting point.

LOST SPANISH PACK TRAIN GOLD

Winn Parish, Winnfield: Legend has it that a Spanish pack train consisting of fifteen soldiers and eight mules loaded with gold was headed east through what is now Winn Parish enroute to Natchez. Northeast of present day Winnfield, near the Dugdemona River, the mules became bogged down in a swamp. The soldiers removed the gold from the mules, hid it nearby, and continued on with the intent of returning for the gold. The soldiers never returned, and the gold remains buried in the swamp awaiting some lucky person.

EARL K. LONG'S MISSING MILLIONS

Winn Parish, Winnfield: At last count there were three governors of Louisiana from Winn Parish. The most notorious of all of the governors born in Winn Parish was Earl K. Long. When "Uncle Earl" died, a modern gold rush started. Rumors have persisted that Earl left over $1,000,000 buried at his farm the "Pea Patch." Some believe that before he died Earl gave the money to Blaze Star. Another rumor placed the money in the safe of a famous New Orleans hotel from where it disappeared shortly after his death.

THE BALLOWE TREASURE

Plaquemines Parish, Point a la Hache: Supposedly, when Doctor Hewitt L. Ballowe died, he left a treasure cache worth $260,000 buried somewhere on his property near Point a la

Hache. Doctor Ballowe was said to have came into possession of several of Johnny Gambi's treasure maps, receiving them from either Gambi or a member of his family. Some say he may have found at least one treasure near Diamond.

MONSIEUR RICHARDE

Caddo Parish, Shreveport: In the 1890's a very wealthy man named Monsieur Richarde was known to hoard gold coins. Richarde was a wealthy businessman from New Orleans who retired in Shreveport. Richarde was also known as a recluse who liked to work in his garden. Richarde would spend hours each day toiling amid his beautiful flowers. At the time of Richarde's death his residence was searched, but all that was found were a few French and Spanish coins. Because of the fact that Richarde was always seen working in his garden, it is believed that his hoard of gold coins may have been cached in his garden.

THE SOLDIER OF FORTUNE'S TREASURE

A story has been told of a soldier of fortune who cached four iron bound chests filled with treasure in the area of Louisiana Highway 82 and the Vermillion River. In 1978, one chest was found in this area. The chest contained Spanish coins, jewels and documents.

LAKE HULL

Grant Parish, Georgetown: Treasure stories abound at Lake Hull. Reports of treasure caches small and large seem to center around this "bottomless lake".

One story tells of a family of four traveling through the area who stopped for the night near Lake Hull. Soon after dark the father hid the family's valuables near the camp site. As dawn arrived and the family was ready to depart, the father went to retrieve his cache. Before he could reach his hiding place, a band of Indians arrived and drove the family off. The father intended to return for his valuables, but waited too long. When he did return he found that the landscape had changed. He searched in vain for days and finally gave up and returned to his family.

Another story tells of a bank robbery in which the robbers made off with $40,000 in gold and silver coins. The robbers were pursued past Lake Hull by a posse. As the robbers passed the lake they threw the saddle bags filled with the bank loot into the lake. The outlaws were captured and led the posse to the point where the coins were thrown, but they were never found.

There is also the story of two brass cannons being stuffed with gold and dumped into Lake Hull and never recovered.

Another story tells of many plantation treasures being buried during the Civil War in the area around Lake Hull. The plantations were destroyed and most of the caches are still missing.

It has also been said the Wells outlaw gang cached $90,000 in the area of Lake Hull, none of which has ever been recovered.

INDIAN HILL

Grant Parish, Colfax: There is an interesting tale of a Spanish treasure being cached at Indian Hill, but this same story has been told of another hill within the same area. Both hills have been searched and nothing has ever been reported found.

HOLT

Caddo Parish, Vivian: In December, 1963, a man named Holt was said to have hidden several caches of money around his farm before he died.

THE CANNON STUFFED WITH GOLD

Vermillion Parish, Gueydan: There is a story of a cannon having been stuffed with gold and buried approximately three miles north of Gueydan on the south bank of Bayou Queue de Tortue. No one seems to know the name of the man who buried it or the reason behind this story.

HUBBARD

Bossier Parish, Ivan: A man named Hubbard is said to have cached $90,000 in gold coins in the area of Ivan.

CASTOR SPRINGS

Caldwell Parish, Vixen: Castor Springs was an 1800's vacation resort and several treasure caches are believed to be buried in this area.

WEST MONROE

An unknown treasure is said to be buried near the junctions of Chenier Creek and the Ouachita River.

GRANICOA

An unknown treasure has reportedly been buried along the Spanish Trail near Granicoa.

LEVI O. SHOLARS

In the 1750's an man named Levi O. Sholars settled in the area of Saint Francisville. People in the area believed that Sholars had been a pirate. After Sholars' death in 1795, rumors spread of treasure being buried on his property.

NATCHITOCHES PARISH

Natchitoches: $8,000 in gold coins was reportedly buried in 1858 near the banks of the Red River by a shop owner. The man died before he could retrieve or tell anyone of its exact location.

THE SILVER CROSS OF HERNANDO DE SOTO

Avoyelles Parish, Simmesport: As De Soto explored North America, he carried with him an elaborate silver and jeweled cross. De Soto's men felt that as long as the cross was with De Soto the expedition would be successful. De Soto went from Indian village to Indian village and convinced the Indians that he was the son of God, and as such could not die. Wherever the son of God went so did the cross, the symbol of his power. In 1542, when De Soto died, Luis de Moscoso de Alvarado, now in charge of the expedition, had De Soto's body placed in a hollowed out tree trunk, and weighed it down with the heavy cross. Under the cover of darkness the body was then pushed into the Mississippi River, where it sank. The next day Alvarado told the Indians that De Soto had returned to the heavens, but would return at a later date. The expedition continued on. Many people think that De Soto died near Simmesport and that the cross remains in that area. If found the cross could be considered priceless.

GLASS JARS OF GOLD AND JEWELS

East Baton Rouge Parish, Baton Rouge: This is the saga of a Baton Rouge resident. It has its beginnings in 1848, when a man who distrusted banks buried the family jewels and $50,000 in gold coins near the rear of his house. The cache was made in several glass jars placed between two trees. The man once showed his invalid wife the location, but she was too feeble to remember the exact spot. A short time later the man took sick and died. It is believed that this treasure cache has remained in the same spot for the last one hundred forty-seven years.

GALVEZ TOWN

Amite River: A large cache of gold is reportedly buried near the mouth of the Amite River in the area of Old Galvez Town.

METEORITES

Meteorites are not native to Louisiana, in fact meteorites are not native to Earth. Although meteorites do not fall on glaciers only, most of them are found there because their color shows up well against the background of a glacier. Glacial "deposits" in Louisiana contain a myriad of items. Diamonds, gold, silver, almost anything you can think of. What is found most? Sand, rocks and gravel. Almost all deposits of rocks found in Louisiana are usually in the form of a glacial deposit. There are very few forms of rocks that are native to Louisiana.

Many meteorites usually fall in the same area. Why? As the Earth rotates around the sun and through the path of meteors some meteorites will enter the Earth's atmosphere. These meteorites are usually in large quantities and follow the same general path. Most of them will burn up during entry into the Earth's atmosphere. All meteorites have a scientific value in the studies of outer space.

There are several types of meteorites, and most can be found with a metal detector. Sizes vary from microscopic to approximately a meter in diameter, with most being found in the 2 inch to 2 foot range. The largest known meteorite is estimated to weigh approximately 55 metric tons. The largest known crater created by a meteorite is in northwestern Quebec. It is 2.2 miles in diameter.

Meteorites are heavier than other rocks of the same size. They are irregular in shape, seldom round. Some are fairly smooth and featureless, while others may have flow lines, small depressions or deep holes. Some may resemble finger prints. The color of meteorites range from black to brown.

To test for meteorites, grind off a small corner and inspect the surface. You will be looking for either small specks of metal, broken swirls of colors ranging from white to black, or a solid silvery metallic appearance. Anyone who thinks they may have found a meteorite should not attempt to break it open. If you break open a meteorite you could be destroying any value it may have. You may contact The Center for Meteorite Studies, care of Arizona State University, Tempe, Arizona, 85287-2504. They will buy, trade or accept donations of meteorites.

GLACIAL DEPOSITS

Approximately 600,000,000 years ago, a great one-mile thick sheet of ice covered most of North America. As this glacier moved southward like a giant bulldozer, it dug up billions of tons of material and pushed it south. As this same glacier receded, items that were once trapped in the ice were dispersed as glacial deposits. Over the years this same process was repeated several times, in cycles believed to be approximately every 41,000 years, until about 10,000 years ago when the last glacier is believed to have receded.

These glaciers probably deposited within the state of Louisiana a sample of every known natural-occurring object found on the North American Continent.

AGATE

Agate is a quartz mineral composed of concentric layers often of varying colors. Agate can be polished and is used in the manufacturing of lesser grades of jewelry. While not officially a gemstone, amethyst, jasper, opal and flint are often found in layers of agate. Glacial deposits usually contain agate.

DIAMONDS

Diamonds have been found within meteorites, glacial deposits, and stream deposits. Diamonds found in meteorites are opaque, small, and are called hexagonal diamonds because of their shape. It is believed diamonds are created at the very instant some meteorites impact with the Earth's surface.

What do diamonds look like? Cut diamonds are easy to spot, but a diamond in the rough is not. A diamond is the hardest known substance. However do not hit one with a hammer, it will shatter. Diamonds are cold to the touch and have a greasy luster. Animal fat has been used in the mining of diamonds. A diamond will stick to lard, and lard will stick to a leather conveyer belt. Diamonds have a tendency to form in octahedron crystals (eight plane faces) often with curved surfaces. Diamonds are usually colorless (white), but can also be pale-yellow, brown, blue-white, green, orange, pink, black, and red (the rarest).. A company named Craig Industries of Theresa, Wisconsin makes a "Gold-Silver-Diamond Test Kit." The best way to tell if you have a diamond is to have it checked by a gemologist or a jeweler.

Diamonds can also be found in alluvial deposits, sandstone and other sedimentary rocks within the state of Louisiana. Diamonds also occur in kimberlite, but, as far as is known, there are no kimberlite deposits in Louisiana. Diamonds have been reported found in Bossier and Webster Parishes.

GOLD

"Gold is where you find it." Most geologist will tell you that gold is not native to the state of Louisiana, but if natural deposits do exist, they would be found only in the northern part of the State. Webster and Union Parishes have been listed as parishes that may have native deposits of gold. A geologist will also tell you that gold is found in quartz and in alluvial deposits (material deposited by rivers). The Atchafalaya, Mississippi, Pearl, Red, and Sabine River valleys are composed of alluvial deposits. Gold is also found with sulfur, and Louisiana has sulfur deposits.

Gold has been found in glacial deposits within the state. The following parishes all contain glacial deposits: Allen, Beauregard, Caddo, Catahoula, East Baton Rouge, Evangeline,

Grant, Iberia, Jefferson Davis, Lafayette, Livingston, Ouachita, Rapides, Red River, Saint Helena, Saint Tammany, Washington and Webster.

Calcasieu Parish, DeQuincy: The legend of the "Lost Wyndham Creek Gold Mine" has it that the Indians once worked a gold mine on Wyndham Creek near DeQuincy. This mine may have been in Beauregard Parish.

Grant Parish, Colfax: In 1830, it was reported that Edourd Gillard found gold in the hills near Colfax. At $20 an ounce, the gold was not worth recovering, but today it may be.

Union Parish, Turkey Bluffs: In 1971, Gold was panned at Turkey Bluffs along Bayou D' Arbonne. The gold is said to have been washed down from an ancient river bed in the area.

Unknown Parish: It has been written that R. C. Cameron found and worked an old gold and silver mining operation. The mine was located near Bayou Darro (Darrow) and Rocky Bayou.

SILVER

When sulfides are present silver will tarnish, so do not expect it to be shiny. Silver is usually found with sulfur, and Louisiana has sulfur deposits. Most silver is produced as a by-product of lead sulfide.

Calcasieu Parish, DeQuency: A lost silver mine is believed to be in the area of Wyndham Creek near DeQuency. Silver has been found in this area, but the source has never been found.

Natchitoches Parish, Natchitoches: A circa 1757 French map reportedly shows the location of the Duplesis Silver Mine. The mine was located northwest of the 1757 city of Natchitoches, near the area of the current city limits.

Vernon Parish, Anacoco: Early French explorers found silver and lead in the area of Anacoco.

Winn Parish, Winnfield: In 1881, a ledge of almost pure silver was found in a large cave near Winnfield. The exact location is said to have been lost over the years.

URANIUM

Union Parish, Turkey Bluffs: Small deposits of uranium have been found in the area of Turkey Bluffs along Bayou D' Arbonne.

JASPER

Jasper is an opaque variety of quartz and is considered a gemstone. Jasper is usually stained because of impurities and occurs in many colors, such as blue, green, red, and yellow. If the colors are arranged in bands, it is called riband jasper. All types and shades of jasper can be found in glacial deposits.

PEARLS

Pearls are a lustrous concretion usually caused by an irritant within certain shell fish (mollusk) and is valued as a gem. When a small particle of foreign matter enters the body of the mollusk, it coats the particle with layers of nacreous material. The most expensive pearls are spherical and are black. Less expensive pearls are cream, rose, or white.

According to legend, when the early Spanish explores came across the Gulf Coast, they found the Indians with a large quantity of fresh water pearls. The Indians harvested the pearls from a nearby river, which the Spanish named the "Pearl River." The Pearl River borders Washington and Saint Tammany Parishes with the State of Mississippi.

When La Salle explored the area of Rapides Parish in 1682, he found an Indian village on the Red River. The tribe collected pearls from the river and used them for trade among the other tribes. Fresh water pearls are among the most valuable pearls in the world.

OPALS

One of the characteristics of on opal is its brilliant display of colors. Opals can be found in many different colors. White-yellow to red are called fire opals. Bluish-white stones are called girasol opals. Multi-colored stones are called harlequin opals. The deep green stones are called lechosa opals. Black opals can be transparent to opaque. Another type of opal is called moss, because it resembles moss. Hydrophane opals are porous white or cloudy white when dry and transparent when wet. Hyalite opals are transparent.

According to an article in a 1990 edition of The Beauregard Daily News, opals were discovered near Anacoco in Vernon Parish at a place called Monks Hammock. It was reported that the opals coming from Hidden Fire Opal Mine were the best ever found in the United States. The owners were in the process of opening the mine to the public, where, for a price, you could mine and keep the opals you found. A polished, black opal the size of a penny is said to be worth $3,000.

This report also said that in the early 1900's, a man in Vernon Parish was sending a jeweler in New York what he called "rainbow rocks" for $5 each. It is now believed that these rainbow rocks were opals.

FOSSILS

Fossil is a term that refers to evidence of an organism which lived between 570,000,000 and 10,000 years ago. Fossils consist of organic structures, such as bones, trees which have become petrified, natural moles which covered an organism now leaving just an imprint of the organism, casts where the original organism was replaced by sediment and a replica was formed, imprints such as footprints, and organisms trapped inside amber (fossilized tree resin) and coprolites (fossilized excrement). Fossils can be found everywhere within the State of Louisiana. If you have gravel near your residence pick up some rocks and look closely at them. If you see the outline of small prehistoric creatures on the rocks, you have a fossil.

Caldwell Parish, Columbia: Fossilized zeuglodon bones have been found along the Ouachita River. Zeuglodons were prehistoric whales that lived between 54,000,000 and 38,000,000 years ago.

Grant Parish: Fossilized zeuglodon bones, turtles and crocodiles have been found in Grant Parish. Large quantities of fossilized mollusk have been found in the area of Creola Bluff.

Iberia Parish, Avery Island: The fossilized remains of mastodon and mylodon bones have been found on and near Avery Island. Mastodons were prehistoric elephants that lived between 25,000,000 and 8,000 years ago and were hunted by early Indians. Mylodons were prehistoric ground sloths that lived between 10,000 and 2,500,000 years ago and were also hunted by early Indians.

Before beginning any serious search for gems, it is advisable to purchase The Audubon Society Field Guide to North American Rocks and Minerals, by Charles W. Chesterman. Alfred A Knopf, New York: 1978. A real bargain at only $15.95.

Your coffee cup's empty, and your mind is filled with dreams of a major find. If you are like most treasure hunters you may have already purchased your equipment and went to several of the locations listed, and it is now raining outside. But, if if you are a "Real Treasure Hunter," you know there is a lot of research left to do. For all of the "Real Treasure Hunters," I have encluded a bibliography. Keep in mind that clues to treasure can be found anywhere, and the best ones come from talking to people. I am sure that everyone knows at least one treasure story that is not in this book. Get out of the house and take the time to stop and talk to people. I love to talk. When people learned that I collect treasure stories, they are usually eager to tell one that they are sure I have not heard. Quite often they are right. When the story envolves treasure buried by a relative, I usually offer my assistance, and never devulge the details to anyone else. Treasure hunting rule number one, is the golding rule. "Do unto others as you would have them do unto you."

Although most of us will never find a really big treasure, we can still enjoy all the "little" treasures of nature, the fresh air, the beautiful scenery, and the company of friends, relatives, and the chance to make new friends. The real joy is not necessarily in the finds we make, but in the fun we have in the search.

Happy Hunting.

Johnny

THE END

BIBLIOGRAPHY

Anderson, Nina & William. Southern Treasures. The Globe
    Pequot Press, Chester, Connecticut: 1987.
"Aztec." Microsoft Encarta. Funk & Wagnall's
    Corporation: 1993.
Brain, Jeffrey P. On the Tunica Trail. Baker Printing,
    Baker: 1994.
"Bunch, Eugene, John A." Encyclopedia of Western
    Lawman & Outlaws. Crime Data Research News
    Service, Incorporated, Zane Publishing,
    Incorporated, Dallas: 1994, 1995.
Carson, Xanthus. "Col. Frisby's Lost Treasure." True
    Treasure October 1972: 19-24.
Casey, Powell A. Encyclopedia of Forts, Post, Named
    Camps and Other Military Installations in
    Louisiana, 1700-1981. Claitor's Publishing
    Division, Baton Rouge: 1983.
Casey, Tim. "Louisiana's Plantation Treasure Hoards, Part
    One." Lost Treasure December 1992: 26-28.
_____. "Louisiana's Plantation Treasure Hoards, Part
    Two." Lost Treasure January 1993: 6-8.
"Copeland, James." Encyclopedia of Western Lawman &
    Outlaws. Crime Data Research News Service,
    Incorporated, Zane Publishing, Incorporated,
    Dallas: 1994, 1995.
Davis, George B., Perry, Leslie J., Kirkley, Joseph W. The
    Official Military Atlas of the Civil War. Comp.
    Cowles, Calvin D. Government Printing Office,
    Washington: 1891-1895. Arno Press,
    Incorporated and Crown Publishers,
    Incorporated: 1983.
DeHart, Jess. Plantations of Louisiana. Pelican Publishing
    Company, Gretna: 1982.
Dore, Susan Cole. Plantation Homes of Louisiana. Pelican
    Publishing Company, Gretna: 1989.

Duffy, Howard M. "Treasures of the Devil's Backbone."
Lost Treasure July 1976: 18-20.

_____. "Johnny Gambi's Lost Louisiana Treasure."
Lost Treasure July 1977: 28-29.

Francis, Dorothy. "Find A Fallen Star." Western & Eastern
Treasures February 1993: 74.

Henson, Paul Michael. "Lost treasure Answers Your
Questions." Lost Treasure, January 1977: 50-
58.

_____. "Lost treasure Answers Your Questions."
Lost Treasure October 1977: 42-48.

_____. "Question & Answer." Lost Treasure
September 1990: 72-74.

_____. "Louisiana Loot!" Lost Treasure October
1990: 28-33.

_____. "Question & Answer." Lost Treasure April
1991: 60-62.

_____. "Louisiana Loot!" Lost Treasure May 1992:
29-33.

_____. "Questions & Answers." Lost Treasure May
1994: 62-63.

Howard, Ron and Elizabeth. The Untold Story of
Confederate Coins. Brannon Publishing
Company: 1990.

Hothem, Lar. North American Indian Artifacts. Books
Americana, Incorporated, Florence: 1994.

"James, Alexander Franklin." Encyclopedia of Western
Lawman & Outlaws. Crime Data Research News
Service, Incorporated, Zane Publishing,
Incorporated, Dallas: 1994, 1995.

"James, Jesse Woodson." Encyclopedia of Western Lawman
& Outlaws. Crime Data Research News Service,
Incorporated, Zane Publishing, Incorporated,
Dallas: 1994, 1995.

Kiedrowski, Leonard P. "Louisiana's Treasure Island." True
Treasure August 1969: 17-19.

Kildare, Maurice. "Lost Treasure Answers Your Questions."
    Lost Treasure July 1976: 45-51.
Klein, Victor C. New Orleans Ghosts. Lycanthrope Press,
    Chapel Hill: 1993.
Kniffen, Fred Bowerman. The Indians of Louisiana.
    Pelican Publishing Company, Gretna: 1991.
Kutac, C. "Fort de la Boulaye's Treasure." True Treasure
    August 1975: 14.
Lafitte, Jean. The Journal of Jean Lafitte. 1958. Vantage
    Press; Woodville: Dogwood Press, 1994.
Lasco, Jack. "Gulf Coast Gold Rush for Jean Lafitte's
    Missing Millions." Saga's Treasure Special 1975:
    20-78.
Latham, John H. "Treasure Trails Answers Your
    Questions." Treasure Trails of the Old West Fall
    1974: 48-52.
Louisiana. Map. North Kansas City: Midland
    Lithographing. 1992.
"Louisiana." Microsoft (R) Encarta. Microsoft Corporation,
    Funk & Wagnall's Corporation: 1993.
Loup, Robert J. "Letters." Treasure World July 1975:
    63-64.
Martin, Gay N. Louisiana Off the Beaten Path. The Globe
    Pequot Press, Old Saybrook: 1993.
Masters, Al. "Has the Beale Treasure Code Really Been
    Solved." True Treasure April 1972: 15-21.
"Mitchell, William." Encyclopedia of Western Lawman &
    Outlaws. Crime Data Research News Service,
    Incorporated, Zane Publishing, Incorporated,
    Dallas: 1994, 1995.
"Montezuma II." Microsoft (R) Encarta. Microsoft
    Corporation, Funk & Wagnall's Corporation:
    1993.
"Murrel, John A." Encyclopedia of Western Lawman &
    Outlaws. Crime Data Research News Service,
    Incorporated, Zane Publishing, Incorporated,
    Dallas: 1994, 1995.

New Orleans. Map. U. S. A.: Rand McNally.

Kiwanis Tourist Guide of Opelousas, Louisiana and the
    Surrounding Areas. Opelousas Kiwanis Club:
    1984.

Penfield, Tom. "Treasure World Answers Your Questions."
    Treasure World June 1970: 45-53.

_____. "True Treasure Answers Your Questions."
    TrueTreasure October 1970: 49-53.

_____. "True Treasure Answers Your Questions."
    True Treasure December 1970: 56-59.

_____. "Treasure World Answers Your Questions."
    Treasure World November 1971: 55-58.

_____. "True Treasure Answers Your Questions."
    True Treasure December 1971: 48-52.

_____. "True Treasure Answers Your Questions."
    True Treasure June 1972: 51-54.

_____. "Treasure World Answers Your Questions."
    Treasure World January 1973: 65-71.

_____. "True Treasure Answers Your Questions."
    True Treasure April 1973: 66-72.

_____. "Tom Penfield Answers Your Questions."
    True Treasure December 1973: 51-60.

_____. "Treasure World Answers Your Questions."
    Treasure World September 1975: 50-57.

Pitts, Stella. "Dreams Still Do Come True: Kenilworth Is a
    Case in Point." The Times Picayune. September
    1, 1945: sec. 2: 4.

Poesch, Jessie J. The Art of the South. Harrison House,
    New York: 1989.

Ross, Nola Mae Wittler. Jean Lafitte Louisiana Buccaneer.
    Nola Mae Wittler Ross, Lake Charles: 1990.

Rossbacher, Nancy Dearing. Civil War Collector's Price
    Guide 6th Edition. Publisher's Press,
    Incorporated, Orange: 1993.

Roush, Fred J. Chalmette National Park. National Park
    Service, Series No. 29, Washington D. C.: 1975.

St. Bernard Parish Facts. Chalmette: Saint Bernard Parish
    Police Jury, 1978.

Saxon, Lyle. Dreyer, Edward. Tallant, Robert. Gumbo
    Ya-Ya. Pelican Publishing Company, Gretna:
    1991.

Saxon, Lyle. Lafitte the Pirate. Pelican Publishing
    Company, Gretna: 1994.

Segura, Chris. "Fort Proctor: Abandoned to the Marsh."
    The Times Picayune. December 28, 1975: sec.
    3: 10.

Serpas, Paul F. Gulf South Journal. Ad/Copy Service, New
    Orleans: 1973.

_____. Tales of Louisiana Treasure. Claitor's
    Publishing Division, Baton Rouge: 1975.

Smith, John D. "Treasure Q & A." Treasure November
    1991: 14-19.

Smith, Joseph Frazer. Plantation Houses and Mansions of
    the Old South. General Publishing Company,
    Ltd., Toronto: 1993.

Stall, Gaspar J. "Buddy". Proud, Peculiar New Orleans:
    The Inside Story. Claitor's Publishing Division,
    Baton Rouge: 1988.

Sunday Advertiser. "Treasure in the Headlines." Treasure
    February 1991: 32-86.

Swope, Robert Jr. Indian Artifacts of the East and South an
    Identification Guide. Robert Swope, Jr., York:
    1982.

Tallant, Robert. Voodoo in New Orleans. Pelican
    Publishing Company, Gretna: 1994.

Terry, Thomas P. New Orleans Treasure City. Specialty
    Publishing Company, La Crosse: 1980.

_____. United States Treasure Atlas. Vol. 4.
    Speciality Publishing Company, La Crosse:
    1985.

Townsend, Ben. "Lafitte's Lost Faro Cache." Treasure
    World, January 1975: 18-21.

"Treasure Headlines." Treasure World July 1973: 14.

"Treasure in the Headlines." Treasure February 1990: 32-75.

Viemeister, Peter. The Beale Treasure, A History of a Mystery. Hamilton's, Bedford: 1987.

Viviano, Christy L. Haunted Louisiana. Tree House Press, Incorporated, Metairie: 1992.

Ward, James B. The Beale Papers, Containing Authentic Statements Regarding the Treasure Buried in 1819 and 1821, Near Bufords, in Bedford County, Virginia, and Which Has Never Been Recovered. Virginia Book and Job Print, Lynchburg: 1885.

Word, Christine. Ghosts Along the Bayou. The Acadiana Press, Lafayette: 1988.

Yeoman, R. S. A Guide Book of United States Coins, 27th Edition. Western Publishing Company, Inc., Racine: 1974.

Index

Index

To order additional copies of **Treasure in Louisiana**, complete the information below.

Ship to: (please print)

Name _____

Address _____

City, State, Zip _____

Day phone _____

_____ copies of *Treasure in LA* @ $18.95 each $_____

Postage and handling @ $1.50 per book $ _____

Total amount enclosed $ _____

Make checks payable to *John Miller*

Send to: **John Miller**
P.O. Box 3764 • Bay St. Louis, MS 39521

To order additional copies of **Treasure in Louisiana**, complete the information below.

Ship to: (please print)

Name _____

Address _____

City, State, Zip _____

Day phone _____

_____ copies of *Treasure in LA* @ $18.95 each $_____

Postage and handling @ $1.50 per book $ _____

Total amount enclosed $ _____

Make checks payable to *John Miller*

Send to: **John Miller**
P.O. Box 3764 • Bay St. Louis, MS 39521